BOOK
3

WITH
LUCAS

DAILY READINGS
THROUGHOUT
THE YEAR

D1440254

JEFF LUCAS

CWR

Contents

Introduction

TRAVELLING as much as I do, I'm often asked if I enjoy a life that involves a lot of planes, trains and automobiles. My answer is simple: I like arrivals. The hassle of airports, packing, security lines, traffic jams and crowded stations – all of this I could do without.

But *getting there* – meeting new people, seeing new sights, *arriving* – now that's what I love. Like the would-be athlete who wants the body of steel but without the laborious hours of pumping iron, I would love the result without the work involved to get there. Teleportation would be a wonderful invention: I could be here, and then there, in a moment, at will.

I feel the same way about discipleship. I'd like to have greater love, show more consistent kindness, and have deeper understanding and wisdom. But, as with muscle, faith grows as a result of a journey, a lifetime that's made up of thousands of days and hours, spent with Jesus. Sometimes it's a sprint; other times, a plod. There are times when it seems that He is so close; and then, seasons when we wonder if we're even in the same locality. But the journey matters as much as the arrival.

And that's why I'm glad you've got hold of this third volume of daily reflections and thoughts. If you fulfil the will of God by buying this book (I jest), then we're going to spend quite a lot of time together. Far more importantly, I pray that as we wander and march and meander through the coming days, you'll sense Jesus Himself at your side. As we ponder, ask questions and – who knows – maybe even chuckle once in a while, may you be encouraged and strengthened as you continue your life journey with God.

Travel well, and safe. Come on, let's go.

Jeff Lucas

Jailhouse Rock

Jailhouse Rock

IT WAS a long-haired Larry Norman who wailed 'He's the rock that doesn't roll'. He was talking about Jesus. The song lyric seemed corny then, and cornier now, but it's absolutely true. Paul was living proof that when you're overwhelmed by the tides of life or, to put it as the hymn writer did, 'when sorrows like sea billows roll', then Jesus is the trustworthy, dependable friend: in times of ease and crisis both, He's the Rock. And the Rock was able to get Paul through his days on death row, as his prison correspondence to the Philippians shows. Come with me, and let's ask God to be the immovable foundation in our lives, as we consider Jesus in Philippians – the real Jailhouse Rock.

Refrigerator door theology

MANY Christian refrigerators (if a household appliance can be so described!) are decorated with family photos, calendars, Post-it notes – and popular scriptures. I have seen a huge variety of texts on display. 'God is love' is a firm favourite. But despite my scrutinising hundreds of the fridges of the faithful, I haven't yet seen 'In this world you shall have trouble'. 'Judas went and hanged himself' is even less likely.

I worry lest we spend so much time chopping up scriptures that we miss out on the big picture. As we consider Paul's letter to the Philippians, we must remember that that's what it is – a letter, a complete document in and of itself, and it must be read as such. The fact that it was written in another language and culture means that we must break it down to study and apply it carefully, but let's not rush to the dissection.

That's why I'm asking us to read all four chapters of the letter in one sitting. Don't panic, it's only 104 verses – and during the rest of this first week of our journey together we'll consider a chapter at a time – but this will give us a wide-screen view of the book. Paul and his team had planted the church in Philippi in the early AD 50s (see Acts 16). Now writing from prison, he brings thanks, encouragement and warning to the congregation there, who are struggling with disappointment. It was tough being a Christian in a Roman colony. Paul calls the Philippians to joy, unity – and standing firm. Struggling and nervous about what the New Year might bring? You're not alone.

Prayer: Father, as I begin this journey, broaden my understanding, warm my heart and change my life. Amen.

BIG PICTURE
Philippians 1–4

FOCUS
'Therefore, my brothers, you whom I love and long for, my joy and crown, that is how you should stand firm in the Lord, dear friends!' (Phil. 4:1)

… he brings

thanks,

encouragement

and warning …

God *is* good – all the time

BIG PICTURE
Philippians 1:1–30
Romans 8:28

FOCUS
'Now I want you to know, brothers, that what has happened to me has really served to advance the gospel.' (Phil. 1:12)

… God's

purposes

are being

worked out

I CONFESS to being a little irritated by a practice I've seen among some more 'enthusiastic' churches. A worship leader says (with a little too much gusto) 'God is good', whereupon the congregation holler back 'All the time!' I've got a basic aversion to all hype and cheer-leading and I find this unhelpful. But in the first chapter of Philippians, that's exactly what prisoner Paul is saying. He is in chains because of his faith, yet his emphatic declaration (far more than cheer-leading, because slogans can't survive prison life for too long) is that God is good. Mysteriously, overarching the pain and struggle of Paul's everyday existence, God's purposes are being worked out.

That doesn't make God Paul's jailer, nor the architect of the pain that you might be experiencing right now, but it does mean that, however dark our circumstances, God can bring something good out of them. Dear friends who have recently walked through a lengthy battle with cancer told me how their faith has been nurtured, and they were able to bring comfort to others on the oncology ward. Did God strike them with tumours just to put them in that place of shadows? I don't think so. But the One who calls Himself the Redeemer is able to use even the most awful moments of our journey and turn what was intended for evil around for good.

But it is not only for our good, but for the furtherance of the gospel – about which Paul speaks five times in this chapter – that God works. We're not promised a comfortable ride. But God *is* good. All the time.

Prayer: Lord, You are good, when life isn't. Use the struggles of my life for Your glory, and my growth. Amen.

The way up is down

LAST week I met a man in two completely different locations – and he was Mr Angry in both. Travelling as I do to speak at conferences, I often meet members of what looks like a fraternity of exhibitors and ministries, so faces get familiar. This man was one of those hyper-offended types for whom nothing was right. For some people, it is said the glass is always half empty. For this man, the glass was empty, cracked and full of muck. He tutted, complained, huffed and puffed, and it was obvious that, if he could, he would have blown the house down. I wanted to ask him why he had a life-long commitment to rage. It was clear that despite his Scripture-quoting 'righteous' indignation, he had decided that his wishes were king. Not a great way to win friends and influence people.

In one of the finest Christological passages in the New Testament, Paul shares a stunning portrait of Jesus, the Servant King. But it is not an academic lecture, rather an honest plea for this local church to focus more on Christ – and become like Him.

His example reminds us how we should view and treat others. Selfishness, pride, arrogance and throwing our weight around are ruled out when set alongside the humble King who laid aside His majesty and self-interest to travel the way of the cross. People who live like servants turn heads; their attitude gets noticed and contrasts the grabbing, self-centredness that so often characterises modern living. Do you want to 'make a splash' for God? Serve today.

Prayer: Give me opportunities to notice the needs of others today, Lord, and the resources to help meet those needs. Amen.

BIG PICTURE
**Philippians 2:1–30
Isaiah 53:1–12**

FOCUS
'Your attitude should be the same as that of Christ Jesus.' (Phil. 2:5)

Absolute priority

BIG PICTURE
Philippians 3:1–21
2 Timothy 4:9–11

FOCUS
'Forgetting what is behind and straining towards what is ahead, I press on towards the goal to win the prize for which God has called me heavenwards in Christ Jesus.' (Phil. 3:13–14)

… make

journeying

with Jesus

the main thing

AS I write this, yet again I find myself 36,000 feet up in the air, ensconced on yet another long flight home. Home is very definitely where I'd like to be, having spent the last seven weeks travelling in ministry. But I've noticed, having scanned my diary, that the year ahead is loaded with other journeys: a huge privilege for which I'm grateful. I don't mind going places. I just don't like the hassle of getting there.

In Philippians 3, Paul writes as a seasoned spiritual traveller. Despite the epic journey that he had already taken, from being self-satisfied to throwing himself utterly upon the grace of God to save him, Paul is not done yet. As he continues his trek homeward, he is not ambling along. Twice he uses the term 'pressing on' – and insists that he will not hanker after the past or be distracted in the present. Following Jesus is 'the one thing' that he will do: to be a disciple is Paul's absolute priority.

During this last trip, I bumped into a man who had been my best friend in Bible college days. It was a delightful reunion as we had not seen each other in 15 years. But our time was tinged with a little sadness, as we remembered those fellow students with whom we had laughed and cried, who had professed such determination to make a difference for Christ. Many, sadly, have become disillusioned or distracted, and now are not serving God at all. Our conversation created a fresh resolve in me to finish well for God. Today, make journeying with Jesus the main thing.

Prayer: I want progress in my life today, Lord. Strengthen those around me who are losing heart. Amen.

LIFE is full of surprises – both good and bad. I am sad to confess that I am still stunned when prayer is dramatically answered. I say that I believe Jesus is alive, but then my eyebrows rise when He shows signs of resurrection life. And then, negatively, the Church is often a surprise to me. I expect more grace, more kindness than I often see in practice. And in truth, I am frequently stunned by my own ability to act badly.

Philippians 4 is full of surprising stun grenades. Two women in the church have had a major fallout, and intervention is needed. They have been faithful veterans who have served alongside Paul, so their seething hostility comes as a shock. It's all rather disappointing.

But then Paul offers his own little surprise as he describes himself as a man who is contented. He is languishing in prison, facing a very uncertain future. And at the end of the letter is another shocker (good news again), as Paul reveals that there are disciples even in 'the enemy's camp' – Caesar's household.

Perhaps today you are living in that state of shock because life has served you up something unexpected. When you made those vows, you never saw the gathering clouds. When you joined that church, you had no idea that it would become a hotbed of contention. Bad news has taken your breath away and you're dizzy. Hold steady. Don't panic or react, but pause to be thankful that God is truly bigger than your dilemma. He may yet surprise you with a turn-around, with better news tomorrow.

Prayer: God, today may bring surprises, both good or bad. Fill me with peace when panic threatens. Amen.

Surprise, surprise

BIG PICTURE
**Philippians 4:1–23
Psalm 112:10**

FOCUS
'Do not be anxious about anything, but in everything … present your requests to God. And the peace of God … will guard your hearts and your minds in Christ Jesus.' (Phil. 4:6–7)

Saints alive

When we look at Paul's opening greeting, surely we ask – who are the 'saints'? Obviously there are some who believe that there are a few incredibly gifted and holy people who deserve that name – although according to church tradition, you can't be deemed a saint while you're still alive. But the Bible does not use the term 'saints' in that sense at all. As Paul addresses himself to the saints in Philippi, and he uses that term four times in Philippians (and many other times in his other letters), he is referring to all of us ordinary Christians who are set apart for God's use. Just as there were holy objects in the Old Testament that were sanctified (set apart) for God's purposes, so the saints are all those who have determined that their one life on earth will be spent making themselves available to the purposes of God. Sainthood is not something we attain: we *are* saints.

The term 'saint' relates to the dynamic relationship with God that you and I enjoy, and our entire ambition in life – to be available to and used by God. Let's live like saints today.

Let's live like
saints today

Friends and partners

BIG PICTURE
Philippians 1:3–8
Proverbs 27:9–11

FOCUS
'In all my prayers for
all of you, I always pray
with joy because of your
partnership in the gospel
from the first day
until now.' (Phil. 1:4)

LAST week I mentioned my bumping into a long-lost friend who had been my closest companion during my Bible college days. I found a photograph of the two of us together back then. We were dressed in the hideous fashions of the 1970s: I had hair (he still does) – and the lovely photograph shows us both laughing out loud. It captured a moment of real joy in what was a fairly confusing season of my life.

Most human beings are on a life-long safari, avidly hunting the happiness which too often eludes us. Perhaps we fantasise about happiness coming our way if we could just retire early (perhaps before we're 20!) and relocate to a beach somewhere. But as Paul celebrates joy – a consistent theme throughout this letter – he reveals one of the sources of his bubbling attitude of wellbeing – his friendship with his friends in Philippi. Their partnership – the word is sometimes translated 'fellowship' – was substantial. Sometimes the word 'fellowship' is used to describe the superficial small talk over a post-service cup of tea. This was so much more.

Theirs was a robust working relationship, which had cost the Philippians dearly as they had given financially to help Paul in his work. In fact, he says the church there had given 'again and again when I was in need' (Phil. 4:16).

I've discovered that friendship makes me rich. Whatever other blessings we might enjoy, there are few to compare with the easy laughter, the shared tears or the delightful chatter of true, veteran friends. Want joy? Invest in what really matters. Make friends.

Prayer: Father, bless those whom I call friends. Make me a better friend: thank You for the joy of friendship. Amen.

How to pray for those you love

BIG PICTURE
Philippians 1:9–11
Acts 16:12–40

FOCUS
'… so that you may be able to discern what is best and may be pure and blameless until the day of Christ.' (Phil. 1:10)

OK, it's confession time. Sometimes I have been guilty of assuring people that I would remember them in my prayers – only to quickly forget that I have made that promise. Does that happen to you? A friend of mine is currently on a sugar fast, to remind him to specifically pray for a friend who has asked him for his support through some personal difficulties. Now a friend like that is certainly worth his weight in gold.

Paul prayed consistently for those he loved, and a great deal can be learnt from his prayers (Eph. 1:17–23; 3:14–21; Col. 1:9–12). But his prayer for his friends in Philippi is especially enlightening. The Philippian church was composed of a mixed group of people, including wealthy Lydia, the jailer, the slave girl (all found in Acts 16) and other believers, mostly Gentiles.

So how did Paul pray for such a mixed group? He asked that they might grow in love – a familiar prayer. And then he prays for wisdom and insight – that they might know right from wrong – surely that is what causes relationships and indeed entire cultures to survive or crash. The concept of 'discernment' is connected with testing metal to see if it is genuine. That ability to make the right choices throughout life – 'until the day of Christ' – is what secures our legacy. What shall we leave behind when we're gone – the 'fruit of righteousness' – or the bitter harvest of thoughtlessness? Let's pray for the good choices today and the legacy tomorrow for those we love.

Paul prayed consistently for those he loved …

Prayer: Make me a praying person. Show me how to pray both for those I love and those I struggle with. Amen.

Influence through suffering

BIG PICTURE
**Philippians 1:12–14
1 Corinthians 10:11**

FOCUS
'Because of my chains, most of the brothers in the Lord have been encouraged to speak the word of God more courageously and fearlessly.' (Phil. 1:14)

MOST of us live under the impression that it is only the 'powerful' who have influence. But we're wrong. When Paul writes his words of loving encouragement to his friends at Philippi, he is living a life that he would not have chosen, denied freedom by those who held him in chains under house arrest. But rather than dwelling on his circumstances, he celebrates the wonderful result that has come because of them – his guards know that he loves Jesus and other Christians have been strengthened by his inspirational life.

Those who navigate their way through suffering inspire us the most. In 2006, a good friend and colleague, actor Rob Lacey, died after a long battle with cancer. His funeral was packed and, at the conclusion of the service, the congregation spontaneously jumped to their feet and gave a resounding standing ovation as the coffin was taken down the aisle. Rob's gritty, honest faithfulness was his greatest performance, and he earned the applause of both earth and heaven. I feel encouraged and galvanised by the legacy that Rob left behind. He breasted the tape in the race that is life, and his example makes me want to do the same. So it was with Paul – far from being terrified by his imprisonment, his steady perseverance inspired others around him to greater boldness.

Ultimately we live today for an audience of one. Yet let's remember that our choices can depress and disappoint others, or inspire and motivate them. The world – and the Church – is desperate for positive role models. Paul was able to say, 'Follow my example.' Let's live the same way today.

Prayer: I know my choices motivate or discourage others, Lord. Help me to inspire others today – for Your glory. Amen.

So what?

BIG PICTURE
**Philippians 1:15–18
Mark 9:38–41**

FOCUS
'But what does it matter?
The important thing is
that in every way, whether
from false motives or
true, Christ is preached.
And because of this I
rejoice.' (Phil. 1:18)

WHEN you really care about something, you can want to take possession of it as your own. That's why so many churches are debilitated by conflict; they are filled with people who care just a little too much about what goes on. The apathetic can't be bothered to fuss – show me a passionate church, and there you'll find a perfect environment for a fight to break out.

Paul is incredibly passionate about the message of the Christian gospel – so much was it a part of him, he even calls it 'my' gospel, on three occasions in his writings (Rom. 2:16; 16:25; 2 Tim. 2:8).

But despite this, he refuses to take possession of the message in a controlling way, like someone who feels that they alone have the franchise to operate with authority. Even though some are preaching the gospel for selfish motives – and even doing so because they want to 'stir up trouble' for Paul – the apostle shrugs his shoulders. With the light touch of a truly magnanimous man, he effectively says 'So what?' or, more precisely, 'What does it matter?'

Not only do we learn that not everything has to be done our way in order to be right, but we could also emulate that delightfully carefree attitude which says everything doesn't have to matter. I've met Christians who want to make a court case out of every issue: 'it has to be *right*' is their motto for life. But our own emotional wellbeing would improve, if we'd just learn to lighten up a little. Don't make every issue a crusade. Chill out. Paul did.

Prayer: Lord, show me what really matters – and save me from caring too much about what doesn't matter at all.

Don't make every

issue a crusade

A positive outlook – about ourselves

BIG PICTURE
**Philippians 1:19–21
Job 13:1–16**

FOCUS
'I eagerly expect and hope that I … will have sufficient courage so that now as always Christ will be exalted in my body, whether by life or by death.' (Phil. 1:20)

I'VE recently been wondering: do I expect the worst of myself? There are some people who always see the clouds, but never a silver lining. For them, the light at the end of the tunnel is attached to an oncoming train. But I'm not just talking about a negative outlook about life, but taking a pessimistic attitude towards ourselves.

Speaking at a marriage retreat, I asked the question, 'How many of you think that, sooner or later, you are going to make a horrible mistake and that adultery or some other sin is going to destroy your marriage?' Many people assured me that this was indeed their fear. Perhaps we are too well acquainted with the dark thoughts that sometimes stomp their way through the tiny corridors of our minds, and therefore believing the worst of ourselves is all too easy.

But Paul was almost jaunty about the way he would face his dangerously uncertain future. Yet this was no 'it will all turn out all right' glibness. Rather, like Job, he felt that somehow God was going to get him through and give him enough courage, even if he had to lose his life for the sake of the gospel.

If we think that we are programmed for inevitable failure, surely this will weaken us when testing times come. If we convince ourselves that we are doomed to be one of those who finishes life badly, then we probably will fulfil our own negative prophecy. Why don't we practise an attitude of hopeful expectation, and dream and plan of great things done for God's glory?

God got Paul through. And He can do the very same for us.

Prayer: Lord, save me from self-reliance, but grant me a confidence in You, and in Your work in me. Amen.

Ready to go, ready to stay

It's confession time again. Paul's words here tower over me, making me feel inadequate. As he happily celebrates his complete surrender to God, and is willing to live or die, I feel bowed by intimidation – for one very good reason. I can't say Amen to his willing boldness. In truth, I believe that Christ has conquered the power of death, but I have absolutely no desire to die today. The threat of death would send me into a screaming fight for survival.

Before you join me in my cringing, think again. Paul had a sense of completeness about his life and mission. He was hardly living an easy existence, a man in chains. Perhaps, when you feel that you have done your job on this earth, and everyday life becomes a chore, then maybe you're more ready for the home that is life forever with Jesus. I've talked to older people who have lived wonderfully, but are now tormented by pain, and eager to be reunited with loved ones who have gone before: they share Paul's contented ambivalence.

In the meantime, get over that guilt trip that smothers you because you don't have a divinely-fuelled death wish today.

… Christ has conquered the power of death …

20

AT FIRST glance it almost seems a little pompous or even arrogant – the fact that Paul so openly let the Philippians know that his staying on earth would be such a source of joy to them. It sounds like a man walking into a party and greeting the guests there with a smug, 'Hi everyone, you must be delighted to see me. Now I've arrived, the party can really begin. The fun starts here!'

Paul knew that he was speaking the absolute truth: his teaching, lifestyle and encouragement had proved to be a vital contribution to the development of the faith of the Philippian church. His was no idle boast. Do we have a similar selfless ambition – to be a source of joy to others and to serve their needs? Are we a channel of delight to others or a source of frustration to them? The sight of some people brings a smile to my face as soon as I see them coming. Others create a response of weariness in me. I know that their arrival heralds another probable complaint, a tetchy comment or a negative conversation that will invariably be a struggle.

Today, we can be a blessing or a curse to others. We can cheer them on or drag them down. Let's not just amble through the day, the hapless victims of our own moodiness or whatever circumstances the coming hours will bring. Let's decide that we might be the reason for a deeply felt smile today. And more than that, may everyone around us grow in faith today – even those who currently profess no faith at all.

Prayer: Lord, make me a bringer of joy and strength to those I meet today. May I bless and build. Amen.

A cause for joy

BIG PICTURE
**Philippians 1:25–26
2 Timothy 1:3–7**

FOCUS
'… I will continue with all of you for your progress and joy in the faith.' (Phil. 1:25)

Living the gospel

BIG PICTURE
Philippians 1:27–28
Romans 12:1–2

FOCUS
'Whatever happens, conduct yourselves in a manner worthy of the gospel of Christ.'
(Phil. 1:27)

AS AN army cadet in my youth (I was promoted to sergeant because of my big mouth and my skill in telling others what to do: some things never change) I was once injured during some military exercises. To be more specific, I was shot in the rear end by an enthusiastic youth. Apparently I was so well camouflaged, he didn't notice me, hence my uncomfortable and sudden awakening. I've been wondering lately if I stand out any better now. Am I so keen not to be viewed as a weird Jesus freak that I live a life that looks no different to anyone else's?

Philippi was a proud town. Founded by Caesar Augustus with the special privilege of what was called *jus Italicum*, it was considered to be a miniature Rome, even though it was but a colony. The result of this was that the atmosphere of the city was totally Roman and the citizens who lived there were bursting with pride at their lofty status. Later in this letter, Paul reminds his Christian friends that they have a loftier calling as those who have 'citizenship in heaven' (Phil. 3:20). Here he calls them to live up to that incredible calling; they are to conduct themselves as those who live in a colony, not of Rome, but of heaven. The term, 'conduct yourselves' could be translated 'live as citizens'.

So what of us? Are we so desperate to fit in that we're more concerned about being citizens of our culture than citizens of God's kingdom? Are you a Christian but no one notices?

Prayer: Save me from the temptation to blend in. May I be aligned to Your will, not ruled by the crowd. Amen.

… live up to that incredible calling …

Counting the cost

I'VE been challenged this week as I've read about the practices of our Christian ancestors who lived in the period between AD 200–300. Stifle that yawn because I'm not about to bore you with endless historical detail that has nothing to do with your Wednesday, but here's the headline: back then, becoming a Christian involved a long and careful process. At any time, if you decided that 'The Way' (as Christianity was called back then) was not for you, because the price was too high or you didn't feel able to commit yourself for any reason, then you could withdraw with honour. Just as Jesus taught that the decision to follow should involve 'counting the cost', so those who stood for Christ 1,800 years ago did so as a result of a thoughtful, calculated decision.

The problem with quick, emotional choices is that they don't last – whether that involves a quick Las Vegas marriage or a decision to become a disciple of Jesus Christ. Peter was told by Jesus that the end of his life would be far from comfortable, but he was invited to still follow Christ, with the full knowledge of the perilous future that lay ahead. He was under no illusions: his good choices today would cost him his freedom and his life tomorrow.

Perhaps you've reached a stage in your life when knowing Christ is costing you dearly. Friends and loved ones misunderstand you. Work colleagues mock your faith and your moral choices. You feel alone right now, swimming upstream against the tide.

So now what? Will you still follow Him, now that the pressure is on?

Prayer: Help me to reaffirm my vows of love and loyalty to You, on this very day, whatever it brings. Amen.

BIG PICTURE
Philippians 1:29–30
Luke 14:25–35

FOCUS
'For it has been granted to you on behalf of Christ not only to believe on him, but also to suffer for him …' (Phil. 1:29)

Don't stand out for the sake of it

BIG PICTURE
Philippians 2:1–2
3 John 1–9

FOCUS
'… make my joy complete by being like-minded, having the same love, being one in spirit and purpose.' (Phil. 2:2)

SHOPPING in the supermarket yesterday, I noticed a child who was desperate to be noticed by his long-suffering mother. He screamed at a volume usually associated with a passing jumbo jet, stamped his feet and turned so red in the face, he looked like a beetroot with legs.

Have you ever met people who always have a different opinion from the consensus? Whatever the prevailing decision is, they challenge it. Perhaps I'm describing *you*. You are proud of what you have decided is your independent thinking, your refusal to go along with the crowd.

But sometimes our 'independence' is actually thinly veiled insecurity. There are times when we take issue with the consensus, simply because we are desperate to be seen, and our way of drawing attention to ourselves is to shout as loud as we can. I've met people who think that they are being principled, when in fact they just love the sound of their own voices or are opinionated. How can we tell whether we are staunch defenders of principle or just obnoxiously arrogant? The twin abilities to listen humbly and discuss lovingly would be two signs.

While we shouldn't go along with everyone else for the sake of peace and quiet, we can have the opposite programme – being different so as to be noticed. So if you are currently embroiled in a fight to the death over a principle that you hold dear, think again: are you standing for truth, or stomping your feet in a strop, because you 'love to be first' (3 John 1–9)? Sometimes the ability to be like-minded is a true sign of mature character.

… the ability to be like-minded is a true sign of mature character

Prayer: Father, show me when I am campaigning, not over principle, but because of a need to be seen. Amen.

THIS week, my wife Kay sprang a delightful surprise for my birthday and organised a visit to famous super-chef Jamie Oliver's London restaurant, *Fifteen*. We were there for just a moment or two when the famous lad himself walked in. I watched as he then spent the next 30 minutes greeting and shaking hands with his staff. His winning smile and easy manner were an obvious source of encouragement to them: he was showing all the signs of a terrific leader, in his practice of including and empowering others. There was not a hint of celebrity-fuelled haughtiness but rather a natural humility.

Humility is a much misunderstood character trait. There are those who think that being humble means to adopt an attitude where we choose to become a doormat for everyone else to walk over or we cannot accept praise for an accomplishment. Worse still, there are those who think that self-deprecating comments are a sign of authentic humility: but a grovelling approach to life, where we are eager to put ourselves down (strangely, sometimes in the hope that others will build us up) is not true humility.

Humility is about the way we approach others as well as the way we view ourselves. Humility calls us to realise that we are not the centre of the universe; as we are liberated to consider others, we can delight in their strengths, rather than be depressed by forever staring at the horizon of self.

Our lives are loaded with people who are delightful examples of the grace of God. Let's notice others today, and surrender our relentless preoccupation with ourselves.

Prayer: Lord, open my eyes, that I might see others today. Save me from the obsessive need to be seen. Amen.

Considering others

BIG PICTURE
**Philippians 2:3
John 15:12–17**

FOCUS
'… in humility consider others better than yourselves.' (Phil. 2:3)

Living unselfishly

Picking up on our thoughts about selfishness yesterday, we hear Paul exhorting us, not only to *notice* each other, but also to be aware of the concerns of others as well as all the 'stuff' that constitutes our own existence. Allowing myself to be challenged by these words, I confess that too often I am preoccupied. The pressing deadline, the appointment that I'm late for or the project that I'm working on so fills my mind, that I can actually become 'self' occupied. And by my body language, my words and even the look in my eyes, I can communicate that what I'm in is so much more important than the challenges of others that I bump into. It's an art to dismiss what screams at us with urgency, in order to focus on caring for people we meet, but it's a skill that we can and should learn.

Lately I've been trying to close down the 'windows' of my mind before I meet people. Just as my computer takes a few moments to shut down, so I try to shut off pressing distractions so that I can give full attention to people I meet – and do that for their sake, not for mine. Sometimes I succeed, sometimes I fail. How about you?

It's an art to dismiss what screams at us with urgency …

Distant theology or practical servanthood?

BIG PICTURE
**Philippians 2:5–11
Matthew 23:11–12**

FOCUS
'Your attitude should be the same as that of Christ Jesus.' (Phil. 2:5)

LOOKING at what Christ accomplished on the cross, we watch His faithfulness with amazement: the huge distance that He travelled, from the throne of heaven to that vile cross, is the greatest distance covered in history. But we are wrong to simply 'survey the wondrous cross', as if that is enough. Paul calls on his friends in Philippi to emulate Jesus' servant attitude, not just to admire it. In words that were probably an early hymn, Paul captures the incredible selflessness of Christ but then delivers the knockout punch: those who follow Him should determine to live their lives in the same way.

Servanthood is not just a matter of disposition but comes as the result of good, godly choices. Sometimes we can excuse ourselves by saying that we are not naturally meek; but Jesus, who had 'all authority', determined to put the needs of the world before His own comfort. He *made Himself* nothing. Servanthood is not about acting with false humility or stooping to snivelling that we are useless and worthless. Rather, being a servant is about making a daily choice to place the needs of others before our own. One of the challenges, of course, is that you only find out if you truly are a servant when people treat you like one: that doesn't feel so comfortable. But what a contrast we will be, when we refuse to live the 'grabbing' life and let go of that in order to bring blessing to others. What do you grasp that you need to let go of, in order to serve?

Prayer: Lord, please show me where I am clutching what I need to let go of. Amen.

God & Son (& Spirit) – restoration specialists

BIG PICTURE
Philippians 2:12–13
Jude 24–25

FOCUS
' … it is God who works in you to will and to act according to his good purpose.' (Phil. 2:13)

I BEGAN today with a major panic. My life is filled with labour-saving technology, which means that I have a large collection of gizmos that would save me time, if only I had the time to read the instructions. My whole life is on my palm pilot, which contains my diary, address book and a satellite navigation system that tells where I went wrong when I get lost. But I forgot to charge it and if it's left without power for more than a couple of days, its memory gives up and dumps all my information. With trembling hands I plugged the little machine into the power socket, hoping against hope that all was not lost.

It's useless without power. And so are we. Christianity is far more than a wonderful set of ethics to live by; we are called to live God's way in God's power. As we make good choices – 'working out our salvation' – so God's grace meets us – 'God who works in you to will and to act according to his good purpose'. It's a wonderful surprise to discover that there's a force within that nudges us to decide what is good, despite beckoning temptations.

If you're anything like me, you will have been deeply challenged by the teaching about selflessness and being a servant that we've considered. But here is some good news. We're not in the rebuilding business alone: God is committed to making us the way He wants us to be. Join me as I ask God that we will know the filling of the Holy Spirit. Power changes everything. And my palm-top memory didn't die.

Prayer: Work in me, Spirit of God. Transform my heart, and mould my life. I submit to You. Amen.

Power changes

everything

Being a real star

BIG PICTURE
**Philippians 2:14–16
Matthew 5:14**

FOCUS
'… children of God
without fault in a
crooked and depraved
generation, in which you
shine like stars in the
universe.' (Phil. 2:15)

AS I write this, I am staying in the home of some friends who have a house that backs onto a school playground. The windows are open, the birds are singing and I'd love to report that I'm enjoying the happy sound of children playing. But that's not true. Over the last 30 minutes, I've heard just about every swearword that's ever been invented yelled and screamed in what has been a cacophony of obscenity. The kick-around of a football has turned into an excuse for a verbal blood-letting. Without sounding like the proverbial disgusted of Tunbridge Wells, it seems like our culture is rapidly rotting; values like respect and good manners seem antiquated. And let's not rush to pick on the young: business people on trains, 'responsible people', often join in the litany of obscenities. In one sense none of this is new, as Paul described the culture of his day as 'a crooked and depraved generation'. But what remains true is the call to us as followers of Christ to stand out – to shine like stars is the encouragement.

The call for us to be culturally relevant as Christians is not the full story. Putting it bluntly, we are supposed to be as obvious as the stars in the clear night sky, living lives that are as welcoming as a bright city on a hill, a wonderful sight to a weary traveller. Our attitudes, speech, responses to conflict and commitment to purity should enable us to live 'lighthouse lives' that show the way to a world that is floundering on the rocks.

Prayer: May Your life and love be obvious in me today – a light in the darkness. Amen.

Commitment

Philippians 2:17–18
Numbers 28:1–7

FOCUS
'… I am being poured out
like a drink offering …'
(Phil. 2:17)

HUGE discussions have taken place about British workplaces being hit by sickness epidemics whenever major sporting events happen. Apparently World or European Cup Football or Wimbledon signal a flurry of 'sick notes' as thousands stay at home to 'recover' in front of the television. Employers are frustrated at the lack of commitment or concern that too many demonstrate towards their work.

We can have a similar attitude when it comes to the 'work' of the church and our commitment, in broader terms, to be followers of Jesus each day. We can drift into a take-it-or-leave-it attitude where our support and loyalty can never be counted on. We'll use any excuse not to bother: holiness is a path we take only if we feel so inclined. Even marriage has become disposable. While some marriages do break down irretrievably, we've drifted into a culture where some change their marriage partners like cars, a new model always being more exciting.

Being a Christian takes work and sometimes we act out of faithfulness rather than feelings. Paul uses a familiar metaphor (2 Tim. 4:6) borrowed from the Jewish sacrificial system (Num. 28:1–7). His struggle and imprisonment and the price that he and the Philippians are paying because they name Jesus as their Lord is likened to a 'drink offering' – poured out before God.

Our good choices are primarily made as acts of worship – whether others around us applaud is secondary. And there are some things in life worth making sacrifices for. Today is another day of a life of worship for us. Let's not fob God off with a sick note.

Today is another day of a life of worship for us

Prayer: Help me to choose well, not because I feel so inclined but because I know I should. Amen.

'HE – OR she – is a real character.' That's a term normally used to describe someone who has a high-impact personality. I meet lots of people as I travel and as an avid student of humanity, I love to meet people who are strikingly different. I enjoy the so-called eccentrics who refuse to graze with the herd: their special interests, their outspoken opinions and their bizarre behaviour make them 'real characters'. But what would we like to be known for? What would we hope might be the most striking feature of our lives?

Paul writes about a young friend and companion in ministry, Timothy, and his affectionate description shows us that selflessness is a rare quality. It makes a person truly stand out as special. So it is with Timothy who, Paul says, is of such quality that he has 'no-one else like him'.

Paul was not being overly negative when he summarised the way life usually goes – everyone looks out for their own interests. But Timothy, through his genuine care and concern for others and with his unwavering loyalty not only to Jesus but also to his mentor Paul, had shown that he was truly one of a kind.

Sometimes selfishness becomes our normal pattern of life. Not because of great wickedness but because a busy, demanding life sucks us into a pattern of self-absorption where we don't have the time to notice the needs of others and don't have the energy to meet those needs either. Let's slow down enough to care. 'Looking out' for others: that's real character.

Prayer: My interests seem to monopolise my attention, Lord. Break my selfish gaze and develop true, caring character in me. Amen.

A real character

BIG PICTURE
**Philippians 2:19–20
Ruth 3:1–11**

FOCUS
'I have no-one else like him, who takes a genuine interest in your welfare.'
(Phil. 2:20)

Proven

He was 17, carried a Bible big enough to build significant arm muscles and was insistent that he wanted to do exactly what I do – preach, teach and write. I encouraged the eager young man and remembered with gratitude those who, years ago, took massive risks with me as they gave me opportunities, unsure whether I was up to them.

But I also reminded him that Scripture teaches that gifts emerge gradually and the recognition of others is vital. Sometimes Christians hotfoot it home from the latest conference, insistent that they 'have a ministry', but are unwilling to invest carefully in the preparation or development of their gifts. And some are indignant when others want to offer an opinion about whether the gift or calling is really there. I've heard too many Christian songs that 'the Lord gave' the singer and wondered if maybe the Lord hadn't wanted those songs in the first place …

Timothy had proved himself through his hard work and willingness to keep going, when life proved tough. He was utterly trusted by Paul, who knew his life. Tread carefully when you think you 'have a ministry'.

Tread
carefully …

What do people catch from us?

BIG PICTURE
Philippians 2:25–27
1 Thessalonians 3:1–2

FOCUS
'For he longs for all of
you and is distressed
because you heard he
was ill.' (Phil. 2:26)

I'VE noticed that attitudes are catching. Travelling on a recent flight, I realised that the purser – the senior flight attendant – set a wonderful example with her warm, caring attentiveness and engaging smile. One or two of her crew had begun the flight looking mildly irritated and disinterested, perhaps because of exhaustion, but as the long trip continued, they began to emulate her winning ways, and kindness spread through the plane like a positive virus. The passengers were more polite than usual, too. Without giving the impression that the plane turned into a grinning *Pleasantville*, it certainly was a nice place to be – and all because of the good attitude of someone with influence. Of course the reverse is true: anyone who has worked in an office knows that habits are catching. Where carelessness, lack of punctuality or off-colour humour go unchallenged for long enough, soon the culture will be detrimentally affected as sloppiness becomes the norm.

The Philippians were so concerned about Paul's welfare, they sent Epaphroditus to look after him. And then when Epaphroditus falls ill, far from worrying about himself, he is concerned what effect the news of his illness will have on those who have sent him. Paul also speaks of how the death of Epaphroditus would have created 'sorrow upon sorrow' for him. There is a lot of unselfishness flying around here …

A culture of genuine selflessness and care had developed – a wonderful place to be. So if attitudes are toxic – for good and for ill – what viral effect will you and I have today?

Prayer: Father, as Timothy strengthened others' faith, may I be a source of Your life and love today. Amen.

Honour

BIG PICTURE
Philippians 2:28–30
John 15:13

FOCUS
'Welcome him in the
Lord with great joy, and
honour men like him,
because he almost died
for the work of Christ,
risking his life …'
(Phil. 2:29–30)

I ENJOY eavesdropping on other people's conversations – and so does Kay. Sometimes when we go out, we don't actually talk – we just tune in to everybody else's chat! We were sitting in a restaurant in Dover, when we noticed a group of older gentlemen, probably in their 80s, bidding each other goodbye. It was obvious that they had been long-term companions and I listened in. They were members of the same British Army regiment that had defended the white cliffs of Dover during the Second World War. This was their annual reunion; obviously, their numbers were gradually going down.

I seized my moment and approached one of the men who had got up to refill his coffee cup. I confessed to listening in and then spoke a simple sentence to honour him and his comrades. 'Sometimes my generation hasn't been too good at honouring you for the great sacrifices you made, sir,' I said. 'So I wanted to say a simple thank you.' His eyes shone, we chatted for some minutes and when he got back to his table, he shared our conversation with his friends, to their delight.

The art of honouring has been lost in our culture. I'm not talking about the fawning that goes on around so-called celebrities or the near religious adulation – and vilification – of sports heroes. But as Paul goes out of his way to ensure that the faithful Epaphroditus will be honoured and welcomed – he had literally gambled his life for the gospel – so we learn to offer deep respect to others. It usually costs little, but is priceless.

Prayer: Grant me the opportunity to give thanks and honour to whom honour is due. Amen.

The art of

honouring has

been lost in

our culture

TODAY, I'm asking that we pause for a moment to reflect on our journey over the last month. The psalmist uses a word, 'Selah', which most commentators believe means 'Stop and think about it'. Let's do the same as we consider Paul's inspirational words to the church at Philippi. As we do, I realise that just about everything that we have learned about life from popular thinking is wrong. Paul's words are loaded with surprises.

We have learned that pain and suffering don't mean that God is distant or dead; that the way to really make your mark is to serve. We drew breath as we saw that contentment is possible in the most harrowing of circumstances, that it is relationships, not cash in hand, that make us truly rich. Most importantly for us passionate-about-principle Christians, we saw that there are times when we just need to lighten up and follow Paul's easygoing attitude to his opponents who were preaching the gospel. We realised that radical living doesn't happen as we proverbially stand on our own two feet but that God's mighty power is ready to meet us as we make good choices. We saw the essence of true character: looking out for the interests of others, a rare commodity. And ultimately, we saw that Jesus is not only our Saviour but our example.

Take time to allow those verses to wash over you again. Don't be tempted merely to add their content to your information bank, but pray that God will make their surprising callings a reality in your life.

Prayer: May what I have learned be transferred from my head to my heart and into my lifestyle. Amen.

Remembering

BIG PICTURE
Philippians 1–2

FOCUS
'Your attitude should be the same as that of Christ Jesus.' (Phil. 2:5)

How many times?

BIG PICTURE
**Philippians 3:1–2
2 Timothy 3:1–9**

FOCUS
'Finally, my brothers, rejoice in the Lord! It is no trouble for me to write the same things to you again, and it is a safeguard for you.'
(Phil. 3:1)

IT'S a mantra often trotted out by frustrated parents: 'How many times have I told you?' Sometimes God must feel the same exasperation. History not only repeats itself but, all too often, trouble is caused in our lives by the same tired old problems that just keep resurfacing over and over – yet they still cause devastation each time they arise. The Early Church repeatedly had to battle with a recurring virus of false teaching; so it is that Paul takes a 'better safe than sorry' approach and addresses the so-called 'circumcision' party.

The first believers were Jews who had turned to Christ and as they sought to spread the good news, they found it difficult to know how to approach those outside the Jewish fold (note Acts 10) – it was some time before a true mission to Gentiles began (Acts 11:20). Paul believed that if Gentiles turned to the Lord they were to be accepted as members of God's people, without having to become Jews, so he didn't demand that the men should be circumcised. There were Jewish Christians, however, in Antioch (Acts 15:1) and in Galatia, who insisted that these Gentile Christians should become Jews. The Jerusalem Council of Acts 15 was called and Paul wrote his letter to the Galatians to deal with the same issue. Yet years later this was still a problem: religious ideas that are an attack on grace seem to circulate and take hold so easily.

As we hear Paul treading the same ground again, are there issues in our lives that God has already specifically and clearly addressed?

Prayer: Father, help me to learn and move forward. Save me from falling into the same old snares. Amen.

… are there issues

in our lives that

God has already

… addressed?

SOME of us Christians are so nice that we actually rarely tell the truth. We confuse meekness with blandness, seem incapable of holding an opinion and would go to almost any lengths to avoid confrontation. Paul was obviously not one of those drippy types. He was so angry with those who pressed for Gentiles to become Jews that he called them *dogs*, the derogatory name that Jews gave to Gentiles. These people liked to prowl round the Christian congregations, seeking to win Gentile converts over to Judaism. With their growling and mumbling, they were 'evil workers' (RSV), turning people aside from truth and freedom (Matt. 23:15; 2 Cor. 11:13; Gal. 1:7–9). Because circumcision had no spiritual value, they were just *mutilators of the flesh* and Paul expressed a hope that they might go the whole way and actually castrate themselves: hardly a warm pastoral comment …

So was Paul just being rude, calling a spade a spade? I don't think so. He rightly insisted that the freedom bought for us by the sacrifice of Christ on the cross, should be rigorously defended. Often we hesitate to call legalism what it is, lest we offend those who create their endless lists of human regulations; but when we tiptoe around or refuse to speak out, innocent believers are held in religious chains. Those who declare war on legalistic religion, are usually accused of being woolly liberals and told that they should keep silent in the interests of 'unity'. But, as Paul's robust example shows, some issues absolutely demand that we make our voices heard and risk whatever accusations might follow.

Prayer: Save me from blandness that disguises itself as kindness. Help me to be a person of loving conviction. Amen.

Beware the dogs

BIG PICTURE
Philippians 3:2–3
Galatians 1:6–9

FOCUS
'Watch out for those dogs, those men who do evil, those mutilators of the flesh.' (Phil. 3:2)

Religious superstition

I have a vivid memory from my childhood of a furtive little procedure that I would go through on the few occasions that I went into a church building. Somewhat overawed by the musty smells, the pristine altar and the shadows created by flickering candles, I would cross myself, quickly, hoping that my parents hadn't noticed. Looking back, it was an act of superstition rather than devotion. I hoped to be in God's good books so felt that a little religious gesturing wouldn't go amiss. I didn't have any relationship with God at all: my practice was little more than the rubbing of a religious rabbit's foot.

Paul summarises his impressive religious credentials and history – and unceremoniously lobs them all into a skip. Any of us who take confidence in our family background, in the religious ceremonies that we have gone through or in our commitment to moral goodness, will be seriously disappointed as we hear Paul insist on putting his hope and trust in Christ alone.

Today, we are saved exclusively and totally by Jesus Christ. He has done it all: all we can do is gladly be beneficiaries of His magnificent sacrifice. Worship Him – and junk any false hope or confidence.

Worship
Him …

A PROFIT and loss statement can make sobering reading. When companies publish their annual reports, stockholders and the markets wait with baited breath for the results – did they come out 'in the black'?

Paul is able to publish the interim report of his life freely and to consider his enormous losses: his reputation, livelihood and his place of respect as a senior Jewish leader – all these are gone. Humanly speaking, he is bankrupt, having 'lost all things'.

But then Paul considers his gains – and they are quite marvellous because he is able to report that he knows Christ. These words, familiar as they are to us, call for another look. These are not the words of a man who has signed up for a mild dose of religion. Rather, he is privileged to affirm that he has now found the source and the answer to life; that his purpose has been set; his ambitions fixed, in a wonderful relationship that is so fabulous, all other contenders for his affections pale into insignificance by comparison. He has discovered the very essence of what life on earth is all about: our time spent connected to the Creator of it all, living His way, in friendship with Him.

If we share Paul's appraisal of what is truly priceless, then we will make sure that our lifestyles reflect our priorities. We can worry and sweat our way through our days, forever chasing what is a mirage, desperate for 'bread that doesn't satisfy' (Isa. 55:2). Or we can join Paul and decide what really matters – and what is just rubbish.

Prayer: Lord, help me live for what matters and bid farewell to what I must lose as I gain Christ. Amen.

Paul's primary agenda

BIG PICTURE
Philippians 3:7–9
John 17:2–4

FOCUS
'… I consider everything a loss compared to the surpassing greatness of knowing Christ Jesus my Lord, for whose sake I have lost all things.'
(Phil. 3:8)

Thoughtless words

BIG PICTURE
Philippians 3:10–11
Luke 14:28–33

FOCUS
'I want to know Christ
and the power of his
resurrection and the
fellowship of sharing in
his sufferings …'
(Phil. 3:10)

YEARS ago, I stood at the front of a church, and exchanged marriage vows. I recall that the minister, as part of the ceremony, warned us that the promises we were making 'should not be entered into lightly'. His words were more than just a part of the liturgy: they were a solemn warning that we should not just be moved by the beauty of the day or the romantic atmosphere. We were making real promises.

I'm worried that there are times when we rush to affirm promises to God that we haven't taken time to think through seriously. More than once recently, I have found myself choosing silence rather than song because I was nervous about rushing to declare something with my heart that my head hadn't been able to process. And I have found myself reticent about rushing to respond to a stirring sermon, wanting to weigh up the possible results of my making a vow to God (Eccl. 5:5–6).

As we hear Paul announce his desire and determination to suffer with Christ, I find myself backing away once more and being slow to add an amen to his words. But Paul knew what he had signed up for (Acts 9:16). From the beginning of his Christian life, suffering had been a major part of his experience.

Jesus taught a thoughtful approach in His teaching about tower building and battlefield tactics. That isn't to say that enthusiasm and moments of decision should not be a part of our gatherings; but let's also make space for reflection so that our vows are real and considered.

Prayer: Save me from hasty words and vows, where I offer what I have never properly considered. Amen.

… make space

for reflection …

IT MUST be the sobering occasion of a 50th birthday, once an impossible date on the distant horizon, now very much here, but I've been thinking more about retirement. Whatever our 'day' job, in some sense Christians never step aside from actively serving God. We may choose a change in pattern in our working schedule and certainly we may drop our swift march through life to a more relaxed amble, but none of us can ever say that God's purposes for us are over.

If anyone might have been tempted to rest on their laurels, it was Paul. He was a seasoned veteran who had planted and nurtured churches, who had given himself tirelessly to the development and mentoring of others. Paul had proven his loyalty to Christ by his willingness to languish on what, for all he knew, was death row. And yet Paul, having done so much, was not done yet and still was in hot pursuit of the headline life-purpose that Jesus had called him to. Putting it bluntly, he wanted to grab that for which God had grabbed him.

The sad truth is that more people begin the Christian race than finish it. Like the Galatians, who 'began well' we can surge down the track as new Christians, powered by the joy of new discovery and unhindered by the bone-aching weariness that disillusionment and cynicism brings. We make great strides but then settle down and sometimes, ultimately, totally drop out of the Christian journey.

Whatever miles we have covered, let's commit to joining Paul in his determination to breast the tape as a winner.

Prayer: May I finish well, and help others do the same. Amen.

Pressing on

BIG PICTURE
Philippians 3:12
Galatians 5:1–15

FOCUS
'Not that I have already obtained all this, or have already been made perfect, but I press on to take hold of that for which Christ Jesus took hold of me.' (Phil. 3:12)

All our yesterdays

BIG PICTURE
Philippians 3:13–14
Isaiah 43:14–28

FOCUS
'But one thing I do:
Forgetting what is
behind and straining
towards what is ahead …'
(Phil. 3:13b)

I'M SOMEONE who spends his life jumping between time zones – my commuting between Colorado and the UK means that my mind and body are usually seven hours behind each other (at least that's my excuse). But while that is an occupational hazard, I have also discovered that I can long to live in two different time zones that are actually utterly beyond the reach of us all: the past and the future. At times, the past becomes a wonderfully enchanting place, time having edited out its harsher days. I can view it as a warm resort where the sun always shone. I want to be back there. But there are moments when yesterday screams at me and causes a downpour in my soul today. I cower before the memory of harsh words I've spoken, foolish actions I've taken and a host of failures that I can remember well but never reach and undo. Then the future becomes an easy place in which to be contented: it is easy to imagine how disciplined and committed I will be in the future.

Paul was a man with more trophies and regrets than most. He'd known the esteem of religious position and the grip of being a fire-breathing persecutor of Christians. The death of Stephen must have lingered in his memory. But he was determined – using the phrase 'this one thing' to describe his utter singlemindedness – to grab today by the scruff of the neck and then stretch out for (he uses an athletic term here) what was to come.

We could all long for another time, another place. But flights to those locations are unavailable. Live today.

Prayer: Thank You for the gift of today. As I live it with You, may I loosen my grip on the past. Amen.

| Live today

IT'S old news now but the movie *The Da Vinci Code* starring Tom Hanks caused quite a stir when it was released and Dan Brown continues to earn truckloads of money from the worldwide sales of the book that spawned the craze. Christians have been quick to wonder about the gullibility of people who seem so ready to swallow such a wild tale: it was G.K. Chesterton who commented that our problem is not that people will not believe in something; rather it is that they will believe in anything.

But we Christians should be careful about pointing fingers when it comes to gullibility. I'm amazed at our capacity seemingly to kiss our brains goodbye because we want our hearts to be warmed. Christians often rush to accept miraculous claims of healings that aren't, turn books about the second coming into massive bestsellers (even though they are based on speculative and even ridiculous eschatology) and nod our amens to 'prophecy' that is fantastic and even totally incomprehensible. Faddism is a constant problem for the Church; we are forever looking for the latest trend, the locality of the big breakthrough or the elusive revival that will solve all of our mission challenges. Paul considers maturity of thought as important; the believers at Berea were noted for their 'nobility' because they earnestly reflected on the Scriptures, seeking authenticity over the latest fad. Brains are given so that they might be used and an atmosphere of questioning debate is a sign of a healthy church. For God's sake, let's think.

Prayer: Help me to develop a faith that is informed and thoughtful, that has depth and reflection at its heart. Amen.

Think!

BIG PICTURE
Philippians 3:15
Acts 17:11–12

FOCUS
'All of us who are mature should take such a view of things. And if on some point you think differently, that too God will make clear to you.'
(Phil. 3:15)

Legacy

In January 2006 we lost the incredible man that was Selwyn Hughes and a pause to reflect and remember his legacy is surely appropriate. Selwyn made an impression upon me, not only because of his writing skills and visionary leadership, but because of his consistent living. He set out upon the Christian pathway at a young age and was not to know that the trail he was on would have some dark twists and turns, with the death of his wife and the loss of both his children – surely every parent's nightmare. But through it all, Selwyn kept the faith, and left a legacy that we can admire, emulate and give thanks for. He lived up to his youthful vows and followed Paul's advice to us all, to live up to what we have already attained.

Sadly, too many of us end up tarnishing our lives and destroying any possibility of an enduring legacy because of poor choices made in the closing episodes. And so, especially to older readers, let's hear Paul's advice. You've come this far. Don't back off now and spoil all that has already been accomplished in the name of Christ.

Don't … spoil all that has already been accomplished in the name of Christ

A model

BIG PICTURE
**Philippians 3:17
1 Corinthians
10:23–33**

FOCUS
'Join with others in
following my example,
brothers, and take
note of those who live
according to the pattern
we gave you.' (Phil. 3:17)

KAY and I have just taken delivery of some shiny new gym equipment. Mocking friends have suggested that this is just sophisticated machinery to hang our washing on but we have actually been using the stuff. Daily we run, lift weights and even hang upside down like bats on something called an inverter, which stretches out the spine and makes blood rush to the head. This is apparently good for us.

Notwithstanding all this exercise, it is unlikely that we will be releasing a work-out exercise video soon: so don't hold your breath for *Praise Him in the Perspiration*. We want to live a little longer and to be healthier, not to set ourselves up as examples for the world to follow.

In the work-out of life, Paul was able to set himself up as a model. There's no arrogance here, just a quiet assurance that Paul's character was worth emulating. We've no idea whether the great apostle was blessed with muscles, charisma or charm: but he did have what counts: character.

Elsewhere, however, Paul adds a caveat to his call to others to model themselves on his life – to the Corinthians he says, 'Follow me as I follow Christ'. He is only worthy of emulation while he himself is still actively pursuing Jesus: there's no demand for respect 'for old times' sake', or because of the position Paul had gained. Leaders are only worth following while they are still followers.

In our lives, what areas could be made into a video to help others along the way – and which facets of our character would make painful viewing?

Prayer: May I be an example worthy of imitation, for Your glory. Amen.

Heavenly citizenship

BIG PICTURE

**Philippians 3:18–21
Matthew 6:19–21**

FOCUS

'Their destiny is destruction, their god is their stomach, and their glory is in their shame. Their mind is on earthly things.' (Phil. 3:19)

THERE are times when being a Christian means trudging a lonely pathway. When I worked in the city years ago, there were times when I was asked to leave the office for a moment while an ultra-blue joke was told. My work colleagues didn't feel comfortable about sharing their gags in front of a Christian and I didn't want to listen so the solution they came up with was to ask me to step outside. I remember how it felt to wait in the corridor for the peals of laughter to pass, so I could make my reappearance. Obviously, I felt excluded and isolated, not only by the more extreme aspects of my colleagues' behaviour, but simply by what dominated their thinking. Some of them seemed to have little concern about the value and meaning of life; their horizons apparently stretched only as far as a good night out on Saturday. Still, there were moments when I desperately wanted to join them, because the loneliness was too great.

The Philippian Christians must have felt the same way, in a city where Roman citizenship was highly prized. Paul reminds them of the small ambitions of those around them – filling the stomach with the latest delicacies is hardly a worthy purpose in life and celebrating cheap behaviour (as our culture does) is a pathetic way to live. Paul is stripping away the veneer of sophistication that so frequently cloaks sin and showing it to be a hollow lifestyle. But then Paul reminds his brothers and sisters of their high calling, their heavenly citizenship and their incredibly wonderful future. Don't step down from your high calling.

Don't step down from your high calling

Prayer: Lord, 'earthly things' can be very alluring. Help me to see through superficiality, and live well. Amen.

Love, actually

EACH year on Valentine's Day millions of cards are sent professing undying love and loyalty – not a bad thing. The cynical side of me wants to dismiss the whole event as a conspiracy by greeting card manufacturers and florists to help us part with yet more cash, which is partly true. But any excuse to express our gratitude, affection and even passion for those we love is one that we should take advantage of. Particularly in the British culture, we can be inhibited about expressing our love, for fear of superficiality. How tragic it is that for some, the news of how much they were loved and appreciated is suspended until the one event that they cannot attend – their funeral service. The husband who announces 'I told my wife I loved her on our wedding day and if I ever changed my mind, I'd let her know' is sadly not fictional.

Consider the contrast as Paul uses strong language to demonstrate that he views *his* relationships as priceless jewels. Twice in one verse he uses a word which literally means 'beloved'. The Philippians are the source of his joy. He sees them like a crown on his head (see 1 Thess. 2:19). He loves and longs for them (1:8). Far more than a gushing outburst of sentiment, Paul is unafraid to bare his heart and let his Christian siblings in Philippi know how much they are loved.

Are there people in our lives who we cherish, but have forgotten to remind of how much they mean to us? Put that right today.

Prayer: Help me to express love and encouragement, without fear and with meaning. Amen.

BIG PICTURE
**Philippians 4:1
John 13:1–17**

FOCUS
'Therefore, my brothers, you whom I love and long for, my joy and crown …'
(Phil. 4:1)

Whatever

BIG PICTURE
Philippians 4:2
Matthew 5:21–26

FOCUS
'I plead with Euodia and I plead with Syntyche to agree with each other in the Lord.' (Phil. 4:2)

I'M SAD to confess that today I watched some British daytime television, which is surely a government ploy to get people who usually stay at home back into the workplace. Alongside the usual fodder involving selling houses and discovering priceless antiques in one's bathroom, was a relatively new 'reality' show; a British version of Jerry Springer. In it families and former friends savage each other, gladiator-style, for the wondrous prize of 15 minutes of fame – or notoriety. One lady responded to a tearful outburst from her husband by putting her hand up to his face and constantly saying 'Whatever.' She was the master of complete indifference: her contempt for the man she had once loved was skilfully communicated by her utter lack of interest in his tears. She couldn't have cared less.

As Paul addresses the painful fall-out between two former allies, he is on his knees begging for reconciliation between them. The word 'plead' suggests the urgency of his appeal. Some think these two ladies might have been deaconesses in the Philippian church: whatever their past, neither are living up to the meaning of their names – 'Euodia' means a 'prosperous journey' and 'Syntyche' means a 'pleasant acquaintance'. Notice Paul doesn't discuss the reason for the fall-out – often the issue of contention isn't what really matters; it's the way we deal with it that counts.

Perhaps we find ourselves in a position of tension and we're tempted, because of weariness, fear of confrontation or just the simple desire for a quiet life, to mutter 'Whatever' and allow the conflict to drag on. Let's live up to our names. We're called 'Christians'.

Let's live up

to our names

Prayer: Lord, I pray for all with whom I share in Christ's community. May we live up to our names and to Your name. Amen.

Help needed

THERE are a number of well-known sayings that sound wise and almost biblical, but actually are not scriptural at all. These include 'Always let your conscience be your guide' (not a phrase coined by the apostle Paul, but Jiminy Cricket) and 'Love means never having to say you're sorry' (not found in 1 Corinthians 13 but delivered in the weepy movie *Love Story*). And there's 'An Englishman's home is his castle' (I don't know who coined that, but it's a great excuse to make sure that the more personal and embarrassing struggles of our lives are kept hidden safely away from the eyes – and the help – of others).

With the conflict between these two feuding ladies, Paul realises that some outside help is necessary. And so he appeals to Syzygus, 'the loyal yokefellow' (we're unsure as to whether the Greek word here is someone's actual name or a description of their character – and it doesn't matter) to get alongside this sparring pair and help them sort things out.

Sometimes it's nothing less than pride that makes us refuse to ask for help, even though we know we're drowning. How many alcoholics could have found freedom? How many marriages might have been saved? And how many churches might have been spared painful division, if pride had been ignored and help sought?

Perhaps it's time to call in an expert to help with an area of your life. To do so is not an admission of defeat, but a simple recognition that we're designed to live in community, to bear each other's burdens and to discover resources beyond our own horizons. Shout for help and let the drawbridge down, before the castle collapses.

Prayer: Help me to call for help when I need it. Save me from privacy fuelled by pride. Amen.

BIG PICTURE
**Philippians 4:3
Galatians 6:1–5**

FOCUS
'… help these women who have contended at my side in the cause of the gospel, along with Clement and the rest of my fellow workers …'
(Phil 4:3)

Don't worry, be happy?

Another one of those non-biblical statements of popular wisdom is 'Don't worry, be happy'. It sounds so very liberating, just to cast off your concerns and grin. But just exactly why should I abandon fretting and replace my anxiety with a cheerful smile? If the mantra is to have meaning, there must be a reason for the switch.

Paul does not call the Philippian believers, under huge pressure as they were, to some kind of superficial smile – although we all need to laugh more. But he calls them to something more solid – rejoicing – and is emphatic in his command that they rejoice, repeating it for effect. Here is an invitation to know something deeper than happiness, which so often depends on happenings. Rather, as we reflect on the privilege of knowing God's power and love in our lives, and enjoy friendship with Him today, we can know calm and gladness, even when circumstances are against us.

That doesn't mean that we ignore our problems or pretend they don't exist. But we affirm that there is someone bigger and greater than life or death itself, and we can know calm in the midst of storms.

… we can know calm in the midst of storms

Gently does it

BIG PICTURE
Philippians 4:5
Galatians 5:22–25

FOCUS
'Let your gentleness be
evident to all. The Lord is
near.' (Phil. 4:5)

IT'S sad to say it, but for some people religion is a dangerous additive that not only messes up their lives but can also bring destruction to others. I think of a couple of ministers that I know who are fiercely embroiled in the ongoing tensions of Northern Ireland. They relish the description 'hardliners' since they have concluded that this means that they absolutely reject all compromise and that they are faithful to the truth. But the sad reality is that they are difficult to converse with (most chats turn into a monologue and occasionally a diatribe). The possibility that they might ever change an opinion or hint that they might be anything other than utterly right, is very rare indeed; and they are extremely rude. They are what we call 'difficult' people. 'Painful' is a better if slightly less kind description, because confidence is only a short step away from arrogance.

I can think of others – one friend comes to mind right now – who disagrees firmly with many of my views on charismatic Christianity, and would prefer an approach to preaching that certainly isn't mine. But he is known for his graciousness, kindness, winning smile and warmth of spirit. I admire him enormously.

Paul calls the Philippians to gentleness – a trait that he insists Christians should be known for, as it's something that should be displayed by all. The word that he uses literally means 'sweet reasonableness'. People like us, who hold our convictions with passion, should remind ourselves of that call, lest we be right in our beliefs and utterly wrong in our lifestyle and manners – or lack of them.

Prayer: Father, 'sweet reasonableness' is a character trait that I ask for. Amen.

Reasons to be cheerful

BIG PICTURE
Philippians 4:6–7
Matthew 6:25–34

FOCUS
'Do not be anxious about anything, but in everything, by prayer and petition, with thanksgiving, present your requests to God.' (Phil. 4:6)

PAUL has plenty to worry about. The churches that he planted and nurtured are constantly under threat from false teachers. Divisions and spats threaten to tear the fledgling communities apart. And there is the little detail of his own life; despite the confidence and hope that he has for a release, Paul can't be sure of his future. His next day could be his last, a fact that would have weighed on anyone's mind. But he invites us to join him in refusing the shadowy pathway of anxiety. Notice, though, that he gives a very solid reason for our rejecting nail-biting worry – and that is his belief in the power of prayer. Christians don't calm their fears with natty little slogans. We know that horoscopes have no influence over us and our lives are not dominated by either lucky numbers or good luck charms.

Our security is based on this reality that changes everything: there is a God and He is very interested in us indeed, hence the call to prayerful petition and grateful thanksgiving. Not only that, but He's the God of the detail so that *in everything* we can come to Him.

My capacity to worry is directly linked with my discipline in prayer. When I forget to tell God about my little or huge concerns, I end up hoisting them onto my own back and dragging them around, with exhausting effect.

Of course, the Bible is blunt about the uselessness of worry – it achieves nothing – and the effectiveness of prayer – it can change everything and leads to a peaceful heart. What will today be about for us – worry or prayer? Choose one.

… there is a God and He is very interested in us …

Prayer: Deliver me from anxiety: develop in me a solid trust. Help me to pray, not fret. Amen.

Your mind matters

I WAS in Sicily, the sun was blistering and I was forced to eat the worst meal of my life. Deep fried sea snake and live mussels were part of the yuckiest feast that has ever passed my lips. I shall not return to that menu again and only ate what I did for fear of offending my hosts. I'm careful about what I eat.

Unfortunately, I'm not always so diligent about what I allow in through the gate of my mind. It's all too easy to take such a relaxed view about what we read, watch and ponder, that our heads become like an expensive house, where the front door is left wide open, an open invitation to any passing malicious intruder.

Clearly, our thinking directly affects our behaviour. Those who say that violent or pornographic images have no effect on the way people live are lying. Why else would advertisers part with millions in order to buy a few seconds of prime time to grab our minds and convince us to buy their stuff? If image, music and words don't influence us, the whole advertising industry is a con: clearly it is not. When I listen to endless profanity and swearing, I find that those words remain and quickly reform in my head. Can it be good for our children to watch the thousands of on-screen killings that they do?

The sea snake/mussels banquet affected me in ways I shall not describe. And what we allow into our heads will also lead to some kind of result/results (Rom. 12:1–2).

Prayer: Give me discipline and diligence to guard the gate of my mind. Amen.

BIG PICTURE
**Philippians 4:7–8
Colossians 3:1–4**

FOCUS
'Finally, brothers, whatever is true, whatever is noble, whatever is right, whatever is pure, whatever is lovely, whatever is admirable – if anything is excellent or praiseworthy – think about such things.'
(Phil. 4:8)

Do it

BIG PICTURE
Philippians 4:9
James 1:22–27

FOCUS
'Whatever you have
learned or received
or heard from me, or
seen in me – put it into
practice. And the God of
peace will be with you.'
(Phil. 4:9)

AS I travel, I've been blessed and encouraged by bumping into numbers of you that use *Life Every Day* regularly: many of you have been kind enough to write, email or personally comment that you find the notes helpful, for which I'm grateful. Some of you have asked how you could best pray for me as every 60 days, another writing deadline comes around – and here's my prayer request.

There's always a danger for anyone who is dealing with a lot of Christian material – Bible study and reflection or sermon preparation – that a familiarity can develop so that the text becomes something to study and comment upon, rather than the wisdom of God that must be applied and obeyed daily. The discovery of a wonderful truth can tempt the preacher or writer to sermonise about it rather than apply it: we can become those who challenge God's people with God's Word, rather than allowing it to impact us first. Paul encourages the Philippians to 'put into practice' what they have learned. Elsewhere James paints a bizarre word portrait of a man who sees, on looking into the mirror, that some changes need to be made – he needs a shave, his hair is unkempt – but then he walks away without changing a thing.

So pray that I might be someone who always puts the Word into practice – and while you're at it, pray for those in your life who are involved in the privileged but perilous work of teaching and preaching. May we all truly be practisers of what we preach.

May we all truly
be practisers of
what we preach

Prayer: Save me from becoming a theorist. May all those who handle Your Word have their lives shaped by it. Amen.

WARREN Buffett is one of the world's richest men – he's currently worth around 44 billion dollars, give or take a million or two. He is an investment genius and so his advice is worth a great deal. Recently an auction was held to sell off the opportunity to have lunch with Warren – a buffet lunch (ouch!). Contenders parted with tens of thousands just for the chance to spend 60 minutes with the mega-mogul. Apparently what Buffett can teach is worth a huge amount of money. The secrets that he carries in his heart and head are worthy of a king's ransom.

But what Paul has learned is priceless. He has learned to be content whatever the circumstances, which makes him truly one of the richest men in history. He needs no toys, no sunshine, no perks or celebrity status in order to delight in life – he was one of the most alive people that ever lived! I can't say that I have even started in the school of contentment. But I do want to learn. Helpfully, Paul's so-called secret of contentment is no secret, because he openly shares it without an auction: his source of strength for everything is Jesus Christ.

Living in friendship with Jesus, knowing that He cares for us (1 Pet. 5:7), trusting rather than worrying and refusing to allow our circumstances to dominate our emotions – these are lessons that perhaps take years to learn but are certainly the very best of educations.

Prayer: Teach me how to be content. Be my strength, my life and my all. Amen.

Contentment

BIG PICTURE
**Philippians 4:10–13
2 Corinthians 12:7–10**

FOCUS
'I know what it is to be in need, and I know what it is to have plenty. I have learned the secret of being content in any and every situation …'
(Phil. 4:12)

No lone rangers

All that talk of being contented, whatever the circumstances, and being able to do everything in the strength of God makes Paul sound like some kind of spiritual superman, a dynamic hero, turbo-charged by the Spirit, invincible and triumphant …

But in the very next verse, Paul speaks tenderly about how much the friendship of the Philippians has meant to him. He is no insular lone ranger who will battle through with Jesus at his side. He knows that God has designed him for relationships, and part of the all-sufficiency of Christ in his life is God's provision of trusted companions like those in Philippi.

Perhaps you're going through some really tough circumstances right now, and you're tempted to go it alone with God, shutting friends and loved ones out of the picture. You may even feel that it's more spiritual or brave to do so. Or perhaps you think it's a sign of weakness to be on the receiving end of help – you're usually so strong, that it's *you* who does the helping. Think again. God's strength and comfort often come through God's people: we were created to be together. Let others in on your pain.

God's strength and comfort often come through God's people …

Giving

IT'S the subject that makes some ministers tremble when they have to preach about it, because any mention of this word often signals trouble. You've guessed it – I'm talking about money. Some Christians have a super-sensitivity to the subject, and scream when the offering plate comes around, or complain that it's not spiritual to discuss matters of finance and giving – and they couldn't be more wrong. The Bible talks about money repeatedly, in bold and specific terms, and for very good reason. Our money is the key to the lives that we lead: the way we spend it, give it or refuse to give it are clear indicators of what matters to us, and show what we think of God in a way that singing worship songs never will. After all, to sing a song only costs us the air in our lungs.

So Paul is open about the Philippians' support of his ministry – but he is no health and wealth huckster who tries to make giving to God into some sure-fire investment programme, where we give to get. When he talks about their giving 'being credited to your account' there's no suggestion here of buying God (all that we have comes from Him anyway) or making some investment in a get rich quick scheme organised by the bank of heaven. Simply, he is showing them that God sees and notes their giving: it is an offering, not just to Paul, but to God Himself, and one that is recorded with joy. Let's come to God with open hearts – and open wallets and purses.

Prayer: All I have is Yours, Lord. May my giving always outweigh my taking. Make my lifestyle a generous one. Amen.

BIG PICTURE
**Philippians 4:15–19
2 Corinthians 9:6–15**

FOCUS
'Not that I am looking for a gift, but I am looking for what may be credited to your account.'
(Phil. 4:17)

To God be the glory

BIG PICTURE
Philippians 4:20
John 14:1–4

FOCUS
'To our God and Father be glory for ever and ever. Amen.' (Phil. 4:20)

AS PAUL comes towards the end of his letter to his friends in Philippi, he points them and us to the very core of what the Christian life means, as he happily expresses his worship to the Lord: to God be the glory. No longer are we to tinker with trivial living where, as Neil Postman puts it, 'we are entertaining ourselves to death'. The life that Paul has described in his epistle – where serving matters, and position and status don't, where unity is worth pleading for, and where self-sacrifice is a daily choice – is a noble life lived in such a way as to please God and point others to Him.

Paul, mindful that he might have only days left before death comes for him, reminds us all that eternity is a reality, with his words, 'for ever and ever'. It's been said that some Christians are too heavenly-minded to be of any earthly use. The fact is that there has never yet been a Christian who has been so preoccupied with eternity that they have been of little use in this life – on the contrary, it has always been those who have been thrilled by the future who have made a radical difference in the here and now.

It seems almost clichéd to say that, if life is tough now, eternity will be bright and beautiful; and yet it is so true. God's people have always found comfort from looking up and out into eternity when life on earth was difficult. Let's live today with purpose, for His glory, and be grateful for a wondrous tomorrow that is yet to come.

Prayer: In my life, Lord, be glorified today. Amen.

Let's live today

with purpose …

Called to be saints

WE HAVE already seen that there's a lot of confusion about this word 'saints', and we reminded ourselves that Paul was a saint, and his colleagues and comrades in Philippi were saints (1:1) – and so are we, as those who have decided to follow Jesus Christ. We remind ourselves that the word 'saint' simply means 'set apart one' – and that's us. As we saw yesterday, we have decided to live our lives for the purposes of God – and so just as the various utensils in the Temple and the tabernacle were 'holy' because they were used for the work of God, so our lives too are consecrated for God's glory.

Notice that the 'saints' and 'brothers' are everywhere – even in Caesar's household. This probably referred to the slaves and dependents of Nero who had been converted through Paul's teaching while he was a prisoner in the Praetorian barracks attached to the palace. And that is the wonder of the gospel – whatever our social background or ethnic identity, we are now first and foremost Christians, citizens of heaven.

So as we conclude, let's offer ourselves once again to the God who has graciously decided to get His will done through the likes of ordinary us. God usually uses those who freely and willingly offer themselves – volunteers rather than conscripts. And that choice – to be used by God – is one that is worth reiterating as each new day dawns: life, truly, every day.

Thanks for taking this journey back to Philippi with me. And, based on what the Bible teaches, I'm signing off, as yours truly …

… Saint Jeffrey.

Prayer: I belong to You utterly and totally, my Lord and my God. May I live as a true saint always. Amen.

BIG PICTURE
Philippians 4:21–23
Ephesians 1:15–23

FOCUS
'Greet all the saints in Christ Jesus. The brothers who are with me send greetings. All the saints send you greetings, especially those who belong to Caesar's household.'
(Phil. 4:21–22)

Peter – How to
fail successfully

Peter – How to fail successfully

I LOVE the story of Peter, because he's a gifted, flawed, sensitive, insensitive mixture of brilliance and muddle. In so many ways, I'd like to be like him – he jumped in with both feet when he saw an opportunity to please Jesus, and for all his flaws, he was greatly used both as a disciple and an apostle. As we look at snapshots both from his life in the Gospels and his words in 1 and 2 Peter, there's much we can identify with. Not every mention of Peter is included here, and I've not taken these in any supposed exact chronological order – think of this as 'snapshots from Peter's life – a rough guide'.

One further note before we begin: these notes were written during an extended ministry trip to Australia, Singapore, Indonesia and France – and so I have 'flavoured' our journey with some international insights.

I hope you enjoy the ride!

Rock Idol

TELEVISION shows like *Pop Idol* may be entertaining to some and excruciating to others, but they do offer 'the public' the opportunity to decide who their favourite is. And sometimes it's the bumbling, tonally challenged crooner whose voice sets your teeth on edge that wins the vote – at least they are giving their best, even if their efforts are not the greatest. When they sing, dogs join in with the howling, but their flawed attempts are sometimes more winsome than the slick delivery of the more accomplished.

Ask any congregation who their favourite Bible character is, with the obvious exception of Jesus, and more often than not they'll pick Peter. And why is that?

Surely it's the sheer earthiness, the humanity of the man that makes him the people's hero. As Scripture unfolds his story, we see a warts-and-all portrait of a real person, just like us, capable of epic achievements and spectacular blunders. Perhaps we love Peter the most because his life is testimony to the truth that we all need reminding of – that failure doesn't have to signal the end. With Jesus, the Redeemer, our bad days can become stepping stones to something better. Peter's flaws don't give us a licence to sin – but they do remind us that God wants to pick us up when we fall, rather than leaving us to wallow around in the mud of our mistakes. We'd better learn how to fail, and accept grace when we do; if our commitment to God only lasts as long as we can go without messing up, our Christian journey will be brief.

Prayer: Thank You, Lord, for the real-life portraits of people in Your Word. Encourage me in *my* ups and downs. Amen.

BIG PICTURE
1 Peter 1:1–2
1 Corinthians 1:26–31

FOCUS
'Brothers, think of what you were when you were called. Not many of you were wise by human standards; not many were influential; not many were of noble birth.' (1 Cor. 1:26)

With Jesus …

our bad days

can be stepping

stones …

What a day can bring

BIG PICTURE
Matthew 4:18–22
Psalm 31:1–15

FOCUS
"'Come, follow me,"
Jesus said, "and I will
make you fishers of
men." At once they left
their nets and followed
him.' (Matt. 4:19–20)

SOME Christian leaders give the impression that the Christian life is like living in a theme park. They skip from one breathless roller-coaster experience of God to another. God seems to be very, very busily engaged in almost constant conversation with them, and miracles apparently accompany their every waking hour. Bluntly, I don't find the life of faith thus; God is wonderful, and my life has been punctuated with probably more than my fair share of wonders, but many of my days fade into grey and should be filed under the heading of 'Nothing much happened'.

But there *are* those life-changing days – perhaps a handful in a lifetime – when everything *does* seem to change. The ancient Jews had a saying: 'If not for that day …' These epic days are like rudders on the ship of life; sometimes bright, sometimes tragic, we know that we will never ever be the same again because of them.

So it was with Peter. He was not to know what was ahead of him, when his eyes blinked open on surely another ordinary day; fixing nets, cleaning fish, selling the catch to local traders – all much like every other day of his adult working life. But a revolution was on the immediate horizon and everything was about to be turned upside down – or perhaps the right way up – for Peter, because he was about to bump into Jesus.

Perhaps today doesn't so much threaten us, but is more likely to inspire a yawn as we consider its possibilities. Think again. *Our* times are in His hands (Psa. 31:15). This might be one of *those* days.

Prayer: What will You do today, Lord? Help me to have eyes open to see You at work, through me and others. Amen.

Potential

I gave the long-suffering saint who was my RE teacher a hard time. On my signal, the whole class would take a dive off their chairs, landing on their backs, kicking their legs in the air like helpless insects. We thought it very funny. She probably wanted to cry. But through it all, Mrs Richardson extended a loving grace to me that changed my life. She refused to be thwarted by my idiotic behaviour, and seemed to believe that somehow, even though I made her life quite difficult, I had potential – obviously hidden very deeply. Her kindness mined that potential out, and it was due to her that I finally became a Christian. She is now with Jesus, but I owe my life to her: her warm smile is a happy memory.

Jesus looked at a rough and ready, impetuous fisherman called Peter, and saw that one day he would be the leading spokesperson for the newly formed Church, on the Day of Pentecost. Jesus scribbled, as it were, 'has potential' over the exercise book that was Peter's life. Is there anyone close to you who also has potential, despite all appearances to the contrary?

Jesus scribbled, as it were, 'has potential' over … Peter's life

It's about people

BIG PICTURE
Matthew 8:14–17
Mark 1:29–34

FOCUS
'When Jesus came into Peter's house, he saw Peter's mother-in-law lying in bed with a fever. He touched her hand and the fever left her, and she got up …' (Matt. 8:14–15)

I'M NOT a great fan of those large meetings where one 'celebrity' Christian personality with a healing ministry is the focus of attention. God obviously *does* raise up certain individuals and grants them a gift of faith, and undeniably spectacular things do happen – often we see that God comes running when He catches a hint of faith – and people *are* healed. But what makes me uncomfortable is the way that people can become objects in these gatherings. In a dash to get as many people prayed for as possible, they become little more than the ailment they possess.

As we consider some of the miracles that Peter witnessed, we see that Jesus *did* heal large numbers of people in en-masse gatherings, as we note from our reading today. Peter's house – probably Jesus' residence in Capernaum – was mobbed by desperate people. But the miraculous recovery of Peter's mother-in-law shows something about the marriage of tenderness and power in Jesus' ministry. Matthew tells us that Jesus touched the woman who was so feverish, she was bedridden. Dr Luke, ever the medical eagle eye, tells us it was a 'high' fever (Luke 4:38). And Mark, in his account, adds the detail that Jesus 'took her hand and helped her up' (Mark 1:31). This is not about loud-voice theatrics or performance pomposity – Jesus saw a person, not a fever.

Peter would have been moved as he watched a miracle unfold in his own home, and saw the recovery of his wife's mother. And he would have seen kindness as well as authority in that moment. Today, we'll meet people – not just objects. Let's notice them.

Prayer: Open my eyes to see the uniqueness and beauty around me, as I look into the eyes of others. Amen.

THERE are moments in life when we realise that almost everything that we have come to know is completely wrong. Perhaps we are hit by tragedy, and we always thought that we would crumble under such pressure. But we discover an unexpected reservoir of grace that carries us through, strong in faith. Then those of us who have been 'on the road' with God for a long time come to a junction in our relationship with Him, a crossroads of surprise: we thought we had Him all figured out, but we were wrong.

The day that Peter walked on water was a day when he realised that life doesn't always work according to the same pattern, especially when Jesus is around.

Water is not solid. It's completely impossible to walk on it. Every day of his working life, Peter had dipped his strong arms into that clear, blue Galilean water. He'd enjoyed the feeling of its coldness running through his fingers as he hauled bulging nets over the side of his boat. And this was no flat, shimmering millpond – on the contrary. These seasoned sailors were battling to row their way through this sudden storm, and so the waves would have been a frightening, boiling cauldron.

What did it feel like for Peter to swing his legs over the side, and plant his feet on water that, unbelievably, supported his weight? For a few moments at least, before fear mugged him, Peter knew that God was bigger than his understanding of life itself. Obviously this is an extreme example, but it challenges us still: are there laws of life that we need to unlearn?

Prayer: God, not only could I be wrong about some things, but I frequently am. Teach me. Amen.

Solid water underfoot

BIG PICTURE
Matthew 14:26–36
Mark 6:47–52

FOCUS
"'Come,' he said … Peter got … out of the boat [and] walked on the water … But when he saw the wind, he was afraid and … cried out, "Lord, save me!"' (Matt. 14:29–30)

… we thought we had Him all figured out, but we were wrong

Orders in chaos

BIG PICTURE
Luke 8:40–48
Isaiah 26:1–3

FOCUS
'As Jesus was on his way, the crowds almost crushed him.'
(Luke 8:42b)

JUST as the waves were chaotic, so in this episode in the life of Jesus, it seems pressure and chaos were surging around Him on every side. Crowds are noisy and sometimes frightening – when a crowd stampedes, its centre can be a terrifying place. And that's where Jesus found Himself. Jairus, the synagogue ruler, has raised the alarm for his daughter – and Jesus is eager to help him out. But then, in the press around Jesus, a woman who has suffered from a 12-year-long menstrual loss, grabs Jesus' cloak, prompting Him to enquire – who touched me?

It's Peter, of course, who volunteers the obvious answer – why ask which person touched you, when you're almost being trampled by a herd of need? But none the less, in the midst of the chaos, Jesus brings a fabulous miracle to the long-suffering woman. The clamour, noise and incessant demands didn't throw Him off His purpose. The supernatural can break out in the middle of what seems a mess.

Perhaps your life is currently loaded, crammed full of pressure. The schedule is overwhelming, and your unfinished tasks tower over you. Maybe there's no end in sight for a while, and you've decided that the possibility of God intervening in your life is at best an appointment that's a long way off. While peace and quiet is vital, and solitude can help us meet ourselves and God again, let's not fall into the trap of believing that God is far from the madding crowd. He's the Lord of the waves – and He's the Lord of the crowds too.

Prayer: Meet me in the press of life, and help me to find a pause today too. Amen.

Kindness again

BIG PICTURE
Luke 8:49–56
Isaiah 63:7

FOCUS
'Her spirit returned, and
at once she stood up.
Then Jesus told them to
give her something to
eat.' (Luke 8:55)

A FEW days ago we considered that Peter had wonderful opportunities to learn that miracles are not fireworks for the excitement and entertainment of onlookers, but come from the heart of our compassionate God who cares so much about people. As Jesus moves on from healing the woman with the issue of blood, He walks into a situation that seems utterly hopeless. The child that He has been called to help has already died. He is now visiting a deathbed, not a sickbed.

But let's give attention to *how* Jesus raises this girl to life. Remember that He is now the darling of the crowds. What better way could there be to make a huge impact than let as many of them as possible have a ringside seat? Yet Jesus refuses to allow the girl to become exhibit 'A' for the crowds to gawp at. Only those closest to Him at the time – Peter, James and John – are allowed into the bedchamber, and the child's parents are admitted too, Jesus tenderly responding to the heartbreak that they have been through. And, when she comes back from the dead, He reminds the stunned parents to feed the little girl, not forgetting the important in the midst of the incredible.

Sometimes I meet Christians who are zealous, highly dedicated people, but who aren't kind or thoughtful. Conviction has made them dogmatic: a fear of any kind of compromise has made them rigidly inflexible and opinionated. No finger-pointing here; I'm sure I've had more than a few days like that myself. Believe God for great things – and show great kindness as you do.

Prayer: Loving Father, Mighty God, give me a heart filled with faith, mingled with kindness. Amen.

Believe God for

great things …

High cost commitment

BIG PICTURE
Luke 18:18–30
Matthew 16:24–28

FOCUS
'Peter said to him,
"We have left all we
had to follow you!"'
(Luke 18:28)

I'VE just spent the last 12 days with a brilliant young couple who have the world at their feet, but who choose to serve God and the world He so loves at considerable personal cost. He could earn many times more than he does now; she has plenty of opportunities to have a significant career. Their home is in the affluent South of England.

But right now, they are spending their lives building a community centre in Banda Aceh, Indonesia, where the Boxing Day tsunami in 2004 claimed around 200,000 lives. Mass graves abound.

Here these two young professionals are living in stifling heat, with no hot running water and no flushing toilet, because both of them love God and they feel His call to bring a smile again to the faces of children who have been so bruised by the onslaught of that wave. The grins that greeted us from so many children are created by costly choices.

Christianity is no hobby, habit or insurance policy for the afterlife. Being reconciled to the God whose heart is breaking for a lost world will cause us to feel His pain and may even break our hearts too, costing us everything. Peter had a large home in Capernaum where his brother Andrew and his mother-in-law lived, along with his own family (Mark 1:29; Matt. 8:14). But he bade farewell to security and a safe income to follow Jesus.

That young couple are Kelly and Ben, my daughter and son-in-law. Am I biased about the beauty of their lives? Definitely. But I'm still inspired by those who pay a high price.

Has following Jesus cost us much lately?

Prayer: Help me to make costly choices when I have the opportunity to change my world, Lord. Amen.

But Lord …

Peter often either argued with Jesus, tried to steer the one he called 'Master' away from His central purpose, or made ridiculous suggestions. Peter was just like us – sometimes we think we know better than God.

Here we have a flashback to the beginning of Peter's adventure with Jesus. As an experienced fisherman, Peter could think of any number of reasons why he shouldn't bother with casting his nets again. For one, a whole night's fishing had produced nothing; moreover, fishing in the deepest water was done at night-time; the fishing industry focused on the shallower waters during the day. Didn't the carpenter's son know that?

To his credit, Peter's response meant that Jesus was proved right again, and another miracle unfolded with the provision of a bumper catch of teeming fish.

Perhaps God is asking you to do something that seems a little strange. I write this with some hesitation, because some Christians seem to think that strangeness is a sure sign of spirituality, which is wrong. Nevertheless, there are times when God's commands to us defy our logic or conflict with what we'd choose to do. He does know best. Let Him win the argument.

He does
know best

What really matters

BIG PICTURE
Matthew 17:1–5
Romans 1:21–23

FOCUS
'After six days Jesus took with him Peter, James and John the brother of James, and led them up a high mountain by themselves. There he was transfigured before them.' (Matt. 17:1–2a)

I'VE just been thumbing through one of those celebrity magazines that follows the antics of the rich and famous, as well as some of the more 'disposable' celebrities who appear in reality TV shows, are recognised faces for a few weeks, and then disappear back into anonymity. I was stunned at the unbelievable obsession with the mundane: one 'celeb' took up nearly a page of photos and prints because she had forgotten to shave her armpits and had turned up at yet another party sporting a very bad hair day. Repeatedly I found myself asking the same question: Who cares? We seem to be a culture endlessly engaged in trivia, leaving the deeper questions of life unresolved.

It is preparation time for the inner circle of Peter, James and John, and they retire to a mountain top for a retreat that will leave a lifelong imprint on their minds – the transfiguration of Jesus. They are about to walk through a season when there will be more questions than answers, and so they need to know what matters; a solid foundation that will hold them steady during the chaos that is to come. Bright lights and bright clouds show them that Jesus is far more than a prophet. The guest appearances of Moses and Elijah reveal that He stands in the noble line of those that God used remarkably to save His people. Both were popularly expected to return to inaugurate the Messianic age, so their appearance here proclaims Jesus as the Messiah. If there was any doubt, the voice from above makes it clear: Jesus is God's Son, greatly loved.

Now *that's* news.

Prayer: God, help me live for what matters and to remember what is vital, especially during the tough times. Amen.

We have to keep moving

I'M WRITING this in Banda Aceh, Indonesia, where, as I mentioned earlier, our daughter Kelly and her husband Ben are working in that tsunami-devastated area to help rebuild the community. Our anticipation is high – it's been too long since we've seen them. But last night I found myself feeling saddened by the reality that in just a few short days, we'll have to say goodbye again, for even longer this time. I wish that I could just make time stand still for a while but instead, life moves relentlessly on, like the endless travellators (flat escalators) that swept us through Singapore's glittering airport this morning.

Peter, overwhelmed by his encounter with the supernatural on the Mount of Transfiguration, wants to park there for more than a while and offers to construct shelters for Jesus, Moses and Elijah. But there was to be no camping on that mountain. No matter how epic and exhilarating the experience, life stretched before them, with all its wonders and disappointments – they would have to go back down into the valley again. Surely we need to heed Jesus' instruction about living one day at a time – grateful for the past but not pining for it: thoughtful about the future but not postponing our joy until tomorrow comes. And let's not try to clutch onto today, which is like trying to catch the wind between our fingers – as soon as we reach out to grasp it, it's gone. Live today. And though the landscape and experiences will surely change as life moves on, decide to live tomorrow too.

Prayer: Save me from living a postponed existence, Lord. I thank You for the unique, irreplaceable gift of today. Amen.

BIG PICTURE
Matthew 17:4–13
Matthew 6:25–34

FOCUS
'Peter said to Jesus, "Lord, it is good for us to be here. If you wish, I will put up three shelters – one for you, one for Moses and one for Elijah."' (Matt. 17:4)

Live today

Engage brain before mouth

BIG PICTURE
Luke 9:28–36
Proverbs 29:20

FOCUS
'… Peter said … "Master, it is good for us to be here. Let us put up three shelters …" (He did not know what he was saying.)' (Luke 9:33)

I DIDN'T know the couple very well, but they had heard that Kay was in hospital, and had rightly assumed that I was alone, either starving to death or slowly killing myself with junk food, and so they invited me for dinner. Over a lovely meal, they asked about my Bible college days: had I preached in any churches as part of my training?

I replied that I had been assigned to a church, which was at the other end of the country, in a different denomination from theirs. They wouldn't know anyone from that church, right? Wrong. I prattled on, and remarked that the church had been very welcoming, but that one of the deacons, when giving the notices, could have bored for England. Some were healed of insomnia when this chap got up to do his bit, I chortled.

They seemed bemused, described a chap they knew from that church, and then named him: was that the boring one? Hapless, I confirmed the identity of our mind-numbing mutual friend. How well did they know him?

The hostess put her knife down on the table, and smiled: the man was her father. Despite my desperate prayers, no ground opened up to swallow me.

Peter, perhaps exhausted, perhaps stunned by the awesome spectacle that was the transfiguration, opened his mouth too quickly. Luke sums up the situation: 'He did not know what he was saying.' Then Peter is told to close his mouth and open his ears a little more – an instruction that perhaps we would do well to follow today.

Prayer: Help me to keep my mouth closed more, Lord. May thinking precede my speaking. Amen.

Heavenly minded

I'M FORGETFUL and would misplace my head if it were not attached. I lose keys, wallets, passports – and even forgot where I'd left my car on one occasion, but that's another story. And I keep forgetting that I'm going to live forever, because of what Jesus has done. Life here and now seems to demand my fullest attention: if I'm not careful, I can lose all perspective on eternity.

At the transfiguration, Peter caught a glimpse of the eternal. As he watched and trembled, Elijah and Moses chatted with Jesus. Step back for a moment and consider how that felt, to have a ringside seat for such a summit meeting. Peter and the others were looking, up close and personal, at the most famous personalities of human history. And then there's an additional detail that would have caused Peter, James and John's collective jaws to hit the floor – these two characters had been dead for a very long time but here they were, larger than life. Peter had seen some stunning sights in his journey with Jesus over the last three years – but this moment would surely sear itself into his memory forever. Surely he reminded himself of this when he was later locked in a prison cell. Perhaps he remembered this when he couldn't sleep at night because he knew that death by execution was out there somewhere on the horizon – Jesus had told him so, and Peter had learned well that Jesus was never wrong. Pause today, especially if today is dark and painful, and remember: whatever this is, this ultimately is not it. There's more.

Prayer: Grant me a sense of the future that sustains me today, Lord. Amen.

BIG PICTURE
1 Peter 1:3–12
John 14:1–4

FOCUS
'In his great mercy he has given us new birth into a living hope through the resurrection of Jesus Christ … into an inheritance … kept in heaven for you.'
(1 Pet. 1:3–4)

… I can lose all

perspective

on eternity

From the heart

BIG PICTURE
1 Peter 1:13–25
John 13:31–35

FOCUS
'Now that you have purified yourselves by obeying the truth so that you have sincere love for your brothers, love one another deeply, from the heart.' (1 Pet. 1:22)

PAK Munir doesn't smile much when he poses for photographs, which may be because of the arrangement of his teeth, which point in all directions. He is universally respected in his village just outside Banda Aceh. Everybody else in his village fled for the hills and refused to return to the village for four days and nights. But Mr Munir is one of those natural leaders who endlessly fusses around, getting jobs done that no one else wants to bother with.

It was a sobering moment when he showed us the log book that recorded his retrieving and burying 221 victims of the tsunami, a feat that took him around ten weeks to complete.

Today he asked how we as a family would say goodbye in our culture. We said that we would hug. Then he asked our daughter Kelly to first of all hug her mother, Kay, and then me. As we did what we were asked, his eyes filled with tears, and he told us that he felt the pain of our being so far apart from our daughter and son-in-law: we live thousands of miles from where they are serving in Aceh. His eyes have seen the most terrible sights; he has learned that time is always too short when it comes to expressing love – we shouldn't need an excuse to share a hug.

Peter understood that principle, as he encourages his readers to 'love each other deeply from the heart', an expression that calls for supreme effort, loving 'with every muscle strained'. Loved like that lately?

Prayer: Lord, help me to love now. Show me where I need to remind others how much they mean to me. Amen.

Very important people

Today we visited one of the barracks that were hastily erected after the Indonesian tsunami swept thousands of homes away. Despite the fact that it is now over two years later, so many still have to call these rickety buildings their home. These buildings were not built to last and they aren't lasting. They are falling apart, a desperate, desolate place to live. And yet one aspect of culture survives here, as strong as ever – the pecking order or sense of hierarchy. We saw the 'chief' of the barracks, and learned that there is an elaborate chain of command here. And those who live in the nearby village want little to do with the barracks people, relegating them to third class status because of their displacement.

One of the vital lessons that Peter had to learn was the disdain with which Jesus treated human hierarchical attitudes. Surely the Master would not leave an important appointment with the religious head-honchos to bless a gaggle of giggling children – would He? Jesus was indignant with the disciples for sending the parents packing. Is there anyone in our lives that we've decided is unworthy of our attention? Perhaps we need to think again.

… think again

Trouble and strife

BIG PICTURE
Matthew 20:1–28
1 Peter 2:1–3

FOCUS
'When the ten heard about this, they were indignant with the two brothers …'
(Matt. 20:24)

THERE'S not a team, church, friendship or marriage that's not under threat from the predator that is envy. Over the last 30 years, I have watched, at times in despair, as churches that I thought were immune to the virus of division have come unravelled, and where close friends who I thought would be together in their twilight years have been irreversibly separated through badly handled conflict.

Some Christians would have a fight right in front of Jesus Himself, as Jesus' own team proved. Real trouble broke out when James and John, using their mother Salome as a mouthpiece, tried to book the best seats in the kingdom to come. The other ten disciples were 'indignant' – a strong New Testament word that describes a major ignition of emotion. Often, when we Christians get angry, we piously rush to defend our ire by calling it 'righteous' indignation – but look closely and you'll see this crowd aren't acting like any righteous brothers. This is the jealousy and pettiness that explodes when someone else takes the pew we've laid claim to, someone else gets the credit that belongs to us, or the place at the front of the line is taken by someone less deserving than our 'good' selves.

As one of the angry 'ten', Peter would have seen firsthand the damaging effects of envy – and so an older and wiser Peter is quick to warn his friends against opening a door to strife. Are you about to light the blue touch paper of conflict in a precious relationship? Think twice: is the issue worth the firestorm that might be harder to stop than start?

Prayer: Save me from the murderous virus of envy. Give me a big, generous heart, loving God. Amen.

Upon the rock

A FEW years ago, a book ingeniously titled *Building with Bananas* was published. It described, in warm and humorous terms, how God is building His 'house' with people – not perfectly shaped bricks, but bananas misshaped and distorted by sin; 'living stones', as Peter puts it (1 Pet. 2:5).

Today we consider one of the most controversial passages of the New Testament, because the whole system of the papacy in Roman Catholicism rests upon the idea that Peter himself was the rock, or foundation, upon which the Christian Church is built. Some have tried to suggest that the 'rock' is not Peter himself, but the revelation that Peter uttered, that Jesus is the Christ. But it does seem more likely that the play on words that Jesus used with Peter's nickname, 'the rock', means that Peter himself was going to play a vital and foundational role in the formation of the early Church – as indeed he did in the early chapters of the book of Acts. None of this leads us to a doctrine of papacy or apostolic succession – but what it does do is affirm that the eternal purposes of God are being forged in partnership with flawed, failed human beings like Peter – and us.

Come to think of it, God only uses imperfect people – He hasn't got anything else to choose from, seeing as 'all have fallen short of the glory of God'. No wonder the Church is so full of imperfections – it's loaded with specimens like us. So next time a fellow Christian disappoints you, be sad but not surprised. After all, you're a banana yourself.

Prayer: Help my knowledge of my own incompleteness and give me patience with other 'irregular' people, Lord. Amen.

BIG PICTURE
Matthew 16:13–20
1 Peter 2:4–8

FOCUS
'And I tell you that you are Peter, and on this rock I will build my church, and the gates of Hades will not overcome it.'
(Matt. 16:18)

After all, you're a banana yourself

We're royalty, you know

BIG PICTURE
1 Peter 2:9–12
Ephesians 4:1

FOCUS
'But you are a chosen people, a royal priesthood, a holy nation … that you may declare the praises of him who called you out of darkness into his wonderful light.'
(1 Pet. 2:9)

MY ENCOUNTERS with the British royal family have been short. I have only ever met one of them, and that conversation was brief. Two words, actually.

Prince Philip was visiting a youth club where I was a member. We were told to carry on doing whatever we were doing when he arrived, as he wanted to see our club in action. I was bouncing on a trampoline and he headed straight for me, which threw me into a panic and taught me a major lesson – it is difficult to bow and bounce at the same time. The great man asked me just one question as I flailed around before him: 'Do you like the trampoline?' I breathlessly said, 'Yes sir' (and messed up, because I was supposed to call him 'Your Royal Highness'), and he moved on to the ping-pong table, where he probably asked the players there if they enjoyed ping-pong. My friendship with royalty isn't that deep.

According to Peter, I may be flawed and ordinary, but I am part of God's royal family. As Christians, we are a combination of *kings* and *priests* – a royal priesthood. Throughout the Old Testament, kings and priests were separate individuals. Only Melchizedek and the Messiah combined both offices. Saul sinned when he tried to discharge both functions (1 Sam. 13:5–15). In Christ, the Christian is both.

Perhaps you're feeling worthless. A recent excursion into sin that shamed you has left you feeling at best insignificant, and at worst, worthy of rejection and judgment. God thinks differently. Accept *His* verdict. And when it comes to life choices, *live* like royalty – walk worthy of your calling.

Prayer: Help me to truly live like a king, or a queen. Amen.

WE TALKED earlier about kindness, and we must consider yet another example of it in the life of Jesus. Here is another episode where Peter specifically participated in the learning experience. The issue here is the payment of the Temple tax, a duty that Jesus, by rights, didn't have to pay, seeing as His Father owned the Temple – and the universe! As the 'Son of the King' He was exempt from the tax. But now He presides over another miracle, and pays His own tax bill and Peter's with it, so that 'we may not offend them'.

If we only look at the life and ministry of Jesus selectively, we could gain the impression that He was a commando personality, who kicked tables over in the Temple and gave the Pharisees a good tongue lashing for their hypocrisy. We can picture Him, erroneously, as someone who relished offending people. But we're wrong to develop such a caricature. While Jesus fearlessly spoke His mind, He didn't go out of His way to create an upset deliberately, and willingly surrendered His 'rights' in order to keep the peace.

Because we Christians are people of principle, sometimes our passion gets a little distorted as we become crusaders for our own rights. Perhaps your 'rights' are being trampled underfoot right now. Is God asking you to grow through surrendering what is rightly yours, and assuming the posture of a servant? Servanthood is the only way to successfully navigate all relationships, especially marriage.

Of course, we never know if we are truly servant-like, until we see how we react when people start treating us like servants …

Prayer: Lord Jesus, You came to serve, and not to be served. Help me follow in Your footsteps. Amen.

Kindness and rights

BIG PICTURE
Matthew 17:24–27
1 Peter 2:13–3:7

FOCUS
'… go to the lake and throw out your line. Take the first fish you catch; open its mouth and you will find a four-drachma coin … give it to them …'
(Matt. 17:27)

Jesus … willingly surrendered His 'rights' …

Read the instructions

BIG PICTURE
1 Peter 3:8–4:19
Luke 17:20–37

FOCUS
'But even if you should suffer for what is right, you are blessed.'
(1 Pet. 3:14)

IN OUR litigation-obsessed culture, manufacturers have resorted to labelling their goods with announcements that are so obvious that they're amusing. Here are a few of my favourite (and genuine) labels: (On a meat pie) **'This pie will be hot when heated.'**
(A label found on the underside of a pie)
'Do not turn this pie upside down.'
(A label located on *children's* cough medicine)
'Do not drive after taking.'
(Helpful words labelled on a bottle of sleeping pills)
'Warning – may cause drowsiness.' And finally, my personal favourite, here is a label found on Christmas tree lights – **'These lights are only for use indoors or outdoors.'**

But if the above make us smile, here's a label that is sometimes slapped on Christianity, even by Christians: 'People who have great faith won't suffer'. Believing we can steer around the turbulent seasons of life is popular with some but, sadly, is a total lie. Peter developed into one of the great faith heroes of the Church, but warned his fellow Christians that the road would sometimes turn rocky. I've watched with sadness when once fervent disciples turned their back on God because suffering struck them, rejecting God because they believed He had broken His promises. But look at the label – or the New Testament, to be more precise. Far from promising five-star ease, the promise is of suffering for doing good.

I'm sorry if this is a time of suffering for you. May you be strengthened, and emerge with greater trust. Don't be surprised, though. It's on the label.

Prayer: You never promised me freedom from suffering, Lord, but You did promise Your presence all the way. Thank You. Amen.

1 Peter 5:1–14 // Ephesians 6:11–17

Battle warning

The idea of the devil can seem a little antiquated. The cartoon image of the red-caped, horned chap with a goatee beard and a pitchfork is easily relegated to mythology. But Jesus clearly warned Peter that he faced an enemy more subtle and devious than the Pharisees and other conspiring religious leaders. Twice 'Satan' is named as responsible for strategic attacks upon Peter's faithfulness and way of thinking.

As a seasoned battle veteran, it is only natural therefore that Peter would later issue his own warning about heightened levels of potential satanic terror. Peter had been told by Jesus to stay alert (Mark 14:38) and so he writes the same admonition to his readers.

Some Christians ignore the reality of the devil. Others think about little else, and see a dark conspiracy theory behind every calamity. Surely we need to ask God to help us to take a balanced view between these two extremes, where we never forget that we live life on a battlefield, but we always remember that the battle is not between two equal forces – God and Satan. We 'resist' the enemy as those who stand on the side of the one who has already won.

Some Christians ignore the reality of the devil

Don't you know?

BIG PICTURE
Luke 22:31
Mark 14:27–28

FOCUS
'Simon, Simon, Satan
has asked to sift you as
wheat.' (Luke 22:31)

DURING the Second World War, people in Britain were taught not to gossip war secrets and so threaten national security. Posters were printed to encourage vigilance, with slogans like 'Careless talk costs lives'. One famous catchphrase declared, 'Don't you know there's a war on?'

Jesus uses an interesting agricultural term to describe the way that Satan wants to attack Peter, and probably the other disciples as well, because the word 'you' here is in the plural – it was not only Peter who was selected for the devil's attention. Sifting wheat in a sieve was done to ensure that small pebbles and grit were removed from the harvest. The grain was placed in the sieve and shaken vigorously, but not too much lest it spilt onto the ground.

Spiritual warfare does not always involve a full-on onslaught. Sometimes there is a dark strategy in the gradual accumulation of the incidental; tiredness here, discouragement there, disappointment with others, all combining to sap our energy and make us more ready candidates for temptation. But most importantly, we must be aware that the power of evil is not just random: there are times and seasons when a specific campaign to bring us down is being played out. Just as the devil sought permission to attack Job (Job 1:8–12; 2:3–6) so similar wording is used here as Jesus warns Peter of a spiritual military campaign to come.

The prayer, 'Lead us not into temptation' assumes a regular recognition that we live in a theatre of war, and shouldn't be surprised when attack comes. Be ready, and resolute. There really is a war on.

Prayer: Give me an awareness of the warfare that rages, but not an obsession with it. Be Thou my vision. Amen.

JESUS is no genie in a bottle, make-a-wish saviour – although some proponents of 'health and wealth' teaching try to turn God into a grinning butler whose major agenda in life is to meet all of our wants and needs. That said, if God offered you just one guaranteed answer to prayer, one 'wish' that would be absolutely fulfilled, what would it be? Would you ask for better looks, a better job, or for fabulous riches? Would a life without pain and suffering be at the head of your list?

Jesus prays on a number of occasions for His disciples, but here He reveals an item that was special to Peter, who would go through more than his fair share of suffering. Perhaps a prayer that the suffering would be avoided would have been good; but instead Jesus prays that Peter's faith might not fail. In Jesus' list of priorities, faith in God and relationship with Him – 'the knowledge of God' (2 Pet. 1:2) come before the circumstances of life. Jesus often pointed out and even celebrated great examples of faith (Matt. 15:28; Mark 2:5), and the word He uses for Peter's faith 'failing' here is 'eclipsed' – the same word that is used to describe the eclipse of the sun that happened on crucifixion day (Luke 23:45). Suffering can do that: shut out the sun, and make us feel bereft of God, and convinced that there is only the darkness. If you're in a chilly season that feels like an endless eclipse, I'm praying for some light and strength for you today.

Prayer: Lord, strengthen all those who struggle, and grant them a special gift of faith for this difficult season. Amen.

Faith and sifting

BIG PICTURE
Luke 22:32a
2 Peter 1:1–2

FOCUS
'But I have prayed for you, Simon, that your faith may not fail.'
(Luke 22:32a)

Jesus …

celebrated

great examples

of faith …

Picking a loser

BIG PICTURE
Luke 22:32
Ezekiel 34:11–16

FOCUS
'But I have prayed for you, Simon, that your faith may not fail. And when you have turned back, strengthen your brothers.' (Luke 22:32)

I'VE often talked in my writing about those days of doing sports at school and the humiliation that took place when the soccer teams were being selected. The two captains would wrinkle up their noses as they looked at the line-up of possible team players. At the very end of the line, and subject to more nose wrinkling than anyone else, stood yours truly, not yet a Christian, yet praying like mad that I wouldn't be the last to be picked.

Most of my prayers apparently went unanswered, and I normally *was* the final pick. How I wished I could have been a better player, a greater athlete, 'sleek and strong', the very first to be selected or even (impossible bliss) one of the two captains.

Jesus was looking for a captain to lead His team into their first major play-off: the kingdom of God versus the powers of darkness. Putting it bluntly, He chose a loser. Jesus always knew that Peter was capable of blundering and brilliance. Peter's denial (which we'll examine in closer detail next week) meant that the Twelve were going to be led by someone who would deny ever knowing Jesus – not because he feared Roman torture, but over a conversation with a servant girl.

Perhaps you're one of the people who rarely gets picked. Your looks, your gifts (or lack of them), or your limited social skills mean that you feel like you're always on the outside, never at the centre. If that's how you feel, I'm so sorry: there are no words to ease your pain quickly. But be assured of this: you're on *His* team.

Prayer: I did not choose You, Jesus – You chose me. And I'm grateful. Amen.

Self-deception

A CHRISTIAN leader and dear friend was recently caught in a situation where he had made some disastrous moral choices. He was dismissed from his job and placed on a two-year programme of discipline and restoration. But more than once I found myself squirming with discomfort when the news of his failure got out. Some of those who heard the news were shocked, and announced that they could 'never ever do such a thing'. While I hope that we would all make the right choices if tempted, I'm convinced that the stance of 'I could never do that' is an actual step to failure. Mark's Gospel has Peter 'insisting emphatically' that he would never fail Jesus (Mark 14:31) – and the other 11 joined in the chorus of self-certainty. Matthew and John have Peter pledging allegiance until death (Matt. 26:35; John 13:37). Peter would later encourage his friends to allow a depth of character to grow in them, and escape the corruption in the world caused by evil desires (2 Pet. 1:4). He knew that it took more than wordy aspirations to stand firm in the more difficult challenges of life.

Putting it bluntly, if we feel we have never failed – say, for example, in our sexuality – it may not be because we are so strong. The reason may not be so much moral muscle as a lack of opportunity. Who knows how any one of us might react given the right set of circumstances (which we'll consider in Peter's life next week)? We might find ourselves not only falling, but taking a willing dive. Let's be mindful of our weaknesses. And never say, 'I could never …'

Prayer: You know me, God. Show me the truth about myself, that I might be faithful where I am weak. Amen.

BIG PICTURE
Luke 22:33–34
2 Peter 1:3–11

FOCUS
'But he replied, "Lord, I am ready to go with you to prison and to death."'
(Luke 22:33)

Let's be
mindful of our
weaknesses

Managing God

BIG PICTURE
Matthew 16:21–23
Job 38:1–41

FOCUS
'Peter took him aside
and began to rebuke him.
"Never, Lord!" he said.
"This shall never
happen to you!"'
(Matt. 16:22)

OUR trip through Asia continued yesterday with a brief stopover in Singapore, a beautiful city dedicated to the art of retail therapy – I have never seen so many shops in one place, or so many thousands of eager shoppers, all in hot pursuit of yet more stuff. Like teeming ants around burrows, we hurry in and out, clutching another item to add to our nest, and a piece of cloth or gold to enhance the way we look. Shopping makes us feel in control.

One avid purchaser was wearing a T-shirt that carried a piece of dark humour. It announced in bold lettering, 'When I get to be God, you're all dead'. I really wanted to stop him and ask him how he actually would manage the universe if he became God; so many shake their fists in God's face, especially when bad things happen. So how would we run things, if, like Bruce in the film *Bruce Almighty*, we took over as God for a while?

Peter didn't try to be God, but he did try to manage the Son of God and become His personal choreographer, attempting to dictate what Jesus could and couldn't do. Peter's pushiness was for all the best reasons – terrible ideas often seem entirely logical – but Jesus shrugged off his steering attempt with a firm rebuke.

There have been a few junction moments in my life when I had to choose between what seemed to be like a good idea from my perspective, and what God was actually asking from me. Take it from me: obedience is better. God knows how to do life.

Prayer: Be Lord, God, and show me when I'm attempting a takeover. Amen.

Tales of two failures

Last week I mentioned an old friend who made some disastrous choices in his life. I can think of another dear friend, who sinned with such depravity that he felt the only way to redemption was to take his own life. And how utterly wrong he was.

A comparison between Peter's and Judas's failures makes for interesting but controversial reading. Jesus prophesied both of their betrayals, which doesn't mean they were puppets of prophecy, or just playthings of God, that they had to be on hand so that Scripture might be fulfilled. Jesus' *foreknowledge* of these two tragic events doesn't mean that they were *foreordained*, which is quite different. Both men failed because of poor choices; in Judas's case there was a consistent character flaw. So Peter wept and would have breakfast with Jesus, while Judas threw his 'blood' money back at the priests and killed himself. Could it all have been different? Could Judas have found forgiveness and grace, and served the purposes of the kingdom again? Why not?

Perhaps, for whatever reason, life doesn't seem worth the effort and death seems attractive. I beg you: think again. There yet can be better days and breakfasts with Jesus to come.

There yet can be better days … with Jesus to come

89

Tired out

BIG PICTURE
Matthew 26:36–46
Proverbs 3:24–35

FOCUS
'Then he returned to his
disciples and found them
sleeping. "Could you
men not keep watch
with me for one hour?"
he asked Peter.'
(Matt. 26:40)

SO WHY do people who genuinely love Jesus let Him down terribly? Looking closely at the story of those who slept when they were asked to pray, it seems to me that a lethal cocktail of shame, bewilderment, grief and bone-dead tiredness got these great men down.

I'm starting to get that numbing tiredness feeling. This week I've been insane enough to step foot on four continents: Asia, Australasia, North America and finally Europe. I'm a different chap when I'm tired. It seems that I wear telescopic lenses in my glasses, which make every little incident a huge issue that I need to 'helpfully' comment on. The chap who was niggling about something incidental as we boarded the plane in Sydney today came narrowly close to hearing a little sermonette from me. The tight grip of my arm from my loving and so understanding wife delivered me from yet another embarrassing gaffe. Tiredness makes everything seem dark as well. I've learned not to make major decisions about the future of my life while tired: the weariness sours my joy, blinding me to the good bits of life. Thankfulness seems packed away in the overhead baggage compartment. And I tend to react rather than respond when I'm tired. Energy and wisdom fade and before I know it, I've done something quite insane, which I'd never consider normally.

Mark records that the exhausted disciples fell into a deep sleep no less than three times in the Garden of Gethsemane (Mark 14:41). We were designed to get proper rest. It's no indulgence to sleep, and sleep well. Your friends will thank you for it.

Prayer: Lord, teach me to live well, work hard, rest and relax. Amen.

Impulse

MOST of the things that I've come to regret doing have been done impulsively. Either my brain was in neutral or my heart was stirred by some dubious power, and so, without taking time to reflect, I jumped in with both feet. I live to regret those days bitterly.

Peter had already massively embarrassed himself in the Garden of Gethsemane: first he fell asleep at the hour of his Master's greatest need, and then his 'contribution' to the moment of arrest was to clumsily swing a sword and amputate a young lad's ear. Jesus fixed Peter's botch-up with an impromptu miracle, but nevertheless Peter would have known that, even with his best effort, which was brave but ill-conceived, he'd made a mess of things. He'd wanted so much to defend Jesus, but his action was not what Jesus wanted.

Yesterday I heard of a lady in America who has taught Sunday School in her church for over 50 years, but has just been removed from her post, because her church has decided to 'get more biblical'. There goes another ear. How many people have been damaged by zealous people doing things in the name of God that were actually unhelpful and hurtful?

Perhaps you've been 'chopping off a few ears' lately. Your well-planned tactics have gone terribly wrong, making things even worse than they were, and now you're so crimson-faced with embarrassment at your gaffes, you're reluctant to try again. Please, for everyone's sake, put that sword down.

Prayer: Save me from my well-intentioned efforts that might damage and wound today. Amen.

BIG PICTURE
John 18:1–11
Luke 22:47–51

FOCUS
'Then Simon Peter, who had a sword, drew it and struck the high priest's servant, cutting off his right ear.' (John 18:10)

Please …

put that

sword down

Parting

BIG PICTURE
Luke 22:39–51
Psalm 88:1–18

FOCUS
'When he rose from
prayer and went back
to the disciples, he found
them asleep, exhausted
from sorrow.'
(Luke 22:45)

AFTER 12 days of wonderful friendship and family time with Kelly and Ben, our daughter and son-in-law, we've said goodbye, keenly aware that we go back to Europe and they stay on in Indonesia. At one level, I wouldn't want them to be anywhere else. I know that they are courageously pursuing the purposes of God for their lives, surely the answer to every parent's prayer for their children. But there are times when I don't want them to care about the dispossessed and the marginalised, or to spend their days swatting mosquitoes that carry malaria and the dreaded dengue fever. I don't want them to be where earthquakes are a real, regular threat. Selfishly, I want them sitting on this darkened plane with me. My sadness at parting with them threatens to drape a shroud of depression over the coming weeks. Parting is tough. And as I write these words, I'm aware that some who read them face a greater pain – you would be thrilled if your loved ones were at least alive, even if they were thousands of miles away. Your parting has created a greater darkness.

The disciples were exhausted from sorrow. So distraught were they at the thought of bidding farewell to the most remarkable person that they had ever met, they could only long for the relief that the oblivion of sleep can bring.

As I write, I am pausing to pray for you, dear reader, if grief is draped over your shoulders today. And as you read this, if you'd like (again, to be personal) – then please pray for dear Kelly and Ben.

Prayer: For each one who weeps alone, today, bring comfort, bring hope and ease their fearful hearts. Amen.

WHEN I mess up, I sometimes find myself wanting to put some distance between me and God. Shame and regret can be overwhelming, and instead of running quickly in repentance to find the relief that a reunion with God can bring, I am like Peter – I walk away and weep. This was not the first time Peter had tried to put some space between him and Jesus because of his awareness of his sinfulness. When they had first met, Peter had made a strange request for distance: 'Go away from me Lord; I am a sinful man!' (Luke 5:8). Now, as Jesus is being tormented by the authorities, Peter cannot bear to be in the same place as the Lord he has denied. The sanity and clarity that comes with the realisation that we have failed can be frightening; perhaps Peter was totally overwhelmed by the enormity of his cowardice: all of his promises of love and loyalty to Jesus had crumbled under pressure.

What is it that you think is too much for God to forgive? It's possible that you still name yourself as a Christian – I suppose you'd be unlikely to be reading this if you didn't – and yet there is a distance that remains between you and God ever since you failed Him in some way; you still believe, but intimacy has been lost. We all need to know how to weep over our sin – but walk towards, not away from Jesus.

Prayer: When troubles like sea billows roll, may I be able to say: Lord, it is well with my soul. Amen.

Overwhelmed

BIG PICTURE
Luke 22:54–60
Proverbs 3:21–26

FOCUS
'Then Peter remembered the word the Lord had spoken to him: "Before the cock crows today, you will disown me three times." And he went outside and wept bitterly.'
(Luke 22:61b–62)

… walk towards,

not away

from Jesus

The very best Friday

BIG PICTURE
**Luke 22:61–65
Matthew 27:32–56**

FOCUS
'The Lord turned and looked straight at Peter. Then Peter remembered the word the Lord had spoken to him: "Before the cock crows today, you will disown me three times."' (Luke 22:61)

IT WAS surely the worst moment of Peter's life – and in a sense, the best. All his protestations of love and loyalty had come to nothing. He'd denied even knowing Jesus, not because a burly Roman thug was scourging him, but during a fireside chat with a couple of strangers. And then came the moment that only Luke records – when a bloodied, exhausted Jesus turned and looked over at Peter. The Greek word used here means to glance, so there's no need to imagine a piercing stare: no lengthy gazing was needed, any more than words needed to be spoken. Peter knew that Jesus had been right all along. But this is the best moment too, for Peter now comes to the end of his own resources. Before him stood the Lamb of God, about to die for Peter's sin.

No wonder Peter went outside and wept bitterly. When he first met Jesus, the sense of total holiness about Him had made Peter ask that He put some distance between them, so sinful did he feel (Luke 5:8). Now, he could hardly stand to look at the total love of Jesus for him, contrasted with the fickle affection that had meant that denial – not once, but three times – was what Peter had given back to that love divine.

Today, we pause to grieve over our ugliness and sinfulness, and we wonder at His beauty and grace. We acknowledge that He has seen us at our very worst, and given His very best for us nonetheless. When He went out to die, marvellously, His eyes were upon us. We may weep, but we *must* worship.

Prayer: Thank You for the cross, living Saviour, and that Your look towards me is one of sacrificial love. Amen.

Appearing to Peter

When it comes to Jesus appearing in His resurrection glory, it seems that failed Peter was singled out for some special treatment. According to Luke (24:34), the disciples told the couple who had met Jesus on the road to Emmaus that He had appeared to Peter, and Paul writes to the Corinthians and tells them that Jesus appeared 'to Peter, and then to the Twelve' (1 Cor. 15:5). That appearance was probably sandwiched in between the different events of John 20 and before the life-changing breakfast encounter of John 21.

Perhaps this was because of the strategic and key role that Peter would take in the early leadership of the Church. Maybe the still-shamed fisherman needed special coaxing to be able to understand that he was still part of the kingdom plan. But perhaps Peter's running to the empty tomb gives us a hint too: he was hungry, desperate even, to see the Risen Jesus. He can't contain himself, and even though John beat him to the spot, it was Peter who burst inside to see what – or who – was there. He shoved aside fears about becoming ritually unclean; he loved Jesus and so all the minor details were brushed away, as he sought to know: what had happened to his Lord?

… he was hungry … to see the Risen Jesus

Life before death

BIG PICTURE
John 21:1–6
Luke 5:1–11

FOCUS
'He said, "Throw your net on the right side of the boat and you will find some." When they did, they were unable to haul the net in …'
(John 21:6)

PERHAPS you're thinking that we've looked at the fifth chapter of Luke before – and you'd be right. It was the occasion when, three epic years earlier, Peter had received his call to follow Jesus. A miraculous catch of fish caught his attention – and as Jesus seeks to renew Peter's sense of calling, that encounter is repeated, with yet another bumper catch. In order to take Peter forward, Jesus had to take him back – to the moment that had revolutionised Peter's life in the first place.

We so easily forget what's important. It's not that we throw in the towel when it comes to faith – we can just settle back into mere survival, which is perhaps what Peter was doing when he returned to his chosen profession. He had a family to support, but his primary calling had been to fish for men.

As one who gave his life to Christ as a teenager, I'm being challenged to continue to make radical choices today as a 50-year-old, with a lot more responsibilities and a lot less hair. Sometimes simple survival looks attractive; every now and again, opportunity presents me with a moment to make a radical decision, one that determines whether or not the life of faith remains fact or theory for me.

So which direction would Peter choose? Would he take the pathway where supernatural power backed his word, where the expansion of the kingdom of God was his biggest concern, rather than a healthy catch to pay the bills?

However we work out our calling, every one of us is involved in full-time Christian service. Let's really live, and not just survive.

Prayer: Lord, You have saved me and called me to Your purposes. Help me to live, not just survive. Amen.

Walking *in* water

PETER had walked *on* water once, albeit briefly. Now he has to content himself with splashing through the low tide and finally finding his way up the beach to meet Jesus – walking *in* water. Sometimes I meet Christians who talk endlessly about the 'good old days' – they have actually become imprisoned by an unhealthy nostalgia that means that they seem less effective today. Saying goodbye to Indonesia a few days ago has thrown me into a nostalgic fit. I *so* want my children to be young again, to hear their innocent laughter and enjoy the wonderful times of yesteryear. But just as Peter's experience of being able to defy the laws of physics and water was a one-time event, now he had to meet Jesus in this new phase of his life. He has to bid farewell to one of his moments of greatest exhilaration.

And there, as he meets Jesus, he is also greeted by the sight of a charcoal fire – and the last time that Scripture describes a charcoal fire was when Peter warmed his hands by one, and denied Jesus. But now there are hands moving across the flames, hands with holes in them, cooking breakfast for a famished group of friends. Peter also has to learn that the moment that he most regrets, the denial, is forgiven: the price paid by those hands.

What is it that you most long for in the past, or regret about your personal history? Let it go and meet with Jesus today. Breakfast is ready.

Prayer: Help me to walk *in* water, even if I once walked *on* it. Amen.

BIG PICTURE
**John 21:7–14
2 Peter 1:12–21**

FOCUS
'As soon as Simon Peter heard him say, "It is the Lord!" he wrapped his outer garment around him (for he had taken it off) and jumped into the water.' (John 21:7)

… meet with

Jesus today

Steadfast honesty

BIG PICTURE
John 21:15–17
John 4:21–24

FOCUS
'... Jesus said to Simon Peter, "Simon ... do you truly love me more than these?" "Yes, Lord," he said, "you know that I love you." Jesus said, "Feed my lambs."'
(John 21:15)

I LOVE to worship, but there are times when I struggle to join in with songs about loving God more than anything in the world, or being ready to die for Him. Words like that need some thinking about.

We've already learned that Peter had been the ebullient enthusiast who was quick to express his undying loyalty to Jesus – loyalty that crumbled under the strain of Jesus' trial. Now Peter has changed, as a close look at this conversation will show. When Jesus asked Peter how much he loved Him, He used the word *agape*, the highest form of love, intense and sacrificial. But Peter, in affirming his love, switched the word in the Greek, and used *phileo* – a lesser love between friends. Don't criticise Peter for lack of love, but compliment him for his magnificent honesty. And Peter wouldn't budge from that place of rugged reality. The second time Jesus placed the question, *agape* was used again – with the same *phileo* response from Peter. Nothing could induce Peter to offer cheap, meaningless words that couldn't be fully backed up by his life. The third question from Jesus cut Peter deeply – for Jesus changed *agape* to *phileo* – effectively asking Peter if he really even had that kind of love in his heart. Somewhat wounded, but growing from the encounter, Peter realises that the only person who really knows what's in the heart of a human is God Himself.

So if you struggle to join in with the singalong immediately, be encouraged. Perhaps it's not that you don't love God – you just love Him too much to exaggerate. Let's worship in spirit and *truth*.

Prayer: Help me to offer heartfelt worship to You, not empty, sentimental words. Amen.

I'M ONE of those charismatic type Christians who believes that God still heals today, and that the gifts of the Holy Spirit remain available to us for our nurture and maturity in the faith. But sometimes I'm troubled when the only 'prophecy' I hear is about blessing, growth or the increase of influence for those in Christian ministry. What about prophecy that prepares us for hard times ahead?

Jesus prophesied three details over Peter – the fact that he would betray Him, the truth that he would be sifted by Satan, that Peter's twilight years would be spent in confinement under the control of others, and that finally he would die a martyr's death. But Jesus did not mention the incredible success that Peter would be: there's no prediction about thousands turning to Christ at the conclusion of Peter's sermon on the Day of Pentecost. All those healings that would pulsate out of Peter's passing shadow don't get a look in either. What Jesus does do is spell out the challenges on the horizon, and then invites Peter to reaffirm his love and loyalty regardless of the outcome, as the invitation that Peter heard three years earlier is repeated: 'Follow me.'

An older, wiser, more battle-scarred Peter is invited to sign up for the second half of the journey – but Jesus makes sure that He's clarified the 'small print' before obtaining Peter's signature – and heart.

Perhaps life hasn't turned out to be what we hoped for or wanted, when we gave our lives to Christ all those months – or years – ago. Are we still willing to follow anyway?

Prayer: God, I give You the things that I have hoped for that have not happened, and I ask You to help me to be faithful in unwanted circumstances. Amen.

Dark clouds on the horizon

BIG PICTURE
**John 21:18–19
1 Thessalonians
5:1–11**

FOCUS
'I tell you the truth, when you were younger you … went where you wanted … when you are old … someone else will … lead you where you do not want to go.' (John 21:18)

Are we still willing to follow anyway?

Focus fixed

BIG PICTURE
**John 21:20–25
1 Thessalonians
4:1–12**

FOCUS
'Peter turned and saw
that the disciple whom
Jesus loved was following
them ... When Peter saw
him, he asked, "Lord,
what about him?"'
(John 21:20–21)

PETER had a habit of focusing on the wrong things at critical moments. Remember how he had walked on water – but then 'saw' the wind (Matt. 14:30)? Now, he is enjoying a final stroll on the beach with Jesus, a moment to relish and remember forever, but one that is overshadowed by Peter once again focusing on what was actually none of his concern. Having been given a chilling glimpse into his future, he, like most of us, is concerned about what is fair, and so he asks about John's future – would he also be called to walk a tough pathway which would ultimately lead to death row? Jesus' blunt retort left no room for confusion: 'What is that to you?' means what it seems to mean – mind your own business. The last thing that Peter needed here was subtlety or the gentle touch: he needed to get his attention away from someone else's life – fast.

Sometimes I find that my emotional energy is depleted because I focus on the failings of others, the inadequacies of the Church or the hypocrisies of high-profile leaders who seem to preach like angels on Sunday but live like devils on Mondays. I can become almost obsessed with their flaws. But Jesus calls me away from such a focus. He doesn't answer Peter's question, and often doesn't answer all of mine. To be a follower of Christ demands a single-mindedness and focus which means there is no room to fret about the behaviour of others. Keeping me straight is a tough enough job; keeping others straight is beyond me. Let's learn how to mind our own business.

Prayer: Father, help me to keep my nose – and my heart – out of what does not concern me. Amen.

Empowered doubters

Our journey through Peter's life has shown us clearly that he was a rough diamond, much flawed – yet still God chose to use his life spectacularly. I find real encouragement in the account of the great commissioning, because even as the resurrected Jesus meets the eleven and talks about epic themes like authority, mission and the assurance of His ongoing company with them through the Holy Spirit, still some struggle with doubt.

Doubt has the capacity to make us feel so utterly wretched and worthless. I confess that, while in Banda Aceh, I saw first-hand the constricting power of religion, with the religious police force literally able to arrest people for violating the Muslim dress code, and even administer public canings to warn those tempted to stray from the rigid rules. Surrounded by that much oppression, all done in the name of religion, I found myself wondering how much damage has been done to the earth in the name of God, by people of all faiths, including Christians. For a moment or two, I wanted to abandon belief, seeing it as constricting rather than liberating. But I can rest easy when I doubt – as can you. We're not alone.

… I can rest
easy when
I doubt …

The big story

BIG PICTURE
Luke 24:36–53
Luke 24:13–17

FOCUS
'He said to them, "This
is what I told you …
Everything must be
fulfilled that is written
about me in the Law of
Moses, the Prophets and
the Psalms."'
(Luke 24:44)

THE third film in the *Lord of the Rings* trilogy created quite a stir among J.R.R. Tolkien purists. According to critics, a vital seven minutes of the final cut of the film was edited out, which not only changed the entire story but altered the message of the film. The loss of a story changes everything.

The story of our God reaching out with His saving grace is what Tom Wright calls 'The Big Fat Story'. In a postmodern world that has generally rejected the idea that there is a foundational story, a core reason behind life, we have news. The gospel is not just that Jesus has come to do something to get us into heaven when we die. To suggest such is to minimise the drama of all dramas that is God's story. The story of the people of God is a wide-screen, big picture epic, a captivating blockbuster; the truth of God the Creator insisting on a continued relationship with the world that He has made; of Him intervening to rescue them, in the Exodus and the cross, and calling them into partnership with His cosmos-shaping purposes.

Before being launched into the world, the disciples had to see the wide-screen view and so Jesus connects all that He has done with Moses and the Prophets, to show that they were part of the glorious eternal activities of God Himself. The final chapter of that story is still being penned, and we are in the screenplay.

God's big story: let's not settle for living for anything less.

Prayer: Thank You that I'm in the story. Help me to keep it before me as I live more lines today. Amen.

Taking responsibility

THERE have been endless debates about the appointment of Matthias to the apostolic ministry – mainly because he is mentioned only here and never heard of again. Also, the casting of lots seems to be a strange way of making a decision, but we should remember that this was before the giving of the Holy Spirit in His fullness. Whether Peter was right or wrong in his claim to have biblical support for replacing Judas, we don't know. But what we do know is he has stopped running back to his fishing nets and is now taking responsibility for the work of God. Something has changed about Peter – is it possible that his experience of failure and then restoration was part of a maturing process that enabled him once again to throw everything he had into serving God?

As I travel and talk to church members and leaders alike, I am repeatedly told that there is a desperate need for people to take responsibility in the church, rather than just being spectators or pew fillers. It's too easy to become a consumer, demanding to be entertained weekly, insisting that the church be shaped around our preferences and never actually rolling up our sleeves and *doing* anything. It's tempting to become vocal critics rather than weary workers – anyone who has ever attended any kind of sports game knows that it is the spectators who are the loudest and most expert people in the stadium. Here's a question for all of us to consider – if we left our church, would there be a gap?

Prayer: God, take me from the stadium onto the field, and help me play my part in Your team. Amen.

BIG PICTURE
Acts 1:12–26
1 Corinthians 12:1–11

FOCUS
'… Peter … said, "Brothers, the Scripture had to be fulfilled which the Holy Spirit spoke … concerning Judas … he was one of our number and shared in this ministry."'
(Acts 1:15–17)

… if we left our church, would there be a gap?

To boldly go

BIG PICTURE
Acts 2:14–41
2 Peter 2:1–22

FOCUS
'[He] was handed over to you by God's set purpose and foreknowledge; and you, with the help of wicked men, put him to death by nailing him to the cross.' (Acts 2:23)

THE real test of Peter's mettle had come. It's one thing to be a passionately committed follower of Christ behind closed doors, in the company of others who share your faith. It's quite another to stick your head up over the parapet and make a public stand for Jesus in the marketplace, as Peter does now.

And he doesn't mince his words, as his sermon here shows, and as his words in 2 Peter also demonstrate: he roundly confronts false teaching without fear. He lays the blame for the execution of Jesus right at the feet of those who politically engineered it, and doesn't hesitate to call a spade a spade: wicked men were responsible, even if God's sovereign purposes were unfolding behind the scenes.

But be careful. Passages like this can give some rude people an excuse to be rude in Jesus' name, which is a false use of the episode. What we do see here is a fearless determination on Peter's part to be clearly identified with Jesus: he is no longer the one who denied ever knowing Christ; he is no longer ashamed, knowing that Jesus was not ashamed of him (Luke 9:26).

Evangelism is not about shouting loudly and seeing how many people we can offend with the fewest amount of sentences. It is a call to stand with clarity and grace at Jesus' side. If the world hates Him, sometimes we'll get caught in the crossfire as we insist on identifying with Christ and His great kingdom cause.

Prayer: Great God, grant me boldness and confidence that is never arrogant or bombastic. Amen.

Mixed motives

WE WERE sitting at table in an outdoor restaurant in Singapore when the lady approached us. She made her living from begging, and had become angry and bitter at her lot in life, not surprisingly. Whatever the reasons for her homelessness, it can't be easy watching others enjoying plenty when you have next to nothing.

I was ready to give her some money, but I'm embarrassed to confess that my attitude changed when she loudly demanded not only some help but the actual sum of money that she felt would be appropriate for us to hand over. All of that advice about not giving to beggars on the streets (much of which may well be right) leapt into my mind, and I quickly said that we were not going to give, whereupon she turned really abusive. I asked her to leave us alone, which she finally did, after some spicy language and graphic personal insults.

To be honest, I'm not sure how I would deal with the situation if faced with it again. But what is clear from this miracle account at the Gate Beautiful is that Peter did not wait for the beggar to get his motives pure before helping him. The approach area to the Temple was an ideal place to beg – worshippers were more susceptible to being put on a guilt trip. You could say that this beggar was a strategic expert in manipulation, albeit to survive. But Peter brushed that aside and healed the man.

Let's not wait for people to conform to our expectations before we reach out to help them.

Prayer: Help me to help, even when others seem ungrateful or their motives catch my attention more than their need. Amen.

BIG PICTURE
Acts 3:1–10
Galatians 2:10

FOCUS
'Now a man crippled from birth was being carried to the temple gate called Beautiful, where he was put every day to beg from those going into the temple courts.'
(Acts 3:2)

Let's … reach

out to help …

Surprise, surprise

BIG PICTURE
Acts 3:11–4:22
2 Peter 3:1–10

FOCUS
'… Peter … said … "Men of Israel, why does this surprise you? Why do you stare at us as if by our own power or godliness we had made this man walk?"' (Acts 3:12)

GOD is faithful and consistent, yet not necessarily predictable. But having walked with Him now for over 30 years, I find that I can settle into the kind of malaise that means that I think I have Him all figured out. I have become so adept at providing people with helpful reasons why some people are *not* healed, that I almost come to expect that miracles never happen and prayers are seldom answered.

So it was with the 'Men of Israel' that Peter challenged, who believed passionately in the God who parted the Red Sea yesterday, but whose mouths hit the floor when the beggar at the Gate Beautiful got up and walked today. I find that I can so easily settle into a humdrum daily existence, and become inoculated against the potential of the miraculous by the hucksters who either exaggerate stories about mighty miracles or seek to profit from them personally. All this makes me forget: there is a God. He is mighty. He can do things that are quite impossible. The fact that I seldom *see* the miraculous does not deny the *reality* of the miraculous.

Perhaps you too have settled into a life where you believe in God but don't really expect Him to do much. Maybe cynicism has mugged you or disappointment has made you wary of any expectation. Too many apparently unanswered prayers mean that you have just become too weary to ask anymore. Don't ask for mere fireworks today – but do ask for your capacity to be surprised by God to be reawakened.

Prayer: Great God, renew my faith: give me discernment, but remove cynicism from my heart. Amen.

Extravagant faith

Christians are frequently caricatured as 'safe' people – a euphemism for 'boring'. Some of us were boring before we found Christ, and we've managed to remain so. But there's a red-hot passion about the apostles as they report on the threats that have been made. Plunged suddenly into the furnace of opposition, Peter and his companions display a wildness of commitment which is refreshing and carefree – theirs is an extravagant faith. They pray with energy and simplicity, saying in essence, 'You're so much bigger than our enemies, God – take a look at their fighting talk!' But this is not just zeal – this is mature, grown-up faith at its best.

There is a tide of generous giving flowing too, led by Barnabas. We're watching a people so excited about God that 'little' things, like criticism, persecution, and selfishness are ignored. With all of this comes a white-hot sense of holiness: Ananias and Sapphira die when Peter speaks the word of judgment.

Passion is not the same as energy – it's possible to be passionate about God and feel completely exhausted. Rather, true passion for Christ is demonstrated in our behaviour, as it was in theirs. Been 'wild' for God lately?

Been 'wild' for
God lately?

Miracles and mystery

BIG PICTURE
Acts 5:12–42
James 5:13–20

FOCUS
'The apostles performed many miraculous signs and wonders among the people. And all the believers used to meet together in Solomon's Colonnade.' (Acts 5:12)

I SAID earlier that I believe God still heals today, but I am almost totally mystified by the subject. As we look at the dynamic explosion that was the Early Church, with demons expelled, the sick healed in huge numbers and angels organising an apostolic jail break, it is obvious that the gospel is indeed a supernatural message. I've never understood those people who say that healings ended when the last of the 12 apostles died – not only does the Bible say no such thing, but the thought of it is patently absurd. 'Better pray for those who need healing quick, because the last of the Twelve has been arrested and will be executed tomorrow. We'd better get our prayer requests in soon …'

But I am equally troubled by those who turn healing into a system, with God as a cosmic vending machine of miracles who will obligingly dispense the desired answer if we have the right coins. And although I remain totally convinced that we need to pray for the sick to be healed – that's all part of the marvellous kingdom partnership that we've been invited to participate in – I don't think that there's a prayer meter in heaven. 'We'd like to see Fred healed, but sadly we're 27 prayers short of the 632 petitions needed. If those last few petitions don't come in soon, it's not looking too good for Fred …'

Surely we can hold a view of God's power and healing that doesn't turn everything into a system, or make sick people feel worse when we tell them they aren't healed because of lack of faith' (or sin). Healing as a simplified system won't work. God will be good, but God is still God.

Prayer: Grant me a balanced, sane and biblical faith in You, living, loving God. Amen.

Open, yet discerning

WHEN I was a young Christian, being dogmatic came naturally to me. Even though I had a very limited knowledge of the Scriptures, my lack of insight was matched by feeling very, very right about most subjects. I cringe now when I look back at some of my more aggressive episodes, where I seemed to think that listening to the opinions of others was an unethical compromise. It's one thing to be burned at the stake for the truth, but quite another not to be able to admit that you're wrong.

But there's another extreme, which I think I could be equally susceptible to – where I become so nervous of anything that has the vaguest scent of dogmatism that I refuse to hold any absolute convictions about anything. This woolly tendency is especially easy in our postmodern culture of relativism, where the overriding belief is that any belief is legitimate as long as it satisfies the individual.

As Samaria becomes a place of miracles, Peter exercises a wonderful combination of openness and yet discernment. It was radical and hugely brain-stretching for Peter and his fellow Jewish Christians to think of God at work among these despised Samaritans; Peter had not had his famous 'snack on food that's not kosher' vision that would confirm that the gospel was going to the Gentiles. Yet Peter and John have hearts that are wide open to what God was doing, surprising though it was – but firmly rebuked Simon the Sorcerer for his attempts to merchandise the power of God. Open, yet discerning – that's the balanced place for us all to be.

Prayer: Give me the ability to be a person both of flexibility and conviction – a combination only possible through Your grace, Lord. Amen.

BIG PICTURE
**Acts 8:4–25
1 Thessalonians
5:19–21**

FOCUS
'Peter answered: "May your money perish with you, because you thought you could buy the gift of God with money!"'
(Acts 8:20)

… hearts that

are wide open

to what God

was doing …

Brother Paul

BIG PICTURE
Acts 9:1–43
2 Peter 3:15–17

FOCUS
'When the brothers
learned of this, they took
him down to Caesarea
and sent him off to
Tarsus.' (Acts 9:30)

I DON'T like it when Christians refer to me as 'Brother', or even 'Brother Jeff'. Don't write in, it's just a personal preference. But sometimes the word 'brother' is loaded with love and meaning.

Today's reading includes the story of Saul's conversion, the mighty apostle who was eventually to become such a leading light in the Early Church. I include it here and the account of Peter's continuing ministry, because it does say something about Peter's nature in that he was able to make room for this most unexpected convert. A former persecutor of the Church, Saul had not travelled the road that Peter and the others had taken, and of course he didn't fulfil the qualifications that Peter himself had set out for the earlier appointment of Matthias to the Twelve. But Peter continues to do what he was called to, while not only making room for Paul but speaking warmly of him – he calls him 'our dear brother' and even defends him when others criticised him.

It takes grace to watch others come to the forefront or enjoy a blessing that we can only long for. Peter still had a vital part to play but is beginning to fade from the limelight.

Are there people who have stepped ahead of you, been promoted before you, as if your employer or church leaders have failed to notice your hard work and tireless faithfulness? Is someone else being celebrated for the achievements that actually belong to you?

Ask God for grace, and let it go. Ultimately, what we do in life, wherever we do it, is done in His name and for an audience of one.

Prayer: You see me, in my failures and my faithfulness, Lord. Let that knowledge be enough. Amen.

SOMETIMES I am so slow to learn. I'm grateful that patience is not only a virtue, but one of God's characteristics, because I've been around the block on a few issues that I should have sorted out faster. Sound familiar?

As Peter dreams his famous dream, this is obviously a major turning point in the history of the Church. It becomes clear, both from Cornelius's experience and Peter's revelation, that the gospel really is a message that includes the Gentiles. But look again. Many years earlier, Jesus had clearly taught His disciples that there was no such thing as unclean food, and then had immediately travelled in Gentile country to preach the message of the kingdom (Mark 7:14–19, 24). Now, years on, Peter is stammering out his hesitation about eating unclean food – and it is three times over that God has to repeat the command – 'Arise and eat'. Of course, the sentence spoken three times would ring some familiar bells in Peter's heart – remember how he had been asked the question three times over breakfast with Jesus, 'Do you love me?' This repeated statement spoke emphatically to Peter, who still wrestled with kosher thinking – don't call unclean what God has called clean.

It's a good thing that Peter finally 'got it', because the history of the Church would have been very different if he hadn't. The day would come when Gentiles, like most of us, would read Peter's words, which previously had been reserved for the Jews: 'But you are a chosen people, a royal priesthood, a holy nation, a people belonging to God …' (1 Pet. 2:9).

Where are we being slow on the uptake?

Prayer: Help me to learn, first time around, patient God, loving Father. Amen.

So dull

BIG PICTURE
Acts 10:1–48
Mark 7:14–19

FOCUS
'Then a voice told him, "Get up, Peter. Kill and eat." "Surely not, Lord!" Peter replied. "I have never eaten anything impure or unclean."'
(Acts 10:13–14)

… patience …

one of God's

characteristics …

A soft answer

BIG PICTURE
Acts 11:1–18
Proverbs 15:1

FOCUS
'… when Peter went up to Jerusalem, the circumcised believers criticised him and said, "You went into the house of uncircumcised men and ate with them." Peter … explained everything to them …' (Acts 11:2–4)

I KNOW of a well-known speaker and writer who is so convinced of the authenticity of his insights and revelations that he has commented – in print – that those who don't believe in his particular brand of Christianity are nothing less than 'peanut brains'. I've heard him use this kind of rhetoric while preaching, and some people in the crowd seem to love what is spiritualised arrogance. If God has revealed such mighty things to him, then why hasn't some information about the importance of humility and grace been downloaded too? And I have been guilty of the very same thing; sometimes my youthful passion for Christ, against what I saw as 'mere' religion, meant that I rudely caricatured other people's expressions of Christian faith, obviously implying that the way I and my friends 'did' Christianity was the superior way. Recently someone wrote to me, criticising me for making a somewhat cutting remark in one of my books. They were right, and I'm grateful for their kind correction. The next edition of that book will be revised.

Peter showed great grace as he was attacked for doing only what God had clearly told him to do. Instead of sulking or getting angry, he carefully gives an explanation to his hearers, who hadn't had the benefit of participating in his rooftop dream. What could have been a devastating clash and a potential for schism ends wonderfully, and the gospel continues its impact among the Gentiles.

Are you being called to account by those who exasperate you or just don't seem to understand? Take a deep breath. Be kind and explain. Much pain might well be avoided.

Prayer: Fill my heart with grace when I hear unpalatable truth about myself from faithful friends. Amen.

A ship of fools

I love the Church, but we are a hilarious lot. We get upset over things that don't matter, ignore the issues that do, and sometimes make the most ridiculous statements that at very least must be off-putting to those who are looking in. We are bumbling along. And it's always been that way. The story of Peter's imprisonment and subsequent supernatural release is a marvellous mixture of power, prayer and stumbling incompetence. The Church faithfully prays for their beloved leader, and then someone forgets to actually open the door to let him in to the prayer meeting, because they are so overjoyed to see him. Angels open prison doors, but Christians forget the door to their gathering. And then when the report is shared that Peter is outside, the 'faith-filled' prayer gathering insist that it must be his ghost. Apparently their prayers for Peter hadn't been too hopeful!

As we look at them, and consider our last couple of months glancing at snapshots of Peter's life, we remember that we too are just the same as him, and them – ordinary people who love God, and are capable of greatness and great stupidity. I find that *really* encouraging …

… we too are just … ordinary people who love God …

113

Still learning

BIG PICTURE
Acts 15:1–11
Galatians 2:11–14

FOCUS
'… Peter … addressed
them: "Brothers, you
know that some time
ago God made a choice
among you that the
Gentiles might hear from
my lips the message of
the gospel and believe."'
(Acts 15:7)

AS WE look at two final references to Peter's life in the New Testament, we see that Paul got into conflict with Peter and rebuked him – Paul records that incident in his letter to the Galatians. Scholars have debated what the 'visit to Antioch' by Peter refers to – was it the visit described in Acts 11:29–30, or is Paul actually filling in a little detail on the conference described here in Acts 15?

In a way, it doesn't matter. What counts is that Peter submits himself to the rebuke and counsel of the junior who is Paul, and so demonstrates that, though he has learned many lessons in the school of hard knocks, he is still open to correction when he needs it.

I'd like to grow older like that. Far from being deluded by my Bible knowledge and experience, I'd love to have the character to hear kind correction from the most unexpected sources, as we saw last week. I'd like to keep learning until I die.

Peter ended well, both as a learner and a faithful disciple, even until his painful end. Tradition has it that he was crucified upside down, insisting that he was unworthy to die in the same position as his Lord. While we don't know that this is definitely authentic, we know this: this passionate, thoughtful, thoughtless, faith-filled and doubting ex-fisherman changed the world and showed that he really did love the Lord Jesus. He shows us that failure is not the end and that extraordinary things can be done through ordinary people. May you and I be worthy carriers of the torch that Peter once held.

And, again, thanks for travelling with me!

He shows us that failure is not the end …

Prayer: Lord, may I ever learn, grow old in faithfulness, and be Yours, both now, and always. Amen.

Proverbs – Wise words
for a wild world

Proverbs – Wise words for a wild world

WHEN I was in school, I gathered quite a lot of information that has been quite useless to me in later life. I never got around to using algebra as an adult; the experiments I learned in the chemistry lab have never come in handy; and I can only remember one sentence from the French class. I can ask how to get to the railway station. Having been to France many times since, I've been desperate to ask someone where the trains are, but the opportunity has never arisen and I wouldn't understand the response anyway. I'm grateful for most of my education but precious little of it actually taught me how to cope with the complexities of modern existence. I downloaded data but didn't hear much about values.

Proverbs is loaded with ancient wisdom that is bang up to date. Winsome, funny, insightful and practical, our journey through some of these marvellous sayings will help equip us, right where we live. Enjoy the trip!

Designer living

HERE'S a question that desperately needs an answer: how should we live? Answers on a postcard please and make it quick. Help is urgently needed; a cursory look around us will show that we're not doing too well in the living department. Epidemic binge drinking, turning our cities into noisy danger zones after dark, shows that many are doing their best to *escape* life. If life is so great, why are so many sprinting away from its realities? The cauldron of ethnic tension bubbles away and there is a sense that another massive terrorist strike – or state sanctioned invasion – is just around the corner. As nations joust, we wonder – where will it all end?

Pop into your local bookstore and you'll see shelves stacked with self-help books; no longer do we need to date/negotiate/subdue our inner demons/pay the bills alone; there's a brace of experts standing by. Daytime television serves up an array of life 'gurus' who can also lend a hand, even down to Jerry Springer, ringmaster in a circus of human misery, who then offers his life tips. Thanks, but no thanks, Jerry.

How should we live? Proverbs provides us with a two word answer: with God. When we take God out of the picture, there is no picture – just a load of random paint blotches without meaning. And this is not God the paramedic, ever on hand to help us out with our cuts and scrapes, or God the Santa impersonator, but God the Holy One, the Creator who calls for our love, obedience and worship. We were made by God, for God.

Prayer: Every hour, every moment, I need You, living Christ. Be the centre and the reason for my life today. Amen.

BIG PICTURE
Proverbs 1:1–7
Psalm 2:1–12

FOCUS
'The fear of the LORD is the beginning of knowledge, but fools despise wisdom and discipline.' (Prov. 1:7)

How should

we live?

Wisdom and common sense

BIG PICTURE
Proverbs 1:8–19
Jeremiah 4:22

FOCUS
'Listen, my son, to your father's instruction and do not forsake your mother's teaching.'
(Prov. 1:8)

IT PAINS me to say it, but some of us Christians are rather daft. Sometimes it seems that the more 'spiritual' some people get, the quicker they are to kiss goodbye to any common sense. Over the last 30 years as a Christian, I've witnessed first-hand some of the wackiest behaviour – and I'm sure I've made my own contribution to the collection of odd things that have been done in the name of God. In my first faltering footsteps as a disciple of Jesus, I got it into my head that whatever logic and wisdom I had was fallen and therefore flawed, so I should beware of my own thought-processes – a sure-fire recipe for bizarre behaviour. One example of this was my belief that I shouldn't have non-Christian friends. Throughout the Bible we are warned that bad company corrupts character (1 Cor. 15:33). That doesn't mean we should shut ourselves away from people who aren't Christians (Jesus obviously didn't) but alerts us to the pressure that 'the crowd' might try to exert.

Proverbs uses two words to describe the legacy of good parenting; they are *instruction*, which is about the accumulation of wisdom, godly common sense if you will; the other is *teaching*, which has to do with the commands of the Law, the Torah. (See Prov. 28:7.)

We saw yesterday that we need God to be at the centre of everything in our lives and so I'm not advocating that we just 'figure life out' independently of Him. But we need wisdom as well as revelation: to use our brains as well as our Bibles.

Prayer: Thank You for giving the ability to make good choices. As I read Your Word, renew my mind. Amen.

RECENTLY I prayed with someone who is angry at God because she has not been healed of her liver disease. For years doctors have been warning her that her daily intake of whisky is killing her. Not only does she refuse to stop, she blames God because she is slowly dying.

The marvellous news of the Christian message is that we can be forgiven for the mistakes and sins that we stumble or march into. But sometimes we forget that our actions have consequences; we live in a universe where every cause has an effect and while God cancels out the due penalty and judgment for our sin when we come in repentance to Him, we may have to endure the ongoing results of our bad behaviour. A person can be forgiven for drinking too much, but they'll still have to face the headache – or the pummelling that excess alcohol gives the body. Pardon is available for marital unfaithfulness, but the marriage might still be the major casualty of that straying. Or to quote a biblical example, Peter's rash sword-swinging in the Garden of Gethsemane was forgiven and the amputated ear (one immediate consequence) repaired, but none the less one of the relatives of the unfortunate amputee recognised Peter later – an unexpected consequence of his wild hot-headedness (see John 18:25–27).

Sometimes people sin with the knowledge that they can get forgiveness later, a bizarre and twisted approach to grace. But while pardon is freely available, perhaps there are lifelong consequences that we might have to face if we take that next step into the madness that is conscious sin.

Prayer: Lord, keep me aware of tomorrow's consequences from thoughtless acts that I might be tempted to commit today. Amen.

Consequences

BIG PICTURE
Proverbs 1:20–33
Galatians 6:1–10

FOCUS
'… they will eat the fruit of their ways and be filled with the fruit of their schemes.'
(Prov. 1:31)

… sometimes we forget that our actions have consequences …

Treasure hunting

BIG PICTURE
Proverbs 2:1–22
Ecclesiastes 7:25

FOCUS
'... if you ... cry aloud
for understanding, and
... look for it as for silver
and search for it as for
hidden treasure, then
you will understand the
fear of the LORD ...'
(Prov. 2:3–5)

THE car treasure hunt did not turn out to be the joyful time of family bonding that we had hoped for. For one thing, my mind doesn't work well with oblique clues: I'm one of those sad souls who would prefer a session of Chinese water torture to completing a crossword, so the 'witty' clues that were supposed to tell us where to drive next were way over my head. And then a friend in our party forgot to tell us that she had a tendency towards car sickness. Being utterly lost in the country lanes of Sussex while stopping every three minutes for a vomit break is not my idea of fun. Not surprisingly, we never did find the treasure, even though we hunted for hours. And then it turned out to be a yellow plastic duck, good for livening up bath times but hardly worth chasing around all afternoon for.

We humans tend to dig for what seems like buried treasure but is actually useless. We can use up all of our energy collecting clutter – 'what is not bread ... what does not satisfy' (Isa. 55:2). Proverbs encourages us to be people ever on the hunt for wisdom and truth. Understanding is not something that comes to the casual. As we engage our brains to think things through; as we read, reflect, discuss, ask questions and sometimes agonise over what we believe, then that worthwhile, lifelong treasure hunt pays the greatest dividends.

So are we on a desperate safari, foraging urgently for truth, or are we less concerned about the vital matters of life?

Prayer: Father, give me a voracious appetite for wisdom and understanding; and grace as I continue to search and learn. Amen.

Promises, promises?

Some people treat the Proverbs as sure-fire promises, like the clauses of a legal contract that work in every situation. An example of this is the oft-misquoted Proverb used to make the parents feel guilty: 'train a child in the way he should go, and when he is old he will not turn from it' (Prov. 22:6).

But the Proverbs should not be used in this way. Broadly speaking, they point us to a series of lifestyle choices that will improve the quality of our existence: the man who makes sure that he stays clear of the red-light district, for example, won't end up shattering his marriage or contracting a sexually transmitted disease. Anyone holding fast to the commands of God can expect a longer life, and putting God first in our finances will be good for us, without getting into ridiculous prosperity teaching. Don't make the mistake of seeing Proverbs as a guarantee of plenty.

In the last few months, in a couple of Two-Thirds World situations, I have met Christians whose love for God makes my Christian commitment look pale; yet their life expectancy is not guaranteed because of it. The Proverbs are pointers, not promises.

The Proverbs
are pointers,
not promises

121

Reservoirs of wisdom

BIG PICTURE
Proverbs 4:1–9
Psalm 145:1–4

FOCUS
'Listen, my sons, to a father's instruction; pay attention and gain understanding.'
(Prov. 4:1)

ONE of the greatest regrets of my life is the fact that I do not know more about my own father's life journey. A teenage soldier in the Second World War, he was captured and held in Italy and Germany as a prisoner of war for four years. Finally he escaped and made his way across Europe, arriving back in England just before the war ended. My dad told me about some of his adventures; I knew some of what he did, but never discovered how he felt. I wish I had asked questions about how he sustained hope during those long years in captivity; and what drove him to make the daring break for freedom? What was it like trying to settle back down to a civilian life again? None of the questions can be answered now, as he died over a decade ago. I am the poorer for not having the benefit of his wisdom. I wish I had sat down with him with a tape recorder …

As we repeatedly hear in Proverbs the encouragement to a son to listen to the good advice of his father, we discover that true wisdom is not just found on the pages of Scripture or good books. Let's respect, honour and learn from our seniors. Many of them are frail, don't know the first thing about our high-tech labour-saving devices, and wonder what's happening to the world. But in so many cases they are also reservoirs of great wisdom, having already trekked so much of life's journey; computers may confuse them but they have experienced pressures that we can only imagine. Let's do ourselves a favour. Listen.

Prayer: Lord, thank You for those who have walked ahead of me through life. May I benefit from their wisdom. Amen.

A healthy heart

ONE of the most stupid things I have ever done (and believe me, I have a vast collection of gaffes to choose from in my life) was pouring the contents of a boiling kettle onto the keyboard of my laptop computer. It all resulted from trying to do too many things at once – tap out a sermon, make a cup of tea, with the mobile phone balanced precariously in the human hands-free position, wedged between shoulder and ear. Over went the kettle and scalding water poured into my machine, which literally – believe me – made a high-pitched screaming noise and died. Everything was nuked in a second by my carelessness. I was not a happy person at that moment. I'm a lot more careful these days about what I allow near my computer – too much is at risk.

Sometimes I'm not so careful about what I allow into my heart and of course the heart, in biblical terms, is not that pump that circulates blood around the body, but means our souls, our thoughts and our inner self. When we give access-all-areas passes to envy, bitterness, lust, greed or a host of other bad attitudes, we can expect chaos to result. It really does matter what we think about. A good life is no accident but comes from the setting of a diligent sentry on the gates of our minds. When we set our hearts on pursuing that which God prohibits, not only are we being disobedient, but we stain our lives. To change the analogy, the 'wellspring' is contaminated. Are you pouring anything toxic into your heart?

Prayer: Lord, help me to be proactive about what I allow into my heart. May I not poison that well. Amen.

BIG PICTURE
**Proverbs 4:10–27
Philippians 4:8–9**

FOCUS
'Above all else, guard your heart, for it is the wellspring of life.'
(Prov. 4: 23)

It really does

matter what we

think about

Killer on
the loose

BIG PICTURE

Proverbs 5:1–14
John 8:1–11

FOCUS

'Her feet go down to
death; her steps lead
straight to the grave.'
(Prov. 5:5)

THE health warnings that are printed on cigarette packets
are becoming ever more startling. When legislation was
first introduced in the UK to make the boldly printed
slogans mandatory, they were fairly low-key: 'Smoking
can damage your health.' Now the size of the lettering
is huge, the letters are in bold and the message more
in your face: 'Smoking kills!'; 'Smoking damages the
unborn.' But even these shock tactics fail to get some
people's attention – nicotine is still a multi-billion pound
industry and lung cancer continues its devastating work.

Here Proverbs give us all a no-holds-barred health
warning about adultery, an epidemic habit in our sex-
soaked culture. The warning is stark: adultery may cost
you everything that you value. Last week we considered
that sin carries bitter consequences. Proverbs carefully
describes the carnage that adultery creates, lest we be
left in any doubt. And the warning is needed, because the
pull can be strong and terrible choices can seem entirely
logical. The casualty list is long: adultery can empty
your bank account, shatter the confidence of those who
respect you, load you up to the brim with regret, cause
your once loving home to be an empty place of loneliness,
and bring you public ridicule. It can also mean that your
children have trouble forming long-lasting relationships.

There's forgiveness available for those who've already
wandered down that path, as the woman famously
caught in the act discovered (John 8:1–11), but we'd
all do well to seriously consider these words. Why this
graphic warning? It's because all of us are capable of
making horrendous choices. Look before you leap.

**Prayer: Help me to heed the strong warnings of Your
Word. Lead me not into temptation, loving God. Amen.**

In praise of monogamy

PICKING up of one those celebrity magazines in the hairdresser's today (I was desperate, so I reached for *OK*), I learned that one big name has announced that monogamy – faithfulness to one person – is 'not all that it's cracked up to be'. 'Let's face it, we're all just animals,' she quipped as the flashbulbs popped. The photograph of her and her equally famous boyfriend shows them as the beaming epitome of exuberance and happiness. It's all rather beguiling, but to be blunt, it's a lie. Bed-hopping is not the way to build a life. On the contrary, faithfulness, celebrated here in Proverbs, can provide the secure, trusting environment that allows for true intimacy: snacking in the sexual supermarket never truly satisfied anyone beyond a transient thrill. The joy of being able to share chatter as well as silence, to have a history of memories, through good times and bad, and the knowledge that you are so very known – and yet still loved – comes only to those who prize and pursue faithfulness.

Another celebrity put it well. Michael Palin of *Monty Python's Flying Circus* fame went to a party hosted by Andy Warhol and Truman Capote, both famous for their wild ways. Palin says that he was appalled by the debauchery of the event and, as the madness of the evening unfolded, he realised what was really important: 'What matters is being able to go with my three children to get the newspapers in the morning.' Palin was celebrating a simple, wholesome family act – but one that is better than all the grubby glitz in the world.

Prayer: God, Your pathway is good. Lord, thank You for the blessings that come from walking in Your ways. Amen.

BIG PICTURE
Proverbs 5:15–23
2 Peter 2:14

FOCUS
'May your fountain be blessed and may you rejoice in the wife of your youth … may her breasts satisfy you always, may you ever be captivated by her love.' (Prov. 5:18–19)

… faithfullness …

can provide the

secure, trusting

environment …

Get moving

BIG PICTURE
**Proverbs 6:1–5
Ecclesiastes 10:18**

FOCUS
'Allow no sleep to your eyes, no slumber to your eyelids. Free yourself, like a gazelle from the … hunter, like a bird from the snare of the fowler.'
(Prov. 6:4–5)

DESPITE owning a vehicle well equipped for the Colorado winter, I recently managed to drive my car off the side of the road and into a gully (the road had unhelpfully disappeared under about six inches of snow). Try as we might, there was not a thing we could do to get out of that muddy rut: all our best efforts just made the wheels spin and dug us deeper into the mire. We sat there in a blizzard and we were thrilled when three hours later a man with only three teeth – but importantly, a beefy tow truck – pulled us out. In the meantime, all we could do was wait.

A saying that used to do the rounds in Christian circles is, 'Let go and let God'. It can be overused. There *are* times when we find ourselves in that place where there is absolutely nothing we can do to make a scrap of difference to our plight; all our best efforts just seem to make things worse. But there are many other occasions when the Bible urges us to get ourselves into gear and take radical action fast in order to prevent disaster.

Guaranteeing a loan for an unreliable person is a recipe for disaster and so Proverbs urges us to rush to extract ourselves from such a dreadfully dangerous deal. There are times when we should not just 'leave it to the Lord', when the Lord wants us to take responsibility. Are there areas that we've 'let go of' that God wants us to grab by the scruff of the neck? Postpone that nap and get out of that trap …

Prayer: Father, help me to know when to act and when to wait for Your action. Amen.

No procrastination!

Yesterday I mentioned having to wait for a tow truck. There have been many other times when I have found myself at the mercy of a breakdown service, not because of mechanical malfunction, but because of my own *dysfunction*. I delay putting petrol in my car until the last possible moment. There's no rational explanation for this. Perhaps I believe the car will get better fuel consumption if I wait; or maybe I like to challenge the fuel gauge to a duel. Or maybe filling up with petrol is boring.

As Proverbs advises us to 'Go to the ant', it holds it up as an example of industriousness. It is rather nifty at doing boring, ant-like activities with great diligence. Contrast the person who always leaves the tedious, dirty jobs until last: 'How long will you lie there, you sluggard? When will you get up from your sleep? A little sleep, a little slumber, a little folding of the hands to rest – and poverty will come on you like a bandit and scarcity like an armed man' (Prov. 6:9–11). If we want to avoid being mugged by disaster, let's do today what needs to be done.

… let's do today what needs to be done

127

Seeing clearly about sin

BIG PICTURE
Proverbs 6:12–35
Psalm 45:1–7

FOCUS
'There are six things the
Lord hates, seven that
are detestable to him …'
(Prov. 6:16)

I'M A thoroughbred grace preacher. Too many Christians live under the oppressive heel of a warped view of God who is ever trembling with angry anticipation, just waiting to zap them with 40,000 volts from a well-aimed lightning bolt. They live in eternal insecurity. I long to remind anyone who will listen that God utterly, wonderfully loves them: this is the heart of the good news that is the gospel. But there is a danger that this message of love can imply that God is soft, that our sins don't matter and that, in order to be inclusive and welcoming to all, we must dilute the hard-hitting challenge of the call to follow Christ. There is no actual contradiction between the message of love and holiness; God absolutely loves us and loves us too much to allow us to muddy ourselves up with bad living and – to use the Bible's word – sin. God is not Santa Claus, a smiling chap who only ever gives gifts and makes no demands. But He is the Holy One who calls us, by His grace, to make holy choices.

Proverbs is blunt here about God *hating* certain attitudes and actions. Among them are pride, lies, the oppression of the innocent, and 'wicked' scheming. Other things include that madness where we throw ourselves headlong into sin, and being a lying witness – one that shatters peace and unity because of a love for stirring up trouble. And the latter part of the passage returns once more to the insanity of adultery. Let's not use grace as an excuse to love what God hates.

Prayer: Thank You for love that calls me to make right choices. Be with me today, as I choose again. Amen.

Sex talk

A BAPTIST minister friend of mine once got into serious hot water because he decided to preach about sex. Furious letters from the irate and disgusted hit his letter box at speed; some Christians were appalled that this 'unspiritual' subject should be so openly discussed. How totally wrong they were. Sunday morning preaching that doesn't affect our Monday mornings is not only a waste of time, but perpetuates the notion that Christianity is irrelevant. Sex *is* spiritual simply because every aspect of our lives is spiritual – to carve up our living into 'spiritual' and 'unspiritual' boxes is a recipe for disaster.

If we've got any doubts that God wants us to talk with clarity about sex, consider how much attention is given to it in Scripture and especially the book of Proverbs. Once again the writer returns to the woes that result from adultery. Here is a colourful, graphic description of the seductive techniques of the 'wayward wife' who is hell-bent on straying while her husband is away working. Proverbs is blunt and leaves little to the imagination as we are urged not to be suckered by our urges.

People don't come to church to find out what happened to the Amalekites, and that 47-part series on *Cooking Utensils in Deuteronomy* might fascinate a few but will have little impact on the way we actually live. Let's call for and welcome biblical preaching that tackles tough subjects. And, if we're living contrary to the blunt advice given here, let's not stash that area away under the heading of 'unspiritual' and therefore unimportant.

Prayer: Lord, in my thoughts, in my relationships, in my sexuality, be honoured and glorified. Amen.

BIG PICTURE
Proverbs 7:1–27
1 Thessalonians 4:3–8

FOCUS
'I have covered my bed with coloured linens … I have perfumed my bed with myrrh, aloes and cinnamon … let's drink deep of love till morning; let's enjoy ourselves with love!' (Prov. 7:16–18)

Let's call for …

biblical preaching

that tackles

tough subjects

129

Wisdom and fun

BIG PICTURE
Proverbs 8:1–36
Deuteronomy 16:15

FOCUS
'Then I was the craftsman at his side. I was filled with delight day after day, rejoicing always in his presence, rejoicing in his whole world and delighting in mankind.'
(Prov. 8:30–31)

YESTERDAY I was given a telling off after preaching a sermon that prompted a fair amount of laughter. I don't tell jokes (I'd mess up the punch lines) but love to share stories in a way that allows people to laugh and learn simultaneously. The lady who disapproved ended our chat (monologue, to be honest) by telling me, 'I'm sure God must love you', which was the thinly coded news that she didn't.

'Wisdom' is a very grown-up word, overlaid with notions of seriousness. The caricature of the wise person is the silent soul who lives like a hermit, removed from the hustle of life, never stooping to the frivolity of laughter. Fun and wisdom seem to be unnatural companions. But here, wisdom is described as a woman in the streets, calling for attention in total contrast to the wayward wife of the previous chapter.

Various reasons are given for choosing the wise way. God tells us the truth (vv.4–11). He who invented life knows how it should be lived. God's ways work – wisdom is practical (vv.12–21). Wisdom is literally as old as the hills (vv.22–31); God used it in creation. But buried in that passage is the truth that the act of creation was playful and fun, as in verse 30 wisdom is the *craftsman*: a better translation is 'little child' or 'darling'. The emphasis is on the joyful play of creation rather than the hard work involved in it.

And the 'fun' continues. 'God is always at play throughout the earth,' says Dallas Willard. Smile if you'd like to. You have permission.

Prayer: I'm grateful for the gift of laughter. Help me to take life seriously; but not too seriously. Amen.

Wisdom and rebuke

YESTERDAY I told you about my little post-preaching telling off. If I'm honest, I find those episodes when someone announces they are about to 'tell me the truth in love' draining. All too often I don't hear truth and there's not much love about. When I'm rebuked, I try to smile and take it on the chin, but some of these encounters make me want to give up.

But there's a danger in my weariness, because there *are* times when I get it wrong, speak out of turn and desperately *need* a kindly corrective conversation, even if I don't necessarily *want* it. A rebuke can be like cough medicine, which sometimes tastes like a syrup made of rotting animals, yet is apparently good if you've got a cough. Let's not demonise everyone who disagrees with us or dismiss all conflict out of hand.

Here Proverbs gives us a character profile of the wise person, which includes the ability to not only listen to a critic, but also love them for their criticism; healthy evaluation is a real bridge to growth. As a parent, I didn't help my children when they were growing up if I unthinkingly agreed with everything they wanted to do; they needed a dad, not another compliant friend.

So beware the leader who refuses to hear those who disagree with the path of leadership they are taking. But also beware the 'followers' whose mission in life is forever correcting everyone else, while they themselves can apparently never be wrong. Who has permission to tell you off?

Prayer: I choose to welcome rebuke; I choose to hesitate, to think and pray, before offering rebuke. Amen.

BIG PICTURE
Proverbs 9:1–12
Revelation 3:19

FOCUS
'Do not rebuke a mocker or he will hate you; rebuke a wise man and he will love you.'
(Prov. 9:8)

Who has permission to tell you off?

Sin tastes good

BIG PICTURE
Proverbs 9:13–18
Romans 6:23

FOCUS
'"Stolen water is sweet;
food eaten in secret is
delicious!" But little do
they know that the dead
are there, that her guests
are in the depths of the
grave.' (Prov. 9:17–18)

I'M EMBARRASSED to admit it, but when I was much younger I got into some small-time shoplifting, mainly for sweets (I had a major addiction to those multi-coloured packets of *Refreshers*). Looking back on my furtive little missions into our local store, I realised that I actually had enough money to *buy* the sweets but there was something far more exhilarating about stealing them. Stolen sweets taste better: as Proverbs puts it, 'Stolen water is sweet'.

It's an uncomfortable truth, but there's something inherently attractive about what we can't or shouldn't have. With all that Proverbs says about adultery, we have to ask: why can it be such a temptation? Often those who stumble into it are happily married to partners that they love dearly. Others around them watch the devastation of their bad choices and wonder: what were they thinking? Why did they stray when what was at home was so wonderful?

Here the lingering perversity of the human condition is exposed, as we realise that that which is furtive and off-limits can have an allure all of its own. Perhaps it's the thrill of the chase, the dark pull of the unknown or just boredom with what we can have anytime. We can all be tempted to snack on what isn't ours.

Look again. Shoplifters become thieves who go to jail. Philanderers destroy their families. Secret gamblers lose it all, closet alcoholics pickle their livers; what looks lovely can lead to the grave. Sin can taste very good at first but a bite or two will fill our mouths with what is rotten.

Prayer: Save me from the deceptiveness of my own heart, living God. By Your grace I stand. Amen.

WEEKEND

Proverbs 10:1–5 // 1 Kings 3:1–15

Solomon

'It could be you,' trills the British lottery commercial, with a giant finger pointing out of the sky, signalling that someone today is going to acquire fabulous riches. How would that feel? Probably when only a teenager, Solomon discovered that the finger of destiny was pointed at him. He was chosen by his father, David, to succeed him as king. Moreover, God gave the young Solomon a blank cheque, an invitation to choose whatever he wanted. Here was an offer from the most fabulously wealthy one that there has ever been: God Himself.

Solomon chose to ask for some more of what he already had – wisdom. Already dubbed by his dad as a man of wisdom (1 Kings 2:9), Solomon wasn't satisfied with his own already rich reservoir of understanding and opted to ask for more of the same, to meet the fresh challenges he now faced as Israel's first dynastic king. And some of the answers to his prayers are passed on to us here in the Proverbs.

Solomon shows us that yesterday's grace is insufficient for today's challenges; we need God daily. And his priorities challenge us. Given an open offer from heaven, what would we choose?

Given an open offer from heaven, what would we choose?

Chattering

BIG PICTURE
Proverbs 10:6–32
James 1:19–20

FOCUS
'The wise in heart accept commands, but a chattering fool comes to ruin.' (Prov. 10:8)

I LOVE people and I love to talk. But there have been too many times when I have plunged myself into excruciatingly embarrassing situations and all because of my propensity to chatter away, mouth firmly in fifth gear, brain stuck in neutral. Just this week I only just managed to stop myself from asking a rather overweight lady when her baby was due. As I opened my mouth, it was as if I heard the sound of screeching brakes inside my head and, thankfully, disaster was averted. But too often I'm like the hapless man who attended a party where Queen Victoria was guest of honour. He greeted the most famous face in the nineteenth-century world with a mild expletive and then dug himself a deeper hole: 'I know your face, Ma'am, but I just can't remember your name.' I'm sure he had years to regret that little outburst. He has my sympathies.

The general advice from Proverbs about words is simple to summarise: keep them few. A mouth on auto-pilot is a dangerous thing, unrestrained by pause or reflection, insensitive to the potential damage that can be caused by runaway verbiage. Sometimes, when I'm tempted to share that tasty little morsel of gossip, or that story that might just be inappropriate or unhelpful, I remind myself that I am about to fill just a few seconds of time with words – which I might regret for days later. It's a sobering thought that might just save me – and maybe you too – from too many verbal gaffes in the future.

Prayer: Father, let my words be few, of greater quality and be honouring to You and Your name. Amen.

Dishing the dirt

A FEW days ago I met a lady who shared some wonderful and terrible news about her teenage son. He is a talented soccer player and has been scouted by one of the major league British teams. A bright sporting career beckons; so much for the good news. The tragic twist is that some of his school 'friends' are so jealous that they attacked him, trying to cut his legs and destroy his future. They weren't successful but he lives in fear now.

We might be horrified by their wickedness – yet be guilty of something similar ourselves. Yesterday I mentioned gossip. Have you ever wondered why gossip is such a delicious temptation and one that we so often pick from the menu of conversation? What is it about passing on sad or salacious news about others that can be so satisfying? Surely gossip is sometimes about taking the legs out from beneath someone who appears more successful, influential or spiritual than us? Gossip allows us to exert a whispering power: with carefully chosen words, we can stain their reputation and undermine their credibility. Gossip can be an expression of sheer envy. Let's think before we blab.

Even confidentiality, celebrated here, can be misused by the gossip. I've seen great churches blown apart by people who whisper lies and spread rumours but then cover the bomb with the cover all: 'This is confidential – don't tell anybody.' Then they choose a time to detonate all of the bombs at once by launching a public attack that has already quietly gathered support. To switch metaphors, the tongue of the gossip is the sharpest knife.

Prayer: May the words of my mouth and the meditations of my heart, be acceptable in Your sight, God. Amen.

BIG PICTURE
Proverbs 11:1–13
Romans 1:29–32

FOCUS
'A gossip betrays a confidence, but a trustworthy man keeps a secret.' (Prov. 11:13)

Let's think

before we blab

Only money

Proverbs 11:14–31
1 Timothy 6:17–21

FOCUS
'A kind-hearted woman
gains respect, but
ruthless men gain only
wealth.' (Prov. 11:16)

WE WERE motoring down glitzy 16 Mile Drive, Southern California's famed location for the most incredibly palatial mansions. Here you can pick up a fabulous house with an awesome view if you have a spare $20 million or so. As we stopped to admire one perfectly manicured lawn, we exchanged our usual comment, one often made by people who ponder the lifestyles of the rich and famous: 'Bet they're not happy.'

It's a comment we make with a smile because money *can* help happiness. It's much easier when you know where your next meal is coming from and it must be fun to occasionally shop without caring about the price tags. And extreme poverty is anything but fun; I've heard people in the affluent West justify their ignoring the plight of the Two-Thirds World with the dismissive comment: 'But they're happy that way.' While many who don't have our luxuries could teach us a thing or two about contentment, the fact is that not to be able to afford the basic necessities of life is no laughing matter. To have is easier than to have nothing.

That said, it is possible, according to Proverbs (and common sense) to gain 'only wealth'. If we've grown a fat bank balance at the cost of our parenting time, our marriages, our friendships, then we've paid too much to see figures in black on our bank statements. If we've crawled our way to the top by hurting others along the way, then we leave a pot of cash and a poisoned legacy when we leave this life. In one sense, the saying is true – it is *only* money.

Prayer: Father, thank You for the provision I enjoy; but help me to value that which is truly priceless. Amen.

Being somebody

IN IRELAND during a Ryder Golf Cup, I noted that despite that beautiful country's inclement weather (all that green grass is surely the result of epic drenching for much of the year), a streaker had made a name for himself by dashing across the golf course wearing nothing but a smile. The television commentators giggled, the police pounced and the bemused crowd applauded.

What inspires an adult human being to remove all their clothing and expose what in this case was their considerably overweight frame while the world watches? This was not even 15 minutes of fame – more like 30 chilly seconds. It must be that the glorious possibility of being noticed (if only for removing clothing in public, not evidence of the greatest genius) is alluring to some. Others, like the Pharisees of Jesus' time, dress *up* to impress.

Celebrities hire public relations specialists to ensure they are kept in the spotlight of public attention. Perhaps much of that is for commercial reasons but you don't have to be famous to hunger to be noticed and approved of. We can all succumb to the temptation to drop the names of 'famous' people whom we've met and bathe in their limelight for a while. Surely there's a more important question to be asked: what is it that makes a 'real' somebody? Lest we succumb to the worship of artificial heroes created by celebrity, we should remember that our importance is not measured by how many other people know we exist (fame). Real 'somebodies' enjoy true significance that is anything but superficial. Today I met someone like that: you'll meet her tomorrow.

Prayer: Save me from the empty, treadmill existence where I live desperate that others will notice that I am alive. Amen.

BIG PICTURE
Proverbs 12:1–9
Luke 20:45–47

FOCUS
'Better to be a nobody and yet have a servant than pretend to be somebody and have no food.' (Prov. 12:9)

… our importance

is not measured

by how many

… people know

we exist

Kindness and significance

BIG PICTURE
Proverbs 12:10–28
Ephesians 4:32

FOCUS
'An anxious heart weighs a man down, but a kind word cheers him up.'
(Prov. 12:25)

RECENTLY I was preaching in Belfast, at the beautiful Waterfront Hall there. It was the end of an exhausting day of travel, beginning with gridlocked traffic in Dublin. Traffic jams always seem to turn me into a mild atheist. The Belfast evening went well, almost everyone had left the venue, when I noticed an elderly lady sitting in the foyer waiting for her ride home.

At first glance she looked like a prim, perfectly groomed Ulsterwoman and I confess that my first thought was that she would have struggled with the flavour of the evening. My preaching had included a lot of humour and some religious sacred cows had been publicly slaughtered. She sat bolt upright, dignified and very proper and I wondered: had I offended her? As I approached her to thank her for coming, her face broke into a huge smile, her eyes sparkling. It turned out that she was a retired missionary-evangelist, had travelled the world preaching the gospel. At 89, she had lost none of her passion for Jesus. For two or three minutes she absolutely overwhelmed me with kind words and encouragement. I wiped a tear away, kissed her on the cheek and then immediately asked if she minded a peck from a stranger. 'Do I mind?' she laughed, 'I was widowed two years ago: all kisses are welcome!'

Five minutes later, she was gone, the hall was empty and my heart was full. That beautiful lady had presented me with a bouquet of kindness; the colour of her words and the perfume of her thoughtfulness 'said it' in a way that flowers never could. Be kind.

Prayer: Show me where my kindness could refresh others today; grant me sensitivity to see and time to take action. Amen.

Shining bright

Yesterday I introduced you to the lady who I would dearly love to adopt as my grandmother, if only she had a vacancy. Let me tell you one more thing about this most delightful soul. She shared with me that she had a strange encounter while travelling on a ferry recently. A man in his mid-fifties, sitting across from her, hesitantly approached her and asked if he could have a moment of her time. 'It's your eyes,' he said. 'There's something in your eyes that draws me to want to ask you about what to do with my life.' He went on to explain that he had experienced some recent family tragedy and that he could see warmth and love in her eyes. Then he asked her if she was a Christian. He was not but there was just something about her that shone for God, a beauty from God that transcended words. She prayed with him and introduced him to Jesus there and then.

As Proverbs continues to portray the stark contrast between the wise and the foolish, we read that 'The light of the righteous shines brightly' (v.9). A house brightly lit is a symbol of love, wholesomeness and joy. God help us to 'let that little light shine' in us today.

The light of
the righteous
shines brightly

Friends

BIG PICTURE
**Proverbs 13:12–25
2 Corinthians 1:3–7**

FOCUS
'He who walks with the
wise grows wise, but
a companion of fools
suffers harm.'
(Prov. 13:20)

WISDOM is catching. It rubs off. That's why I will travel quite a long distance to be with certain friends. I love our times of small talk, of easy laughter and shared stories. But I deliberately seek out people who are better at life than I am; their shared experience creates a classroom where life-shaping lessons can be learned.

Right now I am part of a film and prayer group; four of us meet about six times a year. We go out to watch a movie and discuss the content and our responses to the film over dinner, then take time to share where we are at in our own lives. At some point in the evening, we share prayer. This is far more than a good night out because I am able to download wisdom from three other lives, to gather wisdom from their journeys without travelling their roads. In recent months I have gained a greater understanding of how to deal with family illness, bereavement, disappointment in leadership, navigating into retirement and how to make a major ministry transition. A whole library stacked full of books would not have taught me these vital lessons – all this and I have seen a few good movies too!

I've met too many people (mostly Christian leaders) who tell me, perhaps with a tinge of pride, that they are too busy for friendships. That worries me greatly; in their self-sufficiency, they have cut themselves off from the vital resource that we all need. God created us for friendship.

I'm too busy *not* to have friends.

Prayer: Give friends to the lonely and give pause and priority to the busy. May I grow in true friendship. Amen.

THERE are a number of phrases that I'd be glad to never use again for the rest of my days. They include, 'There's not a job for you any longer', 'I'm sorry, she's dead' and 'We've lost the lot'. The circumstances of life have caused me to use each of these phrases recently and the pain of them means I'd prefer to avoid them for the rest of my life. But here's another well-worn expression sometimes used in Christian circles, one that does more damage than good: 'I know how you feel.'

In a genuine desire to empathise and because we long to bring someone who is suffering out of the chill of loneliness, we try to warm them up with words that are rarely true. Bluntly, we never really know how somebody else feels. No two sets of circumstances are ever identical and just as every human being's fingerprints are unique, so is every person's response to suffering. We can go so far as to say that we have trekked a similar trail but that is the limit of our ability to understand.

Poor old Job, so terribly bruised and battered by tragedy, had to further endure the 'helpful' advice of his well-meaning but clumsy friends. Job's 'miserable' comforters were sincere, thoughtful and intended to say something helpful. Sometimes, to say that we don't know what to say but that we love and care – can be enough.

Prayer: Save me from offering words that hurt, even though meant to heal. Grant me the gift of appropriate words and appropriate silence. Amen.

Things I never want to say again

BIG PICTURE
**Proverbs 14:1–10
Job 16:1–5**

FOCUS
' Each heart knows its own bitterness and no-one else can share its joy.' (Prov. 14:10)

… to say … that

we love and care

– can be enough

Good times and bad times

BIG PICTURE
Proverbs 14:11–35
Matthew 6:25–29

FOCUS
'Even in laughter the heart may ache and joy may end in grief.'
(Prov. 14:13)

TODAY I preached a sermon that was well received, had some great conversations with leaders and actually flew on a plane that was on time. I should also tell you that the plane was loaded with children on their way to the national festival of screaming and I drove away from a petrol station without paying for the fuel. It was a good day and a bad day.

Charles Dickens famously began *The Tale of Two Cities* with the words, 'It was the best of times and the worst of times'. In a sentence, Dickens reveals a key truth about life: times of tears and laugher are often co-mingled. Until recently I viewed life as either being on a mountain top or trudging through a valley – personally I prefer summits and cloudless skies. But Rick Warren, whose wife Kay has been battling with cancer recently, affirms that life is more like a railway track with good and bad circumstances running parallel. That's Warren's experience right now: the church he leads is hugely effective, his book, *The Purpose Driven Life* is a multi-million copy bestseller – and his wife is struggling with her health. Life is rarely a summer's day unspoiled by any clouds; Mediterranean seasons are welcomed but rare and if we delay our happiness for those days, we won't be happy very often.

Paul Tournier famously quipped that 'most people spend their whole lives indefinitely preparing to live'. Be it in sunshine, rain, or some of both, live today.

Prayer: Thank You for today. Whatever the circumstances I may have to weather, please help me live to the full. Amen.

Softly, softly

'WE'D like a taxi to pick us up at the South Terminal, please.'

The dispatcher confirmed the details with an authority that was convincing. If only it had been true. Forty-five minutes later cabs had come and gone – but not ours. We called again and confirmed that we were at the South Terminal. 'We'll be right there.' We called again. Twice. Then our mobile phone rang; it was the taxi service. A somewhat grumpy manager demanded to know where we were as our taxi had been circling *the North Terminal* for 30 minutes and apparently we were responsible for this, together with global warming, world hunger and the increase in British street crime.

Exasperated, I was somewhat tetchy in my response, which only served to light the blue touch paper. I was treated to a free lecture about my telephone manner. The wandering taxi driver finally arrived and greeted my unsmiling visage with a warm grin and sincere apologies. The service was terrible, he said, and he knew he had lost his tip because of it. As we got out of the cab, he apologised again and as a parting shot said 'God bless'.

Rats.

My reactionary words on the phone had simply added fuel to the fire, in sharp contrast to the driver, whose calm manner had defused the tension immediately.

Confrontation usually creates confrontation but when we meet an inflammatory moment with gentle measured words, we may avert an argument, a fight or possibly a world war.

The driver got a big tip for a short journey and I got a lesson in life.

Prayer: I want to learn to respond, rather than react, Lord. Show me how. Amen.

BIG PICTURE
**Proverbs 15:1–13
1 Thessalonians
2:1–12**

FOCUS
'A gentle answer turns away wrath, but a harsh word stirs up anger.'
(Prov. 15:1)

Confrontation

usually creates

confrontation …

Dying laughing

BIG PICTURE
Proverbs 15:14–33
James 3:1–12

FOCUS
'A man finds joy in giving an apt reply – and how good is a timely word!' (Prov. 15:23)

APPARENTLY I was very nearly guilty of manslaughter recently. 'My death certificate would have mentioned your name,' said a lady after a morning service. She suffers from a very acute bronchial condition, was reading one of my books and found something so side-splittingly funny that she moved into fits of laughter that edged her into a danger zone. Her face was serious now. 'I was in a bad way and just couldn't breathe. I nearly died laughing, quite literally. Those books should carry a health warning.'

I was worried now. Was I being told off? Should I add being a health hazard to my other sins? I stammered into an apology; after all, I hadn't just offended this woman, I'd nearly killed her. My anxiety wasn't needed; her face broke into a broad, winning smile. 'Just keep the laughter coming, Jeff. I love to laugh. If I had died, I'd have died happy.'

But then I thought again. We've talked a lot about the power of our talking over recent weeks because in Proverbs the level of our wisdom – or folly – is gauged by the way we speak. Think about it: words can kill. They cost nothing and yet have the power to wreak incredible damage and destruction. They also grant us the ability to build up and change the lives of others. 'The tongue has the power of life and death' (Prov. 18: 21). At the cost of nothing whatsoever, we can change somebody's day – and possibly life – today. God forbid that, rather than cause someone to die laughing, we might contribute to their dying feeling desolate and betrayed.

Prayer: Bring life and joy today through the words that pass my lips. Amen.

Told you so

'I told you so.' It's usually an unwelcome phrase that tumbles from the lips of the know-it-all who is thrilled to discover that they were right. But some can 'tell us so' over how to do life. Here we are able to pause and remember how we met Solomon two weeks ago: the king was offered anything his heart desired from the One who could deliver exactly that. He chose wisdom over riches, prompting a delighted response from God. And here, Solomon lets us know that there were no regrets about that choice. Turning down the cash was the right thing to do (and in his case, God gave him both anyway). But listen to his words: 'How much better to get wisdom than gold, to choose understanding rather than silver!' (Prov. 16:16).

The Bible is a story, not just a compilation of theological information. As we travel with those who once lived through the trials, temptations, joys and sorrows that we now face, we can learn from those who've gone before us, rather than having to repeat their mistakes.

Solomon's experience can 'tell us so': choose wisdom. Why don't we take his word for it?

… choose
wisdom

Pride and falling

BIG PICTURE
**Proverbs 16:17–33
Daniel 4:28–37**

FOCUS
'Pride goes before destruction, a haughty spirit before a fall.'
(Prov. 16:18)

IT IS surely the most famous and oft-quoted Proverb of them all. Here we're reminded that pride doesn't just make people obnoxious and tough to be around but can very often be the cause of their downfall. Why?

Pride blinds us. It makes us think that we can live by another exclusive set of rules, that we are so special that we don't have to obey the basic principles of life and goodness – people with an inflated sense of their own importance often see themselves as being above the expected norms of behaviour. Pride makes us arrogant, unwilling to listen to the warnings of those who we think are less 'important' than us. Compound all of this deception with the feeling that, however we live and whatever we do, we have the golden touch – even call it 'the blessing of God' – and before we know it, the haughty high-flier is face down in a ditch. Is it possible that God loves some of us too much to allow us to fly too high? Does He know that success might destroy us and so sets a limit on our progress for our own protection?

'God opposes the proud but gives grace to the humble' (James 4:6). High and mighty King Nebuchadnezzar had to learn that truth the hard way – his temporary insanity taught him to turn from his self-worshipping ways and he finally acknowledged that God was and is able to humble the proud (Deut. 8:3).

Isn't it better to choose to humble ourselves rather than force God's hand and make Him place us in 'humble school'?

Prayer: Grant me success in Your eyes and give me the character to be able to cope well with success. Amen.

Will my children be proud of me?

BIG PICTURE
Proverbs 17:1–13
1 Timothy 3:1–7

FOCUS
'Children's children are
a crown to the aged, and
parents are the pride of
their children.'
(Prov. 17:6)

TODAY I experienced a huge surge of pride in my daughter Kelly. Working in Indonesia, she determined to try to change the thinking of the local people in their overt prejudice against people with disabilities. Often those who struggle with terrible physical challenges have to bear the additional burden of being outcasts as well, rejected because of their perceived weaknesses. A young boy with severe mobility challenges was being denied access to the local kindergarten because of this prejudice. Kelly took some of the teachers to visit him in his ramshackle, post-tsunami 'barak'. It was supposed to be temporary accommodation but nothing more permanent is in sight.

The teachers fell in love with the delightful lad and now his place in the kindergarten is assured. I can't tell you how 'proud' – in the right sense of that word – I am of Kelly and her husband Ben. But reading this Proverb today, I was challenged that I want my children to be proud of *me* – a parent who is 'the pride of their children'. I want to leave a legacy that is more than financial when I die; the choices I make now matter. The thought of them being ashamed of me, of what I have done and of how I have lived, chills my heart. Proverbs celebrates and values a good name as being 'more desirable than great riches; to be esteemed is better than silver or gold' (Prov. 22:1). And Paul exhorts young Timothy to choose leaders of good repute. Sometimes I hear people carelessly say, 'I don't care what people think of me.' Really?

Prayer: Lord, grant me a good name and a wholesome reputation – for Your name's sake. Amen.

I want to leave

a legacy that

is more than

financial

Good medicine

BIG PICTURE
**Proverbs 17:14–28
Deuteronomy
16:13–15**

FOCUS
'A cheerful heart is good
medicine, but a crushed
spirit dries up the bones.'
(Prov. 17:22)

IT WAS the day after Christmas and we were taking a family walk along the seafront in Bognor Regis. That's when the mad idea hit. We wanted to go paddling. A swim was out of the question – icy water and no swimming costumes. So we opted for second best, sloshed our way in up to our calves, splashed around for a minute and made a memory as we did. It was all very pointless, some would say immature, and we shivered all the way home in our soggy, salty car. But I'm glad we did it. It was fun.

The Purpose Driven Life is an excellent book and has proved to be a great inspiration to millions. But I have a confession to make: I can't stand the title – even though that's probably what initially helped sell the book by the truckload. Everyone is looking for purpose. And the thought of everything I do being efficient, productive – purposeful – is terrible. I'd like to have some fun before death, to laugh uncontrollably a lot more than I do.

Some of us Christians are bewilderingly nervous of fun, seeing it as 'unspiritual'. That idea produces a religion that is as inviting as one of those old-fashioned corsets – the fun is gradually squeezed out of us, until there's no freedom to breathe left. But Proverbs makes it clear – laughter is good for us, a fact now scientifically proven as being more than prose: the human body is hugely helped by frequent doses of laughter. We can giggle our way to better physical and mental health. Nervous of laughter?

Think again. Take your medicine.

Prayer: Help me to be fully, completely alive today; fill me with Your joy. Amen.

Don't interrupt!

A DISTANT acquaintance of mine is a wonderful man, has a real passion for God, is generous and kind to a fault – and he almost always interrupts and finishes off sentences for just about anyone that he is 'conversing' with. It's almost farcical, like one of those television game shows, as if he has to fill in the blank with the possibility of a new car as a prize. But all of that blank-filling means that much of the time he's wrong. Not only does he irritate everyone he talks to, but conversation takes longer. Massive confusion reigns as a result.

'I'm off to the …'

'… bathroom?'

'No, the Netherlands, where I'm going to …'

'That's a long way to go to the bathroom, isn't it?'

Why do some of us develop this dreadful social habit that can be more off-putting than a serious dose of halitosis? Sometimes people of great spiritual passion do this; they're so excited about what they're doing for God, they don't have time for others to complete what they have to say. But surely bad manners sit at the heart of this practice: we are impatient and perhaps subconsciously feel that what we have to say is far more interesting than what we are currently hearing. Hence we answer without listening. Proverbs cuts us down to size if we embrace this practice. We're the foolish ones, according to ancient wisdom. Take a break. Pause for breath – and listen.

Prayer: Lord, help me to value the words and wisdom of others. Teach me to be a good listener. Amen.

BIG PICTURE
**Proverbs 18:1–13
James 1:19–20**

FOCUS
'He who answers before listening – that is his folly and his shame.'
(Prov. 18:13)

Pause for breath

– and listen

Stubborn

BIG PICTURE
Proverbs 18:14–24
1 Corinthians 8:9–13

FOCUS
'An offended brother is
more unyielding than
a fortified city, and
disputes are like the
barred gates of a citadel.'
(Prov. 18:19)

MY HOME in Britain is about a mile from a heavily fortified castle. It's an object of great beauty now, but it sobers me to remember that here my forefathers peered out of the turrets and poured boiling vats of fat on any unwelcome callers who had actually managed to broach the massive moat. We Brits do fortification rather well.

And I've met a few Christians – and been to a few churches – that do life the same way. Woe betide the unfortunate soul who makes a comment, uses a Bible version or sings a song that is offensive to them. If the music is a few decibels too loud, or the flower rota is revised without Doris being included (due to her Amazonian jungle-like arrangements), then up comes the drawbridge and the official verdict is handed down by people who, figuratively speaking, have their arms permanently folded in disgust. They are offended.

Often the scripture that exhorts us 'not to offend the weaker brother' is hauled out, even though the person offended may not be weaker at all; they are not suffering from a weak conscience but a prickly disposition. And the problem gets worse. Here Proverbs lets us know that married to offence is stubbornness, using the pictures of a fortified city and a gated citadel to show just how unyielding we can be.

Perhaps you're offended right now. Two questions – is the issue worth being upset about? And are you willing to listen to those who disagree with you? Put down that vat of fat and think again.

Prayer: Father, save me from becoming passionate about what doesn't matter and from stubbornness that deafens me to wisdom. Amen.

Warped zeal

We all know that zeal is one of the most toxic forces in the world today. People of conviction can so easily be hijacked by wrong causes and then end up perpetuating horrendous crimes, the victims of their own misguided enthusiasm. So Proverbs warns us to make sure that we are informed as well as committed – 'It is not good to have zeal without knowledge, nor to be hasty and miss the way' (Prov. 19:2). And before we look to apply this truth to the world scene, we Christians need to allow ourselves to be challenged too. History is littered with terrible things that have been said and done in Jesus' name: crusades, inquisitions and defending the practice of slavery were all perpetuated by Bible-believing Christians.

And misguided zeal is not just a problem of church history. Sometimes I meet Christians who scare me – Christian fanaticism is a very real possibility. When we go overboard on one particular doctrine, interpretation or way of doing church, we can stray into a danger zone.

Just because a person is loud, and even willing to die for their convictions, doesn't make them right. Let's think before we shout.

Let's think
before we shout

151

Bless the poor, bless the Lord

BIG PICTURE
Proverbs 19:16–29
Amos 5:21–24

FOCUS
'He who is kind to the poor lends to the LORD, and he will reward him for what he has done.'
(Prov. 19:17)

OVER the next few days we'll be considering some of the material in Proverbs about our attitude to money in general and to the poor specifically. Jim Wallis describes a graphic illustration of just how much the Bible has to say about the poor. A seminary student took a Bible and cut out every reference to the poor with a pair of scissors.

Wallis commented: 'When the seminarian was finished that old Bible hung in threads. It wouldn't hold together, it fell apart in our hands. This is our Bible – full of holes from all that we have cut out.' Scripture is emphatic: all of our singing, our religious activities, our busyness in local church life – all of this is worthless to Him – offensive, even – if we have no concern or make no practical effort to help those in our area and in our world who struggle with poverty. Amos slams the message home: God *hates* worship when the worshippers take a 'couldn't care less' attitude to the poor (Amos 5:21). And what does God love? 'I, the LORD, love justice' (Isa. 61:8).

Certainly we can try to evade the issue of the poor by complaining that the needs are so great that we feel overwhelmed by them. Or we exempt ourselves from responsibility, insisting that money given to charities won't reach those who need it or will be swallowed up by crooked dictators anyway, so what's the point? But this just won't do as far as God is concerned. Proverbs makes it clear that love shown to the poor is like love shown to God: true worship. These issues are complex but absolutely demand our attention.

Prayer: Lord, show me my part to bring hope and healing, in the world You love, full of need and pain. Amen.

Deal or no deal

I LOVE a deal. I'm one of those sad types who enjoys the cut and thrust of buying. When the airlines, for example, announce a sale, my fingers fly across the computer keyboard at white-hot speed. Given the chance to pay less, I'll take it. I also love to be generous, but if a multi-national corporation is offering me a product at a price too good to turn down, I'll shake hands on the deal.

But I've seen that principle of thrift and stewardship go badly wrong. Visiting a Two-Thirds World country recently, I watched aghast as some well-heeled westerners took the principle of bartering way too far and effectively ground a market trader underfoot as they battled for ten minutes to save 20p. They strode away, all smiles and triumph; and we could argue that the trader didn't have to accept their offer … or did he? Did that sale mean the difference between putting food on the table for his family that day, so that even though the profit was meagre, he was forced to take it? Proverbs rues the tactics of the buyer who casts aspersions on the product in order to force the price down and then prides himself on his conniving handiwork.

Thank God that we are living in days when buying fair trade products is becoming more accepted. But concern for the poor goes beyond our coffee selection and other fair trade goods, important though our buying choices are. Surely the best way to measure a deal is not to ask, 'Did I get the lowest price?' but 'Is it fair?'

Prayer: Let me do what is right, not just what is best for me. Amen.

BIG PICTURE
**Proverbs 20:1–30
Job 31:13–23**

FOCUS
'"It's no good, it's no good!" says the buyer; then off he goes and boasts about his purchase.' (Prov. 20:14)

… concern for

the poor goes

beyond our

coffee selection …

Justice

Proverbs 21:1–31
Micah 6:8

FOCUS
'To do what is right and
just is more acceptable to
the LORD than sacrifice.'
(Prov. 21:3)

IN 1986 Yoweri Museveni became President of Uganda,
when his National Resistance Army overthrew the
military junta. Museveni had attended Christian youth
camps during his teenage years and, while at one of the
camps, had asked that an evening be devoted to prayer
for nearby Tanzania, which, at the time, was engaged
in terrible civil war. He was told that this request was
inappropriate: 'We don't concern ourselves with things
like that.' Prayers were held but they focused on the
needs of the camp and for the spiritual wellbeing of
those attending the event. Museveni made a decision:
Christianity apparently had nothing to say about the
needs of the day, so he would look elsewhere for a guiding
philosophy for real life. But he was rejecting a 'holiness'
message that was actually a tragic misrepresentation;
holiness has justice at its very heart.

God is just: He calls for justice. One of the favourite Old
Testament terms for God is *the Rock*, a symbol of stability
and consistency (Deut. 32:4). When God introduced the
call to holiness to His people, it was a call to a personal
and social ethic that included caring for the poor and the
elderly (Lev. 19:2), looking after those with disabilities,
feeding the hungry, being concerned for the marginalised
and doing business with honesty – a call that mirrored
His own dependable character.

Make no mistake. The cry for justice is not an addendum
to the gospel, or simply a means of attracting attention so
that we can talk to people about heaven. Justice sits at the
heart of God and the heart of God's message.

**Prayer: Bring justice to the oppressed, righteous God.
Use me in the fight to bring relief to the suffering.
Amen.**

We are family

I MET Julie during a recent visit to Ethiopia. She attended a project run by the charity Compassion, which focuses on caring for children in need. Seventeen-year-old Julie served us tea and biscuits when we visited the centre just outside Addis; she was the perfect hostess, all smiles and kindness.

But her smile comes despite incredible hardship. The average income in Ethiopia is just 15p per day; her father died from the HIV virus and her mother is struggling to bring up the family alone. I complimented Julie on her attitude, her disposition and her hard-working approach to fulfilling her hopes and dreams. When she told me about her family history, I said something simple but I will never forget her reply. 'Julie, I'm so sorry that your dad isn't here. If I were your father, I'd be so incredibly proud of you. You're a wonderful young lady.'

She looked down, slightly embarrassed at the compliment, and then responded. 'Thank you, Jeff. From now on, I will always think of you as my father.' There was no outstretched hand with her comment; this was no calculated move to get anything – just the recognition that we are all actually members of the same human family. I'm not Julie's dad – but I am her brother; both of us made in the image of God and now closer still because of Christ.

The faces of those children, emaciated by poverty, that appear on our television screens – to put it bluntly, they are not aliens, people other than us. They are family.

Prayer: Thank You for the family, Father. Cause us to live as family, I pray. Amen.

BIG PICTURE
Proverbs 22:1–29
Ephesians 3:14–15

FOCUS
'Rich and poor have this in common: The LORD is the Maker of them all.'
(Prov. 22:2)

… we are all

… members

of the same

human family

The defender

BIG PICTURE
**Proverbs 23:1–16
Jeremiah 22:16–17**

FOCUS
'Do not move an ancient
boundary stone or
encroach on the fields of
the fatherless, for their
Defender is strong; he
will take up their case
against you.'
(Prov. 23:10–11)

IN AMERICA they're called the public defenders. They are the lawyers who take up the cases of those who can't afford to hire someone to defend them. And they are much needed: sometimes 'justice' is linked to dollars, as the infamous O.J. Simpson trial demonstrated. The civil trial found him guilty but not the trial on which he had spent so much money.

God is the defender of the poor and the oppressed. He took on Uriah's case when David stole his wife and set him up for a battlefield death and, through Elijah, became prosecuting lawyer against evil Ahab and Jezebel when they tried to wrench Naboth's vineyard out of his hands. He 'takes up the cases' of those wronged by injustice.

But when we talk about God having a 'bias' to the poor, that can imply that He doesn't love those who aren't in immediate need as much – which is not true. Tim Chester explains: 'It is not that God is prejudiced in some way, still less that the poor are more deserving because of their poverty. Rather, because he is a God of justice, God opposes those who perpetuate injustice and he sides with the victims of oppression.'*

That said, when we ignore the poor or, worse still, live in such a way that makes their plight worse, we might well find ourselves in the dock. And, in this case, the public defender is very, very good at His job – this defender is strong. Let's stay on *His* side, allow our hearts to be broken with His and play our part in genuinely making poverty history. What step can we take today?

Prayer: Holy God, save me from Your displeasure. Show me where my ways are crooked; help me to walk uprightly. Amen.

*Tim Chester, *Good News to the Poor* (Leicester: IVP, 2004).

Proverbs 23:17–35 // Ephesians 5:18

The anatomy of a hangover

In many churches in the UK, drinking alcohol is
no longer an issue. Earlier attitudes of prohibition
and total abstinence have been replaced by the more
relaxed view that a drink in moderation is certainly
not condemned by the Bible. On the contrary, a
'little wine for the stomach's sake' is encouraged.
The notion that the wine that Jesus drank (and made
during that wedding in Cana) was little more than
grape juice hardly warrants a comment.

But with freedom comes the need for caution.
Proverbs graphically describes the awful symptoms
of a hangover and the serious threat of alcoholism:
'In the end it bites like a snake and poisons like a
viper. Your eyes will see strange sights and your
mind imagine confusing things' (Prov. 23:32–33).
Let's respect those who totally abstain, for reasons
of conscience, because they know they are prone to
addiction or have those near and dear to them who
are weak in this area. And let's realise that a problem
with alcohol doesn't announce itself; indeed a major
element of addiction is often denial. Enjoy wine if you
like – but don't like it too much.

… with
freedom comes
the need for
caution

Gloating

BIG PICTURE
Proverbs 24:1–22
Job 31:1–34

FOCUS
'Do not gloat when your
enemy falls; when he
stumbles, do not let your
heart rejoice …'
(Prov. 24:17)

IT WAS the night of a general election in the UK and voting results were coming in thick and fast. It was becoming apparent who was going to form the next government and a very famous politician who was tipped for a top job in the Cabinet was being interviewed. The look of gloating that took over his whole face was obscene to watch. He was almost licking his lips at the thought of power; his dismissive remarks about the failed contenders in the other parties came not from the heart of a man magnanimous in victory, but from a small man intoxicated by his own triumph. He smeared this epic moment in his history with gloating or, as one dictionary defines this, 'malicious satisfaction'.

A few years later, that same politician reaped what he had sown as he hit the headlines with news of his own scandals: how the Fleet Street hacks gloated over *his* downfall.

Surely gloating is a sign that we thought we were superior to others all along. When we take pleasure in their downfall or suffering, we reveal that we might have been willing to contribute to their pain if we could have, so pleased are we about their agony. Whatever the reason, celebrating the demise of another – even our enemy – is ugly. More importantly, it could provoke the judgment of God, who is disgusted by gloating. Job, in examining his own heart before God, insisted that he would have no part in rejoicing at the perils of others. Let's join him.

Prayer: Give me empathy for those who fall and humility in the midst of success. Amen.

IF I may use the word in a daily devotional, I think that most of us suffer from the 'Does my bottom look big in this?' syndrome. The correct answer to that question would always be a firm *No*. Or would it?

I recently asked a friend's advice about a huge decision I'd made – and one that I'd consulted with them about at the time. 'If you thought I was taking the wrong step, would you tell me?' 'Of course not,' they replied, 'I'm not *that* radical.' All of which is rather worrying. Surely true friendship is about being willing to risk offence and misunderstanding, if honest counsel is sought. It's not as if a contrary opinion would be intrusive – when we genuinely ask for an opinion, we are giving permission for difficult things to be said.

Taking things a step further, there are some people who deliberately hide the truth and heap effusive praise on those who really don't deserve it, in order to gain political and relational capital. The Bible has a word for this kind of humbug: flattery.

I've noticed that sometimes we Christian leaders surround ourselves with folk who agree with us and are really quite like us. We can even view with suspicion anyone who thinks differently, and view honest questions as hostility. To live like that may be comfortable, but it's perilous. If everyone thinks the same, we'll all end up stumbling into the same trap together.

Don't blunder into brutal honesty – make sure that you have permission to tell the truth. But fudging doesn't belong in a genuine friendship.

Prayer: Give me grace and sensitivity to be honest, and grace and sensitivity when others tell me the truth. Amen.

Honesty

BIG PICTURE
**Proverbs 24:23–34
1 Thessalonians 2:1–6**

FOCUS
'An honest answer is like
a kiss on the lips.'
(Prov. 24:26)

… true friendship

is about being

willing to

risk offence …

Still seeking

BIG PICTURE
Proverbs 25:1–15
Luke 24:36–39

FOCUS
'It is the glory of God
to conceal a matter; to
search out a matter is the
glory of kings.'
(Prov. 25:2)

OVER the last 20 years or so, I've been on a perilous journey. At times, I wish I'd never started down this path. There are shadowy seasons when the terrain turns into a solid uphill trek, with no plateau in sight. And there are other days when I feel I am lost in thick fog, with no familiar landmarks. It is frightening.

The trip to which I refer is the journey of questioning my faith. When I first became a Christian, I swallowed whole – without too much chewing – just about everything that I was told about God. Helpfully, I was part of a wonderful, trustworthy church that gave me some terrific foundations for my faith. But about a decade later, I decided that questions were needed. Did I really believe what I thought I believed about evangelism, the way I approached worship and some of the more difficult doctrines of election, predestination, heaven and hell?

Sometimes I mention to fellow leaders that I am on such a journey and they gasp and get nervous. 'Isn't the Bible enough for you, Jeff?' 'Are you turning liberal in your advancing years?' Faith involves questions, struggling, doubt, mystery and the pain of 'searching out matters'. That's why Jesus told parables – not to 'dumb down' kingdom truth, but to activate a search in His listeners' hearts and minds. Faith is not about treating truth as some fragile thing that might crumble if we touch or examine it too closely. Genuine faith sometimes keeps us awake at night, niggles, irritates, liberates and confounds us. Are you on a similar journey? Take heart.

**Prayer: All-knowing God, open my eyes and mind
to see Your truth, even though it will take a lifetime.
Amen.**

IT'S a bad feeling. An enjoyable evening with beloved friends starts to turn into a nightmare – simply because it's gone on too long. You frantically look for a pause in the conversation, so that you can jump in with 'My goodness, is *that* the time?' You announce that you have to be up at 3am for choir practice. You yawn and stretch – repeatedly. And for Kay, who works extremely long hours, there comes a point when her eyelashes blink at high speed, so desperate is she to keep her eyes open. Those furious lashes make her look like a hostess with semaphore skills.

We have a friend who has a rather brutal solution to those guests who stay too late. When he thinks the time has come, he jumps up and announces with a smile, 'Right, everybody, I think sleep is in order. Thanks for coming over and goodnight.' He gets more rest than me but, despite my call for more honesty earlier, I couldn't use his blunt approach.

Once again we see that the Bible is so practical and that the whole of our lives matters to God – including the details of our social lives. But we also realise that self-obsession and failing to notice the needs of others – including their need for sleep – can destroy the deepest relationships and turn love into hatred. So practical is Proverbs, it gives us wisdom to prevent us becoming early morning sleep intruders too: 'If a man loudly blesses his neighbour early in the morning, it will be taken as a curse' (Prov. 27:14). Be sensitive and practical. People will be happier to see you.

Prayer: Lord, help me not to damage friendships with selfishness; close relationships with insensitivity. Amen.

Overstaying our welcome

BIG PICTURE
**Proverbs 25:16–28
Mark 12:28–34**

FOCUS
'Seldom set foot in your neighbour's house – too much of you and he will hate you.' (Prov. 25:17)

Be sensitive

and practical

Never learning

BIG PICTURE
Proverbs 26:1–11
2 Timothy 3:1–9

FOCUS
'As a dog returns to its
vomit, so a fool repeats
his folly.' (Prov. 26:11)

I HAVE had a problem sometimes that comes from meeting a lot of people: I forget names. This is a real malady for one involved in Christian leadership in a large church, especially when people ask me to pray for them. They tell me their name (which stays in my mind for about three seconds) and then tell me that they don't feel valued in the church – can I pray for them? Now I'm sweating. This person who feels unwelcome and unnoticed is about to be treated to a prayer from me where I don't mention their name – which will compound their chronic sense of rejection.

I've tried to bluff with the use of terms such as 'brother' or 'sister', or even 'this dear soul so loved by you, Lord' but I don't think that I got away with it. This amnesia has afflicted me for about 25 years and I'm sad to say that I only just took action to take care of it. Now, when I'm introduced to someone, I spend the first 30 seconds of our conversation shouting their name inside my head: I make up rhymes and do everything I can to remember it. The problem is – why did it take me so long to learn this lesson and take action? Twenty-five years is a long time.

Some of us haven't learned our lesson yet about more serious issues. Our life is a repetitive cycle of unbroken habits and predictable sins. The picture of a dog snacking on vomit should startle us into action – what foolish patterns of behaviour do we need to break?

Prayer: Help me to learn, take action and move on. Save me from meandering in never-ending circles of sin. Amen.

Idle

Our busy culture means that we frequently talk about how much we have to do, with so little time. Everybody seems to be working hard, sometimes too hard. But as Proverbs warns us about the folly of the 'sluggard', we see that laziness is still a massive problem – even for those of us who are busy. We can be lazy in our relationships, forgetting to be kind or demonstrate our love. We can be lazy in disciplining our children, unwilling to face the pain of their disapproval. It's easier to clean their room than demand they clean it – in a sense, that's lazy. We can be lazy in our beliefs: legalism and liberalism can both flourish when we are unwilling to do the hard work of wrestling with Scripture and thrashing out truly biblical convictions. I recently found out that I have a streak of hidden laziness. I tend to leave the boring tasks until last and dive into what I most enjoy – a recipe for trouble.

And laziness is adept at making excuses for inaction: 'The sluggard says, "There is a lion in the road, a fierce lion roaming the streets!"' (Prov. 26:13). What have you been putting off? Do you have your own lazy streak? Get with it: there's no lion outside.

Do you have your own lazy streak?

163

Self-congratulation

BIG PICTURE
Proverbs 27:1–27
2 Corinthians
11:16–33

FOCUS
'Let another praise
you and not your own
mouth; someone else and
not your own lips.'
(Prov. 27:2)

HE REALLY is a brilliant Christian leader, an effective communicator and very adept at sharing his faith one-to-one. And the problem is, he is very aware of all this and just about every time he speaks, he tells everyone how good he is. The self-congratulation is usually thinly cloaked in comments about 'wanting to give God all the glory' and 'of course nothing would happen without the Lord', but the message is clear: God must be thrilled to have this chap on His side, so clever and skilled is he. There's something incredibly uncomfortable about listening to self-praise.

When we are driven to tell people everything we know, who we've met and the strengths we have, we demonstrate a gaping insecurity and an unhealthy appetite for approval. It is as if we are walking around with our record card, frantic that others be aware of where we triumphed. Of course, the opposite of this reveals a similar hankering. People who forever put themselves down and deny the existence of any gifts, exude a snivelling pseudo-humility which is actually a desire to be corrected affirmatively. They are looking for the same praise and just using a different method to get it.

Ironically, self-praise does nothing to endear people to us – it alienates them. They are repelled by our boasting and also feel lessened by our carping on about our accomplishments. Perhaps we'd be better to take a leaf out of Paul's book and boast about the things that show our weaknesses (2 Cor. 11:30). If there's an A+ to be given, let someone else give it to you.

Prayer: Father, free me from the need to prove myself. Deliver me from addiction to approval, boasting and false humility. Amen.

Know God, know about life

I'M A little perturbed. Angry is probably the better word. I've just listened to a televised interview with a man who'd like the world to believe that all Christians everywhere are utterly misguided, pathetic souls who not only need faith as a crutch to lean on, but have basically kissed their brains goodbye and know nothing at all about life. We are naive, uneducated and stupid. Poor old us.

I'm the first to admit that we Christians sometimes say and do rather silly things. We certainly don't have the monopoly on all truth, and there are times when we don't make Jesus look good. But I also discover that Christians often have an understanding of the dynamics of relationships that is rare in a world where so many marriages are falling apart – and the fact that we are not immune to marriage breakdown ourselves doesn't contradict the reality that we have a good understanding of what makes human beings tick. Many Christians have a firm understanding of the real reason for creation care. We worship the Creator and are not just folks lost in space trying to preserve the mother ship. We have much to say about justice, poverty, forgiveness and sexual ethics. Knowing the God who invented life itself is surely the key to understanding life, as Proverbs reminds us.

We're far from perfect and at times bring shame to our amazing Lord. But let no one write off those who know the Lord as a collective of fools. The Bible speaks of those who, rejecting the knowledge of God, profess *themselves* to be wise and have become fools themselves.

Prayer: To know You, life-giving God, is to know life. Help me walk in the wisdom of Your ways. Amen.

BIG PICTURE
Proverbs 28:1–28
Romans 1:18–32

FOCUS
'Evil men do not understand justice, but those who seek the Lord understand it fully.'
(Prov. 28:5)

Christians have a firm understanding of the reason for creation care

Of flying mice and men

BIG PICTURE
Proverbs 29:1–27
James 1:19–20

FOCUS
'An angry man stirs up dissension and a hot-tempered one commits many sins.' (Prov. 29:22)

THIS week, I've been researching the behaviour of bats (don't ask!) and found out that they spend their whole lives yelling. It's how they get around. I used to think that this was because diminutive bats are as blind, as, you guessed it, bats. This is just an urban myth, like the ridiculous notions that Elvis is living in Birmingham, or that the bat is a flying mouse or that the overhead projector is a great invention. Bats actually have rather keen eyesight – but they do rely on something called *echolocation* in order to live. Echolocation enables a bat to emit high frequency sound waves that bounce off an object, such as a tasty mosquito, to produce a type of sound 'echo' that returns to the bat's ears. So bats yell at each other, they yell at their lunch, they yell at the trees, they yell at their neighbours and they yell at their babies. They yell up to 200 times every second. They're born yelling and they die yelling. Their whole understanding of the shape of the world is based on how everything responds to their yelling.

And some people are like that. Angry from birth, or so it seems, they stomp through life simmering, complaining, flying off the proverbial handle, provoking and winding people up, hot-tempered and generally seeing the world as it responds to their yelling.

For them, there's always something to yell about: bad service in a restaurant, the scruffiness of Heathrow airport, the price of petrol, the follies of the church and the interminable delays on the M25.

Yelling through life: great for bats, dreadful for humans.

Prayer: Lord, may I learn to bring peace, not strife. Amen.

Daily bread

IT WAS our wedding day. We were church planters, fresh-faced and naive (I was 22 and Kay was just 18!) – and we had very little money. We were hoping for a few cash wedding gifts so that we would be able to have a few days' honeymoon. And we were deliriously happy. Despite our tiny income, we had enough, and even then we were fabulously rich by world standards. Now, life is easier – but when we have a little more we can always be looking for a little more …

This year has been one of great contrasts. I've been in Ethiopia and Indonesia and have spent time with people who have next to nothing, whose hand-to-mouth existence is a wretched, daily grind. I've seen women bowed down under great stacks of wood – they will carry them for miles for a few pennies, like human mules. And I've also been around multi-millionaires, who are able to spend huge sums without a thought. Both conditions carry their own perils. Poverty is an appalling, hopeless trap to be caught in; but affluence can be a minefield too. Those with much can end up living superficial lives with little faith and no dependency upon God: frankly, for much of life, the super rich don't see any need for Him. And life can become little more than an endless trek to an ever bigger bank balance.

So it is that the writer of this chapter (Agur, son of Jakeh, of whom we know nothing) asks God simply for enough – not too much, not too little, but sufficient. His is a wise prayer and worth adding our 'Amen' to.

Prayer: I take these words as my own: give me neither poverty nor riches, but give me only my daily bread. Amen.

BIG PICTURE
Proverbs 30:1–33
Matthew 6:9–15

FOCUS
'Keep falsehood and lies far from me; give me neither poverty nor riches, but give me only my daily bread.'
(Prov. 30:8)

… not too much,

not too little,

but sufficient

What really matters

BIG PICTURE
Proverbs 31:1–31
Luke 8:1–3

FOCUS
'A wife of noble character who can find? She is worth far more than rubies.' (Prov. 31:10)

PROVERBS 31 is well known for what seems to be a description of the biblical bionic woman: the super-sister who scoops up the kids under one arm while simultaneously churning out gourmet meals, producing crafts and doing a dozen other domestic chores with the other. But look again at this lady – this passage of Scripture provides no support for the idea that women should only ever take a passive domestic role. That's not to diminish the supreme value and significance of the full-time homemaker – it's just that many women rightly want to enjoy other roles and the Bible shouldn't be used to limit them.

This entrepreneurial lady is a skilled businesswoman; shrewd investor (v.16); she trades, manages staff and is a wonderful example in her care and compassion for the poor (vv.15,18,20). In a culture that so often demeaned women (by Jesus' time it was impossible for a woman to teach), this lady is renowned for her wisdom and instructional skills (v.26). She is strong and confident, and is industrious, taking great responsibility for the affairs of her household (v.27).

And all of this reminds me once again of the message that seems to jump out time and time again from the book of Proverbs: *character* is what counts: good life lived with God.

Perhaps, like me, you're all too aware of your failings and you sometimes get discouraged, not so much about the state of the world, but more about the state of you. Keep travelling with Jesus. May we be described as good people who loved God.

… *character* is

what counts

Prayer: Thank You, Lord, journeying with me through life. Keep me on the right path. Amen.

Joseph – Daydream believer

Joseph – Daydream believer

'GOD only uses people who are totally committed to Him.' It's the kind of phrase that preachers sometimes use and one that always worries me greatly. For one thing, with the obvious exception of Jesus, there's never been a single human being who could fulfil that lofty qualification. And then, the Bible is simply *not* full of the stories of nigh-on perfect folks who get it right every time; rather it is the chronicle of some very messy lives that were kissed by the kindness of God's grace and so managed to make some history as a result.

So, take heart, and join me as we watch God redeem one particularly messy story by His grace.

A broken family

Joseph was raised in a hugely dysfunctional family, racked by jealousy, dishonesty and double-crossing – and that's just for starters. Joseph's father, Jacob, is listed in the 'Hebrews Hall of Faith' (Heb. 11:9,20). Yet he was no pristine saint. Jacob was born grabbing at his brother's heel – and literally swindled his brother Esau out of his inheritance. Later, Jacob himself was the victim of a set-up which led him to marry a woman not of his choice, and then he almost lost a lot of money in a dodgy business deal with his father-in-law – but one that he managed to turn to his own advantage.

It was a polygamous family, where there were two wives (Rachel, famous for being beautiful, and Leah, famous for being the opposite), two concubines and enough children to start a football team (including substitutes) from the four mothers!

Here's a family at war, a home that was a cauldron of boiling tension and intrigue; their story includes the rape of Joseph's half-sister, murder, revenge and lies. In this turbulent home, Joseph was born and brought up.

… your past doesn't have to determine your future

Perhaps, as we begin this journey together, you can look back over your shoulder at a family life that has been difficult – or disastrous. But when God is your Father, your past doesn't have to determine your future.

The beginning of sorrows

BIG PICTURE
Genesis 37:1–2
James 3:13–18

FOCUS
'Joseph, a young man of seventeen, was tending the flocks with his brothers … and he brought their father a bad report about them.' (Gen. 37:2)

SOMETIMES it's possible to do what seems to be the right thing in the wrong way or for the wrong reasons. We've all met people who tell the truth religiously but wreak great damage as they do so; my life has at times been bruised by 'good' folks who were sticklers for *principle* but who didn't seem to care so much about the wellbeing of *people*. The Pharisees, who dogged almost every footstep Jesus took, were righteous and religiously scrupulous – with the worst possible results.

At first glance, Joseph seems to be a model of integrity, reporting back to his father what was probably the shoddy work ethic of his half-brothers. But was this faithfulness, or Joseph 'telling tales' on others when, at the age of just 17, he had barely learned about being a shepherd himself? Also, notice that Joseph only reported negatively about his half-brothers: nothing is said about his full brother, Benjamin. We're speculating and it may be that Joseph's brother Ben was doing a fine job in the family business, hence no 'bad report' was due – but we can certainly see possible hints of enmity based on blood here. And had Jacob placed Joseph in an impossible position, fast-tracking and promoting him ahead of his brothers to a place of authority and oversight at such a young age? The 'coat of many colours' was probably given as a symbol of authority.

Acts of integrity and generosity can be ruined by being thoughtless, unwise or clumsy. Even doing something good needs to be handled with prayer.

Prayer: Lord, give me wisdom to do what is both good *and* wise; save me from diligence that does harm. Amen.

The folly of favouritism

JACOB'S great love for Joseph is easy to understand – Joseph had come late in his life, a delight for his twilight years. And Joseph was the result of his union with the great romance in his life, the gorgeous Rachel. Joseph was her much-awaited firstborn and he was born after a lot of anguish and prayer (and conflict between Rachel and Jacob). To Rachel, Joseph's birth signalled the 'end of her disgrace' (Gen. 30:23).

And now, perhaps because he was seen as utterly trustworthy (Joseph's remarkable faithfulness is a feature of his character and story, as we shall see), his father chooses – perhaps unwisely – to honour him with the famous 'Technicolor dreamcoat'. Again, it was a well-meant action that leads to disaster.

Do those of us with children love them all in the same way? The honest answer is 'No'. There is no totally level playing field in relationships – each person will have their own lovable traits and the unpredictable pathway of life will mean that there is no precise uniformity in the ways in which we express our love. But we can treat others *fairly*, ensuring that our love for one doesn't make another feel unloved. Joseph's brothers' complaint is not so much about how much their father loved Joseph – it was more about how little he loved them.

A postscript: beware of preventing leaders from having close friends in the church or accusing them of favouritism. Our leaders need to offer pastoral support for all in their care but should be free to choose their friendships. If they don't, then watch out for the burn-out and disaster that will result.

Prayer: Lord, do I treat others fairly? Help me never to make people feel unloved. Amen.

BIG PICTURE
Genesis 37:3–4
James 2:1–9

FOCUS
'When his brothers saw that their father loved him more than any of them, they hated him and could not speak a kind word to him.'
(Gen. 37:4)

… beware of preventing leaders from having … friends …

Unwise words?

BIG PICTURE
Genesis 37:5–11
1 John 2:15–17

FOCUS
'When he told his father
… his father rebuked
him and said, "… Will
your mother and I and
your brothers actually
come and bow down to
the ground before you?"'
(Gen. 37:10)

RECENTLY Kay and I had to endure a meeting with someone who was only interested in discussing one subject: the same theme dominated our entire conversation with the tiresome repetition of a CD jammed in the CD player, playing the same few bars of music repeatedly to the point of prompting madness.

The subject so sweet to this person's ears was, quite simply, himself. With an obsession that seemed glaringly obvious, we were told every detail of what he had, what God had blessed him with, what the future held and what he dreamed of. I love to hear of the stories and successes of others, but this conversation was turning into a tedious mini-series.

Today we consider a lesson in life that, once learned, could save us all untold grief and ensure that our friendships and relationships are sustained. The simple principle is this: even those who love us the most can only put up with so much selfishness and boasting from us: we will wear out even our closest confidantes fast if we endlessly blether on about ourselves. Perhaps Joseph demonstrates his oblivion to the feelings of his brothers, who were hardly members of his fan club: they 'could not speak a kind word to him' (Gen. 37:4). Now as he shares his 'I'm going to be the top dog' dreams, he exasperates them even more so that their irritation turns to hatred (the word is used three times) and even his doting father gets frustrated with his favourite son.

Share your successes and blessings with those who will celebrate with you. But don't share *too* much.

Prayer: Lord, please may I always be conscious of why You gave me two ears and only one mouth. Amen.

The plot is hatched

DURING a recent trip to Australia, I learned about the Sydney funnel web spider, which is apparently one of the most toxic creepy-crawlies in the world and one that I'd never like to meet in person. There are a number of stunningly toxic creatures wandering the earth, like the black widow spider (I've met one of them and have an enduring hole in my leg to prove it), a green frog whose skin is apparently loaded with poison, guaranteeing final revenge for the frog upon anything that eats it, and certain breeds of snake: one encounter with any of these and you're in serious trouble.

Sadly, there are humans like that – and I'm not talking about the psychopaths who destroy without compunction. The poison of bitterness can turn any of us into dangerous predators, nipping at each other with our careless whispers of gossip, turning cold shoulders and sometimes verbally bludgeoning people, so utterly enraged are we.

So it was with Joseph's brothers. They were no strangers to the idea of a dream from God as Joseph had described it – their father, Jacob, would have told them about his many supernatural encounters, which included dreams about him being greatly blessed (Gen. 28:10–22) and even a wrestling match with God (Gen. 32:22–32). But bitterness blinds us, even to the revealed will of God; we refuse to listen to the message because we have come to despise the messenger. And bitterness causes us to focus only on our anger when we see some people: just the sight of Joseph at a distance was enough to prompt them to hatch their nasty little plot. Beware the toxicity of bitterness.

Prayer: Lord, may I be aware of the seeds of bitterness before they have grown to be trees. Amen.

BIG PICTURE
Genesis 37:12–20
Ephesians 4:31–32

FOCUS
'So Joseph went after his brothers and found them near Dothan. But they saw him in the distance, and before he reached them, they plotted to kill him.' (Gen. 37:17b–18)

Beware the toxicity of bitterness

Reuben: a mixed bag

BIG PICTURE
Genesis 37:21–30
Romans 7:14–25

FOCUS
'When Reuben heard this, he tried to rescue him from their hands. "Let's not take his life," he said. "Don't shed any blood."'
(Gen. 37:21–22)

REUBEN, Jacob's firstborn and therefore senior in the family hierarchy, is a character who demonstrates the truth that we are all capable of great good – and great evil. Sometimes we can categorise others as being either good or bad – and when they disappoint, we write them off. While there are those who consistently live without a care or concern for anyone other than themselves, the truth about most of us is that we are a mixture; nobility and selfishness, self-sacrifice and pettiness, purity and lust jostle around in the same hearts, battling for control.

Reuben is an example. Here, his was the lone voice of protest against the conspiracy to kill Joseph and he proposed a plan that saved the dreamer's life, even if it did backfire initially. Years later, it would be Reuben who would pledge his own life and the lives of his sons as he promised to get Benjamin out of Egypt. Here was a man who took responsibility for sins that he had tried to avoid.

And yet Reuben was a deeply flawed character too; he had slept with his father's concubine, Bilhah (Gen. 35:22), which was technically incest according to Old Testament law; this was a terrible disgrace on the family and cost Reuben his inheritance as the firstborn (Gen. 49:3–4). He would be described by his dying father as a man of honour, strength, power – and turbulence and defilement.

What we were yesterday, for good or ill, does not determine what we will be today. We are all compilations. What element of our character will win the day today?

Prayer: May the good in me win out today, Lord. Amen.

Sin begets sin

It was the Scottish novelist Sir Walter Scott (1771–
1832) who gave us that famous warning: 'Oh what
a tangled web we weave, when first we practise to
deceive.' As Jacob's family make their way home, fully
aware that they've sold their own brother into a life
of slavery, they meander downhill into a quagmire
of further sin. They become heartless liars as they
take the false evidence of the bloodied 'Technicolor
dreamcoat' to the old man; they are forced to watch
his tears and listen to his declaration that his life is
ruined – with stoic cold-blooded determination.
And then they are forced to become hypocrites,
'comforting' their father in turn, feigning sympathy
and support while all along knowing the terrible
truth. In a moment, any one of them could have swept
the tangled web of deception aside, told the truth and
set out to go and rescue their captive brother. Jacob
was inconsolable. They could have brought an end to
his tears. But the lying continued.

It's one thing to make a mistake, but quite another to
go all out to add sin to sin as we continue to cover our
tracks. Sin multiplies in the dark.

Sin multiplies
in the dark

God meant it for good

BIG PICTURE

Genesis 37:36
Romans 8:28

FOCUS
'Meanwhile, the Midianites sold Joseph in Egypt to Potiphar, one of Pharaoh's officials, the captain of the guard.'
(Gen. 37:36)

JUST two verses to read today, enabling us to press the pause button. Joseph is in deep trouble – his life has been threatened, he's been sold into the hand of the Midianites (famous in the Bible for their heartless brutality) and now has plummeted from being a dressed-to-kill son in a well-heeled family to being a slave in a foreign country. Joseph, like many people today, is the helpless victim of people-trafficking.

All this has come about as a result of a cocktail of human evil: his own father's favouritism began all the trouble, coupled with Joseph's own boasting about his dreams. His brothers' hatred gradually distilled into thoughts of murder and a botched solution from Reuben backfires. The whole thing is a hopelessly tangled mess of lies, conspiracy and bitter envy. And yet, somehow, in the midst of all the mess, God is working out His purposes. He is not the architect of the chaotic evil but He is the Redeemer of it. Joseph must have felt swept away, floundering around in circumstances that were stealing his life. But, quietly, God was placing him where he could become the rescuer of a nation.

Perhaps you find yourself somewhere and it's all because of a stunningly stupid decision you made some time ago: bluntly, you were wrong. Or maybe you have been the helpless victim of the madness of others: their folly or thoughtlessness has conspired to land you where you are now. Don't lose hope; ask the Redeemer to do some redeeming. He is bigger than the mess and can bring something beautiful out of it.

Prayer: Take my life, Lord and bring good out of the bad. Amen.

IT'S a well-known saying about the so-called Midas effect: 'Whatever they touch turns to gold.' In the case of the unfortunate King Midas of Greek mythology fame, all that gold didn't turn out to be much of a blessing, seeing as all his food and drink turned to gold at his touch too …

Joseph had that golden touch as well but this was nothing to do with chance, magic or good luck. The favour of God was with him. We skip over the story in Genesis 38 and we find Joseph, now doing rather well for himself in the household of Potiphar. The two salient themes of Joseph's story clearly emerge here and we'll return to them repeatedly: wherever Joseph finds himself, God is with him, faithfully, and Joseph is with God, faithfully. Surely that's the truest definition of authentic success: a human being cared for by God (even in adversity), found in relationship with God and honouring the Lord and his or her fellow humans, entrusted with success and refusing to be spoiled by it.

So it is Joseph who always rises to the top: in his family, he's the celebrated one with the fancy wardrobe; as a servant, he's entrusted with everything; even when he lands up on what could become death row for him, he flourishes. But, far more than being merely successful, Joseph is trustworthy. The corporate scandals of recent years and the upsurge of so called 'white collar crime' show that some will give up everything that is important, including their integrity, in the frantic pursuit of yet more stuff.

True success is not just about having more: it's about faithfulness and about how we act, whether we're down and out, or up and coming.

Prayer: Lord, challenge my thinking where it is all about success and not about faithfulness. Amen.

Golden boy

BIG PICTURE
**Genesis 39:1–6a
Psalm 18:1–26**

FOCUS
'The LORD was with Joseph and he prospered, and he lived in the house of his Egyptian master.'
(Gen. 39:2)

True success is … about faithfulness …

Temptation

BIG PICTURE
Genesis 39:6b–12
1 Corinthians 6:18–20

FOCUS
'And though she spoke to Joseph day after day, he refused to go to bed with her or even to be with her.' (Gen. 39:10)

WE CHRISTIANS need to talk about sex more: everybody else is talking about it, a lot of the time and in our hearing. The notion that we are somehow immune to the multiple temptations that sex brings is nothing short of madness, and the relentless attempted seduction of Joseph gives us a hint about the nature of temptation. Perhaps you're facing a major sexual temptation right now: here are a few of the notions that may be swimming around inside your head.

I'm only human. I can't take the pressure. Joseph had to endure the come-to-bed eyes – and graphic invitation – of Potiphar's wife, every day. Temptation seeks to wear us out with its repetitive demands – but Joseph refused to give in. So can we.

No one will know. I can cover my tracks. When the final move came from Potiphar's wife, no one else was in the house; it was the perfect opportunity. Perhaps you're in a situation right now where you're confident that your secret would never emerge. But Joseph knew that the issue was not his ability to get away with sin, but rather the betrayal of the trust given to him by his employer, as well as his relationship with God.

A little flirtation is harmless enough. But not only did Joseph not trust his would-be seductress; he didn't trust himself, hence his 'doing a runner' – literally. He didn't even stop to retrieve his cloak. There has to come a time when the talking stops and the only sensible option is to head away from the temptation at full speed.

Prayer: Lord, give me the strength to resist – or run away – from temptation of any kind. Amen.

Injustice

I WANT life to be fair and would be delighted if I were rewarded instantly for making good choices, like a large-scale game show: I did the right thing, now where's my prize? (I have to admit that I'm not quite so keen on the idea of instant judgment for *bad* choices …) But, as we know, not only is life not fair but existing on this confused, sin-bound planet means that we often end up having to 'suffer for what is right' (1 Pet. 3:14).

So, in the short term at least, Joseph ends up losing everything for the second time, once more the victim of conspiracy, this time by an angry, spurned woman. Sharp-eyed commentators have noted that Potiphar may not have fully believed his wife, because the standard punishment for attempted rape was death, whereas Joseph just ends up in the prison. Not only did the slinky seductress have to live with the knowledge that she had condemned a wholly innocent man, but it's possible she had to endure the sideways, questioning glances of her husband too. Notice her manipulative language with her husband: 'That Hebrew slave *you brought us* came to me to make sport of me' (v.17) and, 'This is how *your slave* treated me' (v.19; my italics). It's all her husband's fault, for bringing the Hebrew into the home in the first place. This is no happy marriage but a battleground of control and accusation.

Meanwhile, Joseph is incarcerated. Are you suffering unfairly, the victim of lies and injustice? Take heart – let's see how God turns things around.

Prayer: Lord, give us patience and trust in You when we suffer unfairly. Amen.

BIG PICTURE
**Genesis 39:13–20a
1 Peter 3:8–22**

FOCUS
'Joseph's master took him and put him in prison, the place where the king's prisoners were confined.' (Gen. 39:20)

… life is

not fair …

Living in the gap

BIG PICTURE
**Genesis 39:20–23
2 Peter 1:3–4**

FOCUS
'But while Joseph was there in the prison, the LORD was with him; he showed him kindness and granted him favour in the eyes of the prison warder.'
(Gen. 39:20b–21)

PROMOTED even in prison, Joseph flourishes yet again; even in jail he rises to the top. All this is because God is 'with' Joseph – a statement that is made four times in this one chapter (vv.2,3,21,23). But let's not over-romanticise: Joseph's life could still be snuffed out at the whim of the Pharaoh and as other inmates would discover (and we will see when we look at their stories later) their fate could be an agonising death with even the relief of the afterlife under threat. And to be chosen as the convict in charge is hardly the greatest privilege.

So how did Joseph manage to sustain hope through those 13 years of slavery and imprisonment? Remember those dreams, revelations that Joseph had rushed to share with his envious brothers? Surely God gave them to the young man to sustain him through all that was to come. He had caught a hint of their fulfilment in the favour he had experienced in Potiphar's household, and even in prison, but he must have mulled them over many times as each grinding day unfolded. Greatness and significance were to come; God had said so.

Our maturity – or lack of it – is often revealed by the way we live in the gap between a promise from God and the fulfilment of that promise. My experience to date is that there may be lengthy seasons when circumstances seem to completely deny that something God has promised will ever arrive; then, sooner or later, a new day dawns. But in the meantime, we hold on to hope.

Prayer: Lord, may I hold on to see Your promises fulfilled. Amen.

Genesis 40:1–7 // Philippians 2:1–4

Gift and character: compassion

It was during a training seminar on counselling and deliverance that the speaker spoke some words that chilled my heart. He outlined a particular ministry strategy that he had found helpful and then encouraged us all to 'go out, find someone and try it out'. The thought that we would all search for human guinea pigs to 'practise on' filled me with horror. People are people and their lives are too fragile and important to play with. There are times when I sense that God has given me wisdom about someone's situation but my tendency is to keep quiet until I feel a greater level of certainty – out of concern that what I share may be wrong, and I fear hurting them.

Joseph obviously had a profound ability to discern the voice of God. But look past that gift, to the character of the man who operated it: his prophetic insight flowed from a heart of care and concern for others. Not one who is preoccupied with his own troubles and fails to sense the mood of those around him, Joseph notices that the two imprisoned royal officials are dejected and asks why it is that they are so low. Genuine compassion comes before supernatural revelation.

[People's] … lives are too fragile … to play with

Gift and character: humility

BIG PICTURE
Genesis 40:8
James 4:1–10

FOCUS
'Then Joseph said to them, "Do not interpretations belong to God? Tell me your dreams."' (Gen. 40:8b)

OUR gifts can be our downfall. A sense that we are being used by God, especially in a 'sensational' way, as Joseph experienced, can lead us to an inflated view of our own importance. Our gifts become a way of promoting ourselves rather than glorifying the God who is the Giver of those gifts. How easy it is for a genuine 'testimony' to be a contrived way of us boasting about our usefulness to God. I've been in situations where it was claimed that people were physically healed; sadly more focus was given to the person who prayed the prayer for healing than the God who actually answered the prayer.

Joseph had the opportunity to accentuate his own significance and place himself as the exclusive bridge between God, the cupbearer and the baker. He could have 'struck a deal' with them before sharing the interpretation of their dreams and claimed the franchise on revelation, insisting that the cupbearer would need his help once he was released (the baker, for obvious reasons, would be beyond help). And indeed, Joseph would later ask that he be remembered and released. But Joseph insisted that the ultimate solution to the dream riddles rested with God alone. He ensures that the two confused men know that he is not the source of the much-needed wisdom but merely a channel that God will use.

Let's ask God to use us. And let's ask that, if He does, we'll always remember who is supposed to get the glory.

Prayer: Lord, use me as You wish. May I see Your hand on my life today. Amen.

WE CHRISTIANS can be very driven by our feelings but we must know that sometimes having faith has absolutely nothing to do with what we feel. Obedience may involve us in putting one foot in front of another yet again and making a wooden choice to be faithful. Last week I preached a sermon – and have rarely felt less like preaching. But it was right to fulfil my responsibility, despite my emotional turbulence.

At last we get a glimpse into Joseph's mindset, as he pours out his frustration and grief about the injustice that he experienced at the hands of his brothers and then in Potiphar's house. He is innocent and has ended up condemned to a dungeon. He feels forgotten – 'remember me' – and shamelessly ill-treated – 'show me kindness' and is asking for a little in return for the prophetic insights he had shared: 'mention me to Pharaoh'.

Notice that Joseph has just been used by God to speak into the lives of these two officials – but even in that specific episode of being God's mouthpiece, his heart is overshadowed by sadness. Even though he does not know it, he is right in the epicentre of God's purposes – and yet he still feels profound despair.

Being *outside* of God's will for us is a recipe for serious unhappiness – but being *inside* His purposes doesn't guarantee a spring in our step either. We all have to live with disappointments, unresolved questions, tiredness and, at times, the sheer grind of existence, which can wear us out. Sometimes we just have to faithfully continue to do what is right, as Joseph did, even though our hearts remain heavy.

Prayer: Give me the assurance that I'm where You want me to be, Lord, Amen.

Gift and character: endurance

BIG PICTURE
Genesis 40:9–15
Hebrews 12:1–3

FOCUS
'But when all goes well with you ... mention me to Pharaoh and get me out of this prison. For ... I have done nothing to deserve being put in a dungeon.'
(Gen. 40:14–15)

We all have

to live with

disappointments ...

Gift and character: truth

BIG PICTURE
Genesis 40:16–19
Galatians 2:11–14

FOCUS
'Joseph said. "The three baskets are three days. Within three days Pharaoh will lift off your head and hang you on a tree. And the birds will eat away your flesh."'
(Gen. 40:18–19)

THE news that Joseph brought to the baker was horrible: he was going to die within days. The New International Version's 'hang you on a tree' would be more accurately translated as 'impale you on a pole'. Joseph was predicting that the baker would be beheaded and that, following execution, his body would be picked over by birds – a strategy that, according to Egyptian beliefs, was designed to prevent the soul resting in the afterlife. It must have been traumatic for the baker to hear of his fate and we might wonder what the point was of Joseph's prediction: perhaps, even in the terrifying ordeal that the condemned man was to endure, he would have a sense that there was a God who knew what befell him? But whatever the reason for the revelation, Joseph was faithful to the truth and spoke what was shown to him, even when the sight was so appalling.

Our task is not always to make people feel good because of what we say, as if compliant agreement with everyone is always the Christian way. There are times when we will need to speak solemnly but with kindness, about what is clearly right or wrong. Care is needed here, lest we become impassioned and unyielding about what are merely our opinions rather than God's truth: but we must know that, even though some people's 'ears itch' to hear only the sweet sound of what they like to hear, faithfulness demands that we tell the truth. Tacit agreement isn't always possible: people of faith are people of conviction.

Prayer: Give me courage to tell the truth, Lord, and wisdom to know how to say it. Amen.

JOSEPH was right. For the baker, a banquet turned into a funeral – just as Joseph had predicted. You'd think that Joseph would have been hailed by the cupbearer as a hero, one who had predicted his deliverance so precisely – especially as he watched his poor colleague being dragged away to the gallows. Perhaps the cupbearer made a political decision to keep quiet about his prison encounter with Joseph – why risk upsetting the Pharaoh with the notion that there was someone, a lowly prisoner of all people, who had been able so accurately to predict the great man's actions? Better keep quiet. Let the young prophet rot. Joseph was forgotten.

Ingratitude, for whatever reason, is one of the most difficult wounds that come to us in life. As a Christian leader, I can look back with sadness – and occasional soreness – at people in whom I invested significant amounts of time and care, continuing with them on what seemed to be the extra mile. When they have appeared oblivious to that investment, or even, in some cases, set themselves up as vocal critics of mine, then it's easy to feel terribly used and even abused.

The time would come when the cupbearer's memory would be jogged and he would be part of the process that led to Joseph being set free and appointed to high office. But there's no record of Joseph punishing him for his two years of political forgetfulness; one assumes that, though disappointed, prisoner Joseph guarded his heart and left the matter to God, who Himself is 'kind to the ungrateful'. Let's do the same.

Prayer: Lord, may I forgive the ingratitude of others and not be guilty of it myself. Amen.

Gift and character: facing ingratitude

BIG PICTURE
Genesis 40:20–23
Luke 6:27–36

FOCUS
'The chief cupbearer, however, did not remember Joseph; he forgot him.'
(Gen. 40:23)

Ingratitude … is one of the most difficult wounds …

187

Serendipity

BIG PICTURE
Genesis 41:1–14
Isaiah 42:16

FOCUS
'So Pharaoh sent for
Joseph, and he was
quickly brought from the
dungeon. When he had
shaved and changed his
clothes, he came before
Pharaoh.' (Gen. 41:14)

I DON'T believe in good luck. There's no place in the Christian life for our trusting in chance. But I do believe that God is able to engineer my days and steer me into situations for which, without my being aware of it, He's been preparing me, for some time. I don't want to get neurotic or silly about that and fast and pray about which supermarket to visit today, but I do want to make myself available to God, the great Choreographer.

One somewhat quaint word for this is 'serendipity' – that happy co-ordination of circumstances that means we find ourselves in the right place at the right time, ready to fulfil God's purposes. Joseph had lost his youth to slavery and prison – by now the 17-year-old who was betrayed by his brothers is a man of 30. One can only imagine the mental anguish that he had endured as his life apparently wasted away. And yet as Pharaoh is troubled by an economic revelation from God about the years to come for the nation he leads, the cupbearer's memory is stirred, he repents of his amnesiac negligence and he tells his fearsome boss about a young man who was rather good at dream interpretation …

Enter Joseph, all cleaned up, ready for action, poised to seize his moment and become the architect for the saving of Egypt and the salvation of the Hebrews.

Ignore the black cat, don't worry about your lucky number and don't put your trust in that good luck charm. God is big enough.

Prayer: Lord, I trust You that I will be in the right place at the right time. Amen.

The big break

At last, the pivotal episode in Joseph's life arrives. This is a junction moment, when everything changes – in this case, very much for the better. Perhaps we all have a few 'junctions' in our lives: these might include the time we made a decision about a job or relocation; or the choice of a partner or the decision to really get involved in the life of a local church. And sometimes the junction isn't so clearly marked. What seems like a chance meeting or a casual conversation of little consequence turns out to be vital in the big scheme of things.

As Joseph stands before Pharaoh, he wonderfully avoids what might have been a huge temptation to make himself indispensable in the situation. As he did with the triumphant cupbearer and the tragic baker, Joseph insists that all wisdom comes from God alone: again, he is but the channel.

The 'big days' of our lives don't come announced so that we can prepare for them; Joseph awoke as normal to what seemed like another tedious dungeon-bound day – only to discover that this was the dawning of a whole new life. What might God do for us today?

What might
God do for
us today?

A life learner

BIG PICTURE
Genesis 41:17–32
Exodus 33:12–14

FOCUS
'The reason the dream was given to Pharaoh in two forms is that the matter has been firmly decided by God, and God will do it soon.'
(Gen. 41:32)

HOW do you become a fully qualified dream interpreter? Certainly Joseph was confident in his craft, standing boldly before Pharaoh and announcing that the elusive meaning of his dream, which was beyond the comprehension of a whole gaggle of court magicians, would now be revealed by this newly shaven ex-con. This was risky. As the unfortunate baker had discovered, it was not advisable to irritate Pharaoh – one could lose one's head at the snap of his fingers. Joseph was under some pressure to deliver the goods. So how did he get to the place where he could do that with such uncanny accuracy?

That question is impossible to answer fully but one hint is found in the way that Joseph identified the 'double-hit' dream given to Pharaoh. The same message delivered in two forms emphasised that what had been stated would most definitely come to pass – no negotiation was possible. There are some episodes in the Bible when a course of action may be averted because of repentance and fasting – like Nineveh (Jonah 3:6–10) or intercession, as with Sodom and Gomorrah (Gen. 18:20–32). But here, nothing is going to shift the outcome for Egypt; the need was to strategically prepare for the inevitable, rather than try to change it.

Of course, Joseph had seen this two-time dream strategy before – years earlier, when he caught a glimpse of the place of primacy that would eventually be his, in the dreams that got him into hot water with his family in the first place. Joseph listened to the *words* of God but he also learned the *ways* of God.

Prayer: Lord, teach me not just what You do, but how You do it. Amen.

Ordinary but spectacular

COME with me and, through the eyes of imagination, take a look at this man Joseph. His face is pale, due to years of poor diet; perhaps his teeth are in a mess as well. He owns nothing at all: even the clothes he wears are borrowed, hasty replacements for his prison rags. Since his youth, he has been the property of another. Liberty, sunshine, laughter, love, all denied him, he has suffered hideous injustice, especially from those with whom he should have been safe. His reputation has been shredded. Official documentation shows that he is a convicted rapist, a felon who years earlier repaid the incredible trust and generosity of his employer by attacking and sexually assaulting his helpless wife. He has made no mark on the world: even those few people he has helped along the way have forgotten him.

Look again and see what Pharaoh, wide-eyed with wonder now, sees so clearly. Here is a man so utterly full of the Holy Spirit that he stands head and shoulders above all others. Outwardly he is nothing to look at: inwardly he has been shaped and crafted, mainly through suffering, into a spiritual giant, a man who can be taken from the depths of the dungeon to the heights of the Prime Minister's home, because God is with him.

Today, you and I may well be tempted to interact superficially with people, quickly making surface judgment calls because of how they look or the first impressions they make. Let's look carefully and with discernment: sometimes really great people come heavily disguised.

Prayer: May I see in people today what You want me to see, Lord. Amen.

BIG PICTURE
Genesis 41:33–40
1 Samuel 16:6–7

FOCUS
'So Pharaoh asked them, "Can we find anyone like this man, one in whom is the spirit of God?"'
(Gen. 41:38)

Here is a man so utterly full of the Holy Spirit …

Shaped for success

BIG PICTURE
Genesis 41:41–57
Psalm 105:16–22

FOCUS
'He had him ride in a chariot as his second-in-command, and men shouted before him, "Make way!" Thus he put him in charge of the whole land of Egypt.'
(Gen. 41:43)

SUDDEN success can be destructive. Our television screens and the tabloid newspapers are loaded with the lurid stories of those who become 'overnight' successes – but their being catapulted to prominence so quickly can damage them, sometimes beyond repair. Arrogance, irresponsible binge-spending, an inability to form lasting relationships and reliance on drugs or too much alcohol are often found in the lives of instant celebrities. Joseph survived prison. Could he survive becoming an international VIP?

His was probably the biggest promotion in history, as the prisoner becomes prime minister in an instant and then for seven years tours the nation overseeing the extensive programme of economic preparations that he has proposed. Much pomp and ceremony accompanied his entourage, with plenty of bowing and scraping – literally. But all through his trials and struggles, Joseph knew exactly where his giftedness and therefore his prominence had come from: God. Now he had riches and influence beyond his wildest dreams, but position and prominence did not have him; his heart remained set on God, and, as we'll see, he names his Egyptian children in honour of his God.

You don't have to be a super-rich soccer prodigy or an overnight television celebrity to be damaged by success. A little prominence here and a sense of acknowledgement there can conspire to fill our hearts with conceit. Leadership, even in the small goldfish bowl that is the church, can corrupt, as some get a sense of power and control. The dungeon is a danger zone – but so is the place of success.

Prayer: Lord, help me to handle whatever You have for me – success or apparent failure. Amen.

Learn well while you can

FOR Joseph, everything is utterly different – but back in his homeland, much is the same. The brotherhood are still united in their deceit – for many years now the aging Jacob has believed his beloved, favourite son is dead. His family have watched grief wither him. They could have brought an end to his tears with a word but instead they have allowed him to weep his way towards the grave.

And perhaps Jacob himself is still much the same, in that he hasn't learned much about favouritism and parenting. If anything, his tragic loss of Joseph has caused him to be even more protective of the other great love of his life and fruit of his marriage to the much loved and missed Rachel: Benjamin, Joseph's full brother.

Imagine what it felt like to be one of the ten brothers – the 'B' team – whom Jacob was willing to send off to Egypt. Apparently their father wasn't nearly as concerned about their welfare and would risk their lives without a qualm, as long as precious Benjamin was kept out of harm's way. Jacob hasn't learned a single lesson about favouritism and still continues a pattern of behaviour that only fuels the fires of resentment and jealousy in his dysfunctional family.

Am I still stumbling around in the same idiotic behaviour that ensnared me years ago? To err is human but not to learn from the errors of our ways and so continue in destructive patterns is madness. Let's not be 'always learning but never able to acknowledge the truth' (2 Tim. 3:7).

Prayer: Lord, am I still making the same mistakes as I was ten years ago? Help me to change. Amen.

BIG PICTURE
Genesis 42:1–5
Proverbs 26:11

FOCUS
'… Joseph's brothers went down to buy grain from Egypt. But Jacob did not send Benjamin, Joseph's brother, with the others, because he was afraid that harm might come to him.'
(Gen. 42:3–4)

To err is

human …

The journey of forgiveness

BIG PICTURE

Genesis 42:6–20
Matthew 7:1–2

FOCUS

'And he put them all in custody for three days.' (Gen. 42:17)

JOSEPH, now a husband, father and prime minister, has finally 'forgotten' his Hebrew family and has established his own family unit in Egypt – and it's then that his brothers show up, hoping to buy grain. Considering all the years of pain that they'd sentenced Joseph to when they sold him into slavery, his response to them is mild, but we have to wonder: as he threw them into jail, was Joseph giving them but a small taste of the bitterness of his prison years? As he accuses them of being spies, is he showing them what it feels like to be falsely accused? Then he insists that they return home to bring Benjamin to Egypt, leaving Simeon behind as a 'deposit' against their return. Perhaps Joseph was testing them, placing them once again in a situation where they could take their grain and run, abandoning Simeon as they had dumped him. Had their hearts changed at all over the years?

Perhaps what we see here is Joseph coming to terms with being able to express forgiveness to his brothers. An initial thirst for payback – which led to the brief three-day jail sentence – is gradually replaced by a real desire to bless his brothers and father and enjoy a wonderful family reunion.

I'm nervous when I hear of people being told to 'just go ahead and forgive' people who have hurt them horrendously. To demand that a woman who has suffered rape must quickly rush to forgive her tormenter seems like further abuse to me. Scars may take a long time to heal and forgiving may be a process that takes years. Perhaps even the mighty Joseph had to journey into forgiveness.

Prayer: Lord, may I travel further on the road to forgiveness today. Amen.

Genesis 42:21 // Romans 5:12–19

Human nature

A Christian leader friend, who has been in ministry for over 30 years, recently told me that nothing surprises him any more when it comes to human behaviour. He is grieved when he hears of bad attitudes, church splits and blatant immorality but not surprised. At first I thought he had allowed cynicism to erode his sense of hope: now I realise that he is a realist.

We humans do terribly ugly things. We are fallen. We are capable of wonderful love and yet we can in turn be heartless, self-obsessed and cruel. As the brothers conclude that they are being punished for their past sins, some harrowing details about the viciousness of their actions come to the surface. They vividly recall their own brother literally pleading for mercy, cries that they coldly ignored. It's a stark portrait of just how vicious and calculated we can be.

We won't be able to make sense of church, or indeed any set of relationships, unless we have a clear doctrine of sin. Humanness means messiness; the Bible makes that plain. So let's not be disappointed when people let us down; we humans are rather accomplished – and predictable – when it comes to mess.

Humanness
means
messiness …

195

It's wrong

BIG PICTURE
Genesis 42:22–24
2 Samuel 12:1–13

FOCUS
'He turned away from
them and began to weep,
but then turned back and
spoke to them again. He
had Simeon taken from
them and bound before
their eyes.' (Gen. 42:24)

HERE'S a phrase that isn't too popular these days. Those who use these two little words in the same sentence are in real danger of being written off as intolerant, boring, narrow minded or bigoted. This is an unfashionable phrase: 'It's wrong.'

We live in a culture awash with the deceptive tides of relativism. The popular belief is that truth is what we decide for ourselves. If I feel that a certain moral – or immoral – choice is OK, that's fine. It's my life. So the suggestion that something might be absolutely wrong is deeply unpopular. Couple this with the deceptiveness of the human heart, where we can easily excuse our bad behaviour, and you've a recipe for moral chaos. Sometimes we just have to face up to the facts – we've sinned and we can deny it, or come in repentance and find a better tomorrow. Choose one.

The brothers had barely finished whispering about their sinful treatment of Joseph years earlier being the reason for their present calamity. And now, they have to watch in silence as their brother Simeon is bound with ropes and led away. Look at the fear that widens his eyes. See the tears that glisten on his flushed cheek. The rope chafes at his wrists; the guards push him roughly. Remember?

Joseph is making them relive the moment and see it for what it was: heinous evil. Look, boys. Remember well what you did and weep. Freedom doesn't come when we avoid calling sin what it is, but when we face up to what we have done. Let's cut to the chase and call sin what it is: sin.

Prayer: Lord, where in my life do You want me to face the truth today? Amen.

Outrageous grace

GODFREY Birtill is a worship leader who sometimes composes songs after listening to preaching. A theme emerges from a sermon and Godfrey puts it into song. Listening to me speaking at a conference, he heard me make a comment about God's 'outrageous grace'. The song by that name, which has been sung around the world, is the result of that moment.

But Godfrey has constantly been in trouble for using the phrase I coined; he gets emails and letters from people complaining that it is wrong to describe grace so. I stand totally by the phrase: the cross is a 'scandal' in human eyes, and grace that takes sinners like us and allows us a seat of honour at God's table is nothing less than outrageous to the legalist, to the devil and to the powers of human logic.

Joseph shows some of that stunning grace himself. His brothers had held his life in their hands – and they threw it away, as they had sold him, literally, down the river. Now they were in his hands. What do you do with a herd of scoundrels who have ruined your life?

You load them up with food and put money in their sacks. You overwhelm them with such unmerited kindness that they worry that somehow God is out to get them with a clever trick. You freely give them what they could never afford to pay for.

Like the brothers, sometimes the gift seems just too good to be true. We wonder if God's kindness is only a ruse and He will 'get us' in the end. We've been loaded down with grace. Don't fight it.

Prayer: Lord, thank You for everything Your grace means, in my life and in Your Church. Amen.

BIG PICTURE
Genesis 42:25–28
Luke 15:11–32

FOCUS
'Joseph gave orders to fill their bags with grain, to put each man's silver back in his sack, and to give him provisions …
After this … they … left.'
(Gen. 42:25–26)

We've been

loaded down

with grace

Self-pity

BIG PICTURE
Genesis 42:29–38
Genesis 3:1–19

FOCUS
'But Jacob said, "My son will not go down there with you; his brother is dead and he is the only one left."' (Gen. 42:38)

JACOB threw a pity party when his sons finally returned: the thought of losing Benjamin, with Joseph apparently lost and Simeon held hostage, was just too much for him. Admittedly, it was a grave situation but Jacob became so overwhelmed with his own sadness that incoherence and confusion set in. Self-pity does that: it causes us to lose perspective.

Self-pity means that we whine away about what everybody else has done and fail to see that we have any responsibility for a situation. Jacob rails against his sons but fails to see that it was his own foolish favouritism that had begun the whole sorry process in the first place. He gives way to fear and apparently writes off Simeon as dead. Feeling sorry for ourselves often creates a landing strip for fear to take over our hearts and minds; we succumb to consistent negativity and can only think of the worst possible outcomes.

But self-pity also destroys our relationships. Reuben promises to sort out the whole problem and pledges his own sons too (a massive, heart-rending commitment). That is brushed aside by insensitive Jacob, who makes the stunningly thoughtless comment about Benjamin being 'the only one left'. The brothers must have been terribly wounded: were they not Jacob's sons too? Self-pity means that we can only focus on our troubles and we easily dismiss the needs of others, wounding them as we do so.

Perhaps there's a situation that you're battling right now and it really is bad. Don't allow self-pity to make it worse.

Prayer: Lord, guard my heart against self-pity. Amen.

Straight talking from Judah

I RECENTLY asked a good friend for an honest opinion about something I had done. It took a few minutes to get an answer. He was so desperate not to offend me that he hesitated to say what I knew was on his mind – and he was right in his appraisal; even though his words weren't what I wanted to hear, they were what I *needed* to hear. I'm grateful for a few people in my life who can tell me straight. With them, I have a deal: tell me what you think. No holds barred, no dancing around the issue, just give it to me. It's painful sometimes, but the pain of being left in my own self-deception is a lot worse. I've seen Christian leaders who rise to such prominence that no one feels able to challenge them; a dangerous place to live.

Jacob seriously needed to hear some straight talking. Self-pity was lingering. There are still traces of it in Jacob's heart in this chapter: the grain ran out but the self-pity remained. Finally, perhaps facing up to the very real possibility of starvation, Jacob commands his sons to head for Egypt again but without mentioning their taking Benjamin. Even though the conditions had been clearly set out by Joseph, Jacob seems to have been one of those people who always feel that they are beyond the rules that everyone else has to follow. It takes the straight talking of Judah – and an outright refusal from him to even contemplate a trip to Egypt without Benjamin in tow – to snap Jacob out of his pity-filled daze. In your life, who can tell you straight?

Prayer: Lord, give me the courage to accept the truth, whoever it comes from. Amen.

BIG PICTURE
Genesis 43:1–5
Proverbs 25:12

FOCUS
'But if you will not send him, we will not go down, because the man said to us, "You will not see my face again unless your brother is with you."' (Gen. 43:5)

… who can tell you straight?

Procrastination

BIG PICTURE
Genesis 43:6–10
Matthew 8:18–22

FOCUS
'As it is, if we had not delayed, we could have gone and returned twice.'
(Gen. 43:10)

FINALLY, the problem of a growling stomach focused Jacob's mind, so that at last he instructs his sons to head to Egypt on another grain-buying mission. But while time has ambled on, don't forget that Simeon has continued as a hostage in Egypt. He is perfectly safe under Joseph's patronage, but procrastinating Jacob doesn't know that. Instead of jumping into action to get his son out of jail, once again Jacob displays the favouritism that had created such enmity in this family. Only his own hunger finally prompts him to act.

We procrastinate for a number of reasons: sometimes fear of making a wrong decision paralyses us. We worry that we might step out of God's will for our lives and endlessly fret that the wrong choice might be cataclysmic – a mistake, I believe. God knows our hearts and our future doesn't depend on our being able to make a crystal clear choice about everything. Or we fail to be proactive because we think that a situation left alone might eventually sort itself out – which does happen, but rarely. And there are times when our inaction is simply due to laziness. To do nothing demands nothing; but then often business that we leave unattended creates further problems. Too many people shove that credit card bill – unpaid – into a kitchen drawer, insisting that they'll get around to it eventually. Bills like that actually come looking for us. And sometimes leaders fail to be decisive because they cannot cope emotionally with the reactions they might face if they actually make a decision.

Are you delaying doing something that you know is overdue? Get on with it.

Prayer: Lord, may I have the strength today to tackle that issue that I don't want to face. Amen.

Not everyone is like us

Sometimes I worry me. There are moments, like when I am just about to get up to preach, when I wonder how my listeners would feel if they could see into my heart. Within me is a tangled collection of nobility and pettiness, purity and grubbiness, selflessness and selfishness, which I can barely fathom – but I know enough to know that I am deeply flawed.

Knowing ourselves as we do, we can be guilty of thinking that everyone else is like us at our worst. So the brothers, back now in Egypt and ushered as guests of honour to the Prime Minister's personal residence, begin to wonder if they've walked into a trap and speculate that perhaps they are about to be placed into slavery …

… which is exactly what they had done with their own brother, years earlier. One of the unfortunate fruits of sin is that it makes us cynical about the genuine goodness of others. We tend to think that everybody else is guilty of what we are guilty of.

Perhaps you're convinced that others are going to do something to you … that you've already been guilty of doing. Look again: those around us are not our mirror-images.

… those around us are not our mirror-images

It's true

BIG PICTURE
Genesis 43:19–28
Genesis 37:5–11

FOCUS
They replied, "Your servant our father is still alive and well." And they bowed low to pay him honour. (Gen. 43:28)

THERE'S something that keeps slipping my mind, busy Christian person that I am. It's an unfortunate lapse of memory that I have; sometimes this amnesia seems to affect me for days or even longer. But the truth I so easily forget is the reason that I am alive. It is that Christianity is true. God is real. Jesus really is alive. God can be trusted.

The busyness of life and familiarity with the greatest story ever told means that sometimes the Bible can read a little like highly creative fiction: clever, imaginative stuff, but fiction. Life can seem more real than the God who makes life. That means that the hope of eternity spent forever with Jesus, in what we generically often describe as 'heaven', can seem like a faraway, distant dream; a nice, comforting notion but one that is surely too good to be true.

As the brothers bowed down twice before Joseph, he surely realised that the two dreams he had experienced years earlier had come to pass, just as God had said. And what had brought this about? It was the result of their search for grain, which is surely an interesting link with the 'sheaves of wheat' dream that Joseph had had. There had been years of slavery, heartache and loneliness. But still what God had said came to pass. God was real. It was true.

Pause and think, and pray too, for a moment. Ask God to fulfil His promises in your life. This news makes all the difference: God is for real.

Prayer: Lord, please make Your presence firmly felt today; give me fresh faith and a renewal of hope. Amen.

Not a toy

AT FIRST glance, it seems like Joseph is enjoying a perverse sense of revenge by playing games with his brothers. Is he goading them with his planting silver in sacks, setting out the seating plan for the banquet according to their birthdates (which would have prompted the brothers to wonder how on earth he knew their ages), and then loading Benjamin's plate with a food portion five times bigger than theirs? The brothers had treated Joseph like a worthless commodity – was he now getting his own back with a heartless series of charades cunningly designed to disorientate and bewilder them?

It's difficult to say it so bluntly but there are times when we might be tempted to think the same thing about God. Are we just unimportant pawns on a gigantic chessboard, manoeuvred around at will by a God who only cares about His mission for the earth and therefore treats us as mere playthings, foot soldiers at the disposal of a dispassionate, strategising general?

Look again at Joseph, who is a 'type of Christ' – a person in biblical history who represents some of the wonderful character traits of Jesus. He wants to see reconciliation in a divided family and is so overwhelmed with love, even for those who have treated him so cruelly, that he has to find a place alone to weep. And he just has to pile Benjamin's plate high. His nature is warm, passionate and kind. As we see Joseph weep, know that Jesus cries over us too: at times with joy, at times with frustration. You're more than an instrument of His purposes. You're His child.

Prayer: Lord, may I know that deep inside me, today and every day. Amen.

BIG PICTURE
**Genesis 43:29–34
John 1:10–13**

FOCUS
'Deeply moved at the sight of his brother, Joseph hurried out and looked for a place to weep. He went into his private room and wept there.' (Gen. 43:30)

You're

His child

Passing the test

BIG PICTURE

Genesis 44:1–16
Romans 8:1

FOCUS

"'What can we say to my lord?" Judah replied. "What can we say? How can we prove our innocence? God has uncovered your servants' guilt. We are now my lord's slaves …'"
(Gen. 44:16)

CHRISTIANITY is about growth. We are not all that we will be, but because of God's constant activity in our lives, we are not what we were. Joseph's strategy in secreting his cup in Benjamin's sack gave the brothers the opportunity to discover that they had learned from their past mistakes. Twenty-two years earlier, they had made a terrible, selfish decision. Now, as Benjamin appears to be caught red-handed, they find themselves in the valley of decision once more: will they abandon their brother to slavery in Egypt and head for the hills – or will they stand with him, whatever the cost to them?

Joseph makes sure they know that all options are open, as he insists that only the one caught with the cup will be sentenced to slavery. They have failed before; how will they do now?

Thankfully, they refuse to abandon Benjamin and, to a man, voluntarily offer themselves for a life of slavery rather than turn their backs on him.

We've all said and done things that we regret. No time machine exists to allow us to go back and undo those episodes but we can be comforted by the knowledge that we would not repeat those mistakes again, even given the perfect opportunity to do so. The cup-in-the-sack strategy was an act of kindness as well as a test. Joseph was not sporting with his brothers, but showing them – and proving to himself – that they had changed for the better.

Don't live your life in regret about the past but be grateful that you've moved on to a better place today.

Prayer: Lord, help me to see both how far I have come and how far I have to go. Amen.

JUDAH delivers the longest speech in the entire book of Genesis, pleading to be able to take Benjamin's place as a slave, so that Ben can be returned to his father. His words show us something vital about the nature of sin and repentance. Judah was concerned now, not only about right or wrong but also about the potential terrible effect that losing Benjamin would have on his aging dad. In short, he's worried that the shock would kill frail Jacob.

Pause for a moment. Judah and his brothers had been companions in crime for decades, watching their father weep for poor lost Joseph, able to end his grief in a moment by telling the truth and then going in search of the brother they'd sold into slavery. They had inflicted terrible pain on the old man. But it was enough. The thought of him suffering any more was more than Judah could bear: he would be a slave until death rather than let that happen.

Sin doesn't just hurt God and destroy our potential: it hurts those around us. We need to decide well, not just because we are committed to 'do the right thing' in impersonal moral terms, but because we care too much about others to allow them to be wounded by our selfishness.

Perhaps you are on the brink of making a really bad choice; your spiritual life is somewhat low right now and frankly, you don't care too much about what is right morally. Think again: will what you do bring tears to those who love you so much?

Prayer: Lord, whatever choices I face today, may I make the right decision – the one You want. Amen.

Concern for others

BIG PICTURE
Genesis 44:17–34
Psalm 51

FOCUS
'How can I go back to my father if the boy is not with me? No! Do not let me see the misery that would come upon my father.' (Gen. 44:34)

Sin doesn't just

hurt God …

it hurts those

around us

Wild grace

BIG PICTURE
Genesis 45:1–13
Luke 17:3–4

FOCUS

'And now, do not be distressed and do not be angry with yourselves for selling me here, because it was to save lives that God sent me ahead of you.' (Gen. 45:5)

STRANGE though it seems, it's possible to offer words of forgiveness to someone, while at the same time making them squirm over their actions. We carefully describe the full extent of their dark sin and elaborate endlessly, in great detail, about the pain they've caused us. We tell them how difficult it is for us to forgive but then piously affirm that we have decided to do so, seeing as God has forgiven us. We leave them with an ongoing sense of obligation to us: they are very much in our debt, not least because we have 'freely' forgiven them. We punish even while we speak words of grace. But, as the story of Joseph and his brothers comes now to a climax, as he at last reveals his true identity to his brothers, he also shows some quite remarkable, almost wild, forgiveness.

They have cost him most of his adult life up until recently; yet he tells them not to be distressed or angry with themselves (v.5) and affirms that the sovereign purposes of God have been worked out, as he was 'sent ahead' of them – a gracious way of looking at their selling him out. Finally, he promises to generously provide for them and their wider families.

This is risky grace. It carried the potential of minimising what they did. And, even though Judah's speech was moving and a great demonstration of how the brothers had changed, there was no mention of their betrayal of Joseph. They never did come totally clean.

Perhaps your forgiveness is needed today. Don't ration grace or make a big deal out of being kind. Wildly forgive.

Prayer: Lord, nothing I can do can equal what You have done for me. May I be wildly merciful. Amen.

A real man

I'm one of those chaps who finds it easy to cry. Any time the Lucas family get together, we tend to cry a lot: we cry as we remember, we cry when we talk about how much we love each other; there are times when I cry over a television commercial!

Perhaps the notion is dead these days but there used to be a belief that real men don't cry. Part of being masculine, some thought, meant that you reined in your emotions and kept your tears to yourself, showing what the British call 'a stiff upper lip'.

If that is true, then Joseph was not terribly manly. Consider how often in his story we have watched him weep; these were not just a few tears but often an overwhelming sobbing that meant that he had to excuse himself and find a place alone. The emotion that he showed when he revealed himself to his brothers was loud enough for courtiers outside the room to hear and now we see yet more weeping, kissing and hugging. Joseph was obviously someone who cared deeply and wasn't afraid to show it. Tears aren't a sign of weakness but an expression of a heart moved.

Tears aren't
a sign of
weakness …

Good begets good

BIG PICTURE
Genesis 45:16–20
Luke 19:1–10

FOCUS
'When the news reached Pharaoh's palace that Joseph's brothers had come, Pharaoh and all his officials were pleased.' (Gen. 45:16)

AS I write this, I have just been out and bought a copy of *Woman's Own* magazine, which is not my usual habit. The reason for my buying it was the happy fact that our daughter Kelly and her husband Ben are featured in the magazine because of their work in Indonesia. Regular readers of *Life Every Day* will recall that Kelly and Ben have been working in Aceh, which was so devastated by the Boxing Day tsunami that claimed hundreds of thousands of lives. I read the article with the obvious delight of a proud father but then thought about the effects of such 'good news' stories as theirs. In the midst of all the beauty tips, the agony aunt, the recipes and the celebrity trivia, here is some news about a young couple who have been determined to make a real difference. Is it possible that some of the readers who scan those pages might be inspired themselves to acts, great or small, of kindness and self-sacrifice?

News of Joseph's acts of mercy and generosity reached Pharaoh – the very same chap who had ordered the decapitation of the baker, so he wasn't renowned for his gracious demeanour. The news obviously warmed his heart – and so, quickly, Pharaoh sets in motion a plan to roll out the red carpet for the immigrating Hebrews. Good begets good. Love is catching. When we do something good, we potentially create a ripple effect, and, though we might never know it, others might be moved and motivated by what they see in us. Who knows what kind of positive virus we might pass on today?

Prayer: Lord, thank You for all the good that surrounds me. May I pass some on today. Amen.

THIS week I heard the tragic news of a number of children who had been sexually abused by a paedophile who had used his local church as a place to build trust with young people – and then use them as his prey. What makes matters worse is that the leaders of the church were fully aware of the man's history but in an attempt to make him feel fully included, they allowed him free and unescorted access to the children of the congregation. When challenged about their irresponsible and negligent behaviour, they defended their actions by insisting that the man had been forgiven – and that this was their way of demonstrating that he truly had a new start in life. But they were terribly mistaken and yet more damaged young lives result. Forgiveness was never the issue here; but wisdom was severely lacking in allowing the man into a place where he had so obviously demonstrated such vulnerability. It was like giving an alcoholic a job in a bar.

We've already seen that Joseph had poured out outrageous grace upon his brothers. They were forgiven and now could begin a new life in Egypt, together with their families. They had acted well when tested over the issue of Benjamin. But Joseph shows great wisdom as he warns them not to argue on the way home. Their past history was wiped clean – but Joseph wasn't blind to their weakness, their capacity to scheme and be consumed by envy – hence the parting shot encouraging them not to ruin things with a fight.

Celebrate grace. And be wise.

Prayer: Lord, give us wisdom so that one man's fresh start isn't another one's continuing pain. Amen.

Don't quarrel on the way

BIG PICTURE
Genesis 45:21–24
John 8:10–11

FOCUS
'Then he sent his brothers away, and as they were leaving he said to them, "Don't quarrel on the way!"' (Gen. 45:24)

Celebrate grace.

And be wise

Stunned

BIG PICTURE
Genesis 45:25–28
Psalm 105:1–11

FOCUS
'They told him, "Joseph is still alive! In fact, he is ruler of all Egypt." Jacob was stunned; he did not believe them.'
(Gen. 45:26)

FOR years you've mourned your dearest son, the love of your life. For too many nights you have lain awake, staring at the ceiling, imagining his face and wishing you could have shared more laughter, more play and more conversations together. But he is gone, ripped apart by some ferocious animal. You've lived with a terrible fear that it's going to happen again. You've endured a terrible famine.

And then another day dawns and the impossible comes with it. Your son, dead for over two decades, is alive. Not only that but he is one of the most powerful men in the world: the Egyptian prime minister, no less. You have a five-star invitation, backed up by the Pharaoh himself, to be guest of honour – permanently. Night has turned to day. No wonder Jacob was stunned.

Recently, I've found myself being more than a little stunned by God. That's not to say that this last year of my life has been easy: for various reasons, it has been one of the most challenging seasons of my life, with busyness, family tragedy and sickness, to name a few of the obstacles that I've encountered recently. But I have also been stunned by the sheer kindness and extravagance of God. Just when I think I really know that God is love, He surprises me with yet more tokens and evidence of His huge heart. He really is wonderful and never ceases to amaze me. I'm praying for you today. May you too know what it is to be eyes-wide-open incredulous at this stunning God of ours.

Prayer: Lord, thank You for Your loving kindness – help me spread it around today. Amen.

Don't be afraid

BIG PICTURE
Genesis 46:1–4
Psalm 91:9–16

FOCUS
'Do not be afraid to go
down to Egypt, for I will
make you into a great
nation there … And
Joseph's own hand will
close your eyes.'
(Gen. 46:3–4)

YESTERDAY I talked about being stunned by God. Perhaps the one thing that has impacted me the most in recent months is just the sheer kindness and (if I can put it like this) the *thoughtfulness* of the Lord. Dear old Jacob has been overwhelmed by good news: he hardly has a big choice to make about heading for Egypt; after all, there will be one of the greatest family reunions in history there. Jacob will have the incredible joy of being proud father to a prime minister; he leaves famine behind and heads for plenty. All of this was surely enough to send Jacob scurrying off with a one-way ticket …

Think again. Jacob is old, frail and has walked through more than his fair share of disappointments and turnarounds. Emigration at this stage of his life will be a huge disruption and possible threat to his health. Would he survive the arduous trip?

Enter, once again, the kind God, who appears in a dream, encourages Jacob not to be afraid, gives him hints about the future there and speaks of him dying in peace: 'Joseph's own hand will close your eyes.' God is the God of comfort, of assurance, who at times seems to go beyond what we might actually need and gives us extra help.

That's not to say that big decisions are easy or that dreams and visions are as frequent as we might like them to be. But whether this is a season where God is obviously working overtime in your life, or if it's a time when spiritually, all seems rather too quiet, know this: you are on His mind constantly.

Prayer: Lord, Thank You for all Your reassurances – may I take them on board today. Amen.

God is the God

of comfort …

Taking up the offer

BIG PICTURE
Genesis 46:5–27
John 3:16

FOCUS
'All those who went to Egypt with Jacob – those who were his direct descendants, not counting his sons' wives – numbered sixty-six persons.'
(Gen. 46:26)

WE HUMAN beings often struggle with a great deal. 'If it looks too good to be true, then it probably is', or so the saying goes. The adage works well when it comes to investments: beware the offer that looks ridiculously generous – it usually masks a scam.

But the slogan doesn't work when it comes to the dealings of God. His generosity is legendary and His grace beyond our fathom. He offers so much to us through the shed blood of Christ; now our greatest shame can be healed. It's the greatest free offer in history and the most expensive too, seeing it cost God everything. But we can be reluctant to accept it. Too many Christians spend their lives cowering beneath regret and guilt, affirming a theology of forgiveness but never allowing the marvellous experience of being forgiven to impact them. Ironically, we know that the only way we can call ourselves Christian is through the cross: yet we can be reluctant to allow God to take care of the sins that we've stumbled or marched into since our conversion.

Look at Jacob, staggering around with the wild abandon of a lottery winner. Everyone in the wider family saddles up and heads for the land of promised plenty: this offer is too good to miss and so no less than 66 people travel; not so much a family, more a huge convoy of hope. There's no hesitation or nervousness about how such a crowd will be perceived: rather they rush to take advantage of the wonderful offer.

And so should we.

Prayer: Lord, forgive me for all the times I don't really grasp what You have done for us. Amen.

Reunion 2

Pause and consider what sheer delight relationships
can bring. Nothing can compare with the joy of being
with much-loved family and friends. As we finally see
Joseph reunited with his father, all of the wonderful
elements of relationships at their best are present.
As Joseph prepares his chariot, there is the building
anticipation of time to be spent together. Uninhibited
love is found here too, as Joseph, ever the emotional,
expressive one, throws his arms around his father.
And as we might expect from this remarkable man,
there is extended weeping, tears shed through
overwhelming joy.

Notice too what is missing: Joseph doesn't utter a single
word about Jacob's poor parenting skills which led to
his brothers' terrible scheme. In a sense, the whole thing
had begun when Jacob had flaunted his favouritism
for Joseph. But that was all in the past. Not every single
issue has to be sorted out: some Christians destroy their
friendships because they insist on performing a post-
mortem on every episode. Some things don't need to be
said: a hug is enough.

Invest heavily in relationships: the love of God and
the love of others is all that ultimately matters.

Invest heavily in
relationships …

Blessing Pharaoh

BIG PICTURE
Genesis 47:1–10
Philippians 2

FOCUS
'Then Joseph brought his father Jacob in and presented him before Pharaoh. After Jacob blessed Pharaoh, Pharaoh asked him, "How old are you?"'
(Gen. 47:7–8)

I SUFFER from a bit of a lingering inferiority complex, especially when I get around large groups of Christian leaders. Often they all seem so powerful, so confident (their certainty unnerves me), and, at times, my working class background makes me feel that I don't belong. Many of them come from families that have provided numbers of prominent leaders – and then there's the issue of education: I did go to Cambridge but it was just for a day out. Who am I, I wonder, to be rubbing shoulders with those who are apparently the great and the good?

And then I remind myself that I do what I do because of God's calling and His hand of kindness and favour is all that I need. That's not in any way an argument against a great education but my confidence cannot be based simply on that.

Look at this picture – a foreign shepherd (and shepherds, as we have read in the text, were considered disreputable in Egyptian culture) stands before the most powerful man in the world – and blesses him twice. Pharaoh has all the money in the world (almost literally, as a result of Joseph's deals, as we'll see tomorrow). But old Jacob, who confesses that he has had a rough life, is able to speak words of divine authority and grace to the great one.

Perhaps you find yourself in a situation where everyone else looks greater, more clever, powerful and competent. Ask yourself: has God asked you to stand in that situation? If you think He has, then stand tall.

Prayer: Lord, may I have an accurate assessment of myself – Your assessment. Amen.

AS WE ponder the difficult sight of Joseph wheeling and dealing a whole nation into slavery, we face a temptation: to try to legitimise his actions. Various commentators have done this, arguing that slavery meant something quite different to the more modern expressions that we are familiar with; that to be enslaved meant a secure job for life. I'm no expert on ancient societal customs but I'm not convinced. It does seem ironic and unfortunate to watch Joseph, himself sold into slavery because of envy and greed, now conscripting the whole of Egypt into the service of Pharaoh. And while this programme of enforced servitude (and according to some, wholesale, massive relocation) was unfolding, the Hebrews were prospering and acquiring land in Goshen. None of this seems very equitable. I may be wrong but this seems to be a dark incident in Joseph's life.

But then why do we have to sanitise this event anyway, as if Joseph always has to get it right? Surely one of the many reasons that the Bible is so inspiring is because it is so real and insists on telling us even the less savoury elements of people's stories. Scripture refuses to present us with airbrushed portraits of the heroes of faith but rather presents them, in all their glory and their ugliness.

The man who passed many tests may have flunked this one. We may be incredibly strong in one area of our lives, only to lash things up because of weakness elsewhere.

Thank God for yesterday's triumphs. But today's temptations are another matter. God give us all grace for the next part of the story.

Prayer: Lord, help me to remember that yesterday's triumphs won't remove today's temptations. Amen.

Canny – or oppressive dealings?

BIG PICTURE
Genesis 47:11–27
Luke 16:1–12

FOCUS
'The land became Pharaoh's, and Joseph reduced the people to servitude, from one end of Egypt to the other.' (Gen. 47:20b–21)

God give us

all grace …

Jacob the worshipper

BIG PICTURE
Genesis 47:28–31
Habakkuk 3:17–18

FOCUS
'"Swear to me," he said. Then Joseph swore to him, and Israel worshipped as he leaned on the top of his staff.' (Gen. 47:31)

JACOB spent the last 17 years of his life living in completely unexpected circumstances. At one level, things had unfolded marvellously, with the joy of reunion with Joseph and deliverance from the Canaanite famine. Gone were the years of anxiety and grief, as Jacob grew old with his family around him, at peace at last.

But living in Egypt would have been a huge challenge too for him. For one thing, it was not the promised land pledged to his father Isaac and his grandfather Abraham. No wonder Jacob didn't want to be buried there but insisted that Joseph promise to transport his bones back to Canaan, the land of his fathers. And Jacob had been forced to make this huge transition and emigrate when he was at a great age. Change, even when it's very much for the better, is always hard (ask any minister who has tried to rearrange the pews). But it's even tougher for those in their senior years: as life rushes by, they cling, understandably, to what is familiar. But despite the total change of landscape for Jacob, he remains a worshipper and we are treated to the sight of him 'worshipping as he leaned on the top of his staff'.

Recently someone asked me if I was doing what I always dreamed of in my life, if many of my ministry objectives have been fulfilled. My response was that almost nothing has worked out as I either wanted or expected – it's far better. But perhaps you find yourself where you never thought you would end up – for better or for worse. May you be a worshipper either way.

Prayer: Lord, like Habakkuk, may I rejoice in You regardless of my circumstances. Amen.

FOR a good while now, Joseph had been used to having everything very much his own way. In a sense, he had the whole world in his hands, because Egypt was the most powerful nation on earth and he had nudged many into slavery because of the economic crisis. He had held the lives of his brothers in his grasp too: one word from him and a terrible execution would have followed. And now he was the mighty provider for his entire extended family, flourishing in the land of Goshen. There was no doubt about it: Joseph was the boss, whatever he decided happened – until he took his two Egyptian sons to his dying father for his blessing. Placing Ephraim at his dad's right hand (the place of primary blessing in Hebrew culture), Joseph carefully choreographed the moment so that his first-born would get the lion's share of favour, as was the custom. When old Jacob refused to co-operate, Joseph was irritated and tried to rearrange his hands. But Jacob was determined to do what he had decided to do.

Perhaps you're especially struggling right now, because circumstances that have hit your life mean that you feel out of control. There's not much you can do and your efforts to date have drawn a blank. It's even worse for you if you're well organised at best – or a control freak at worst. Panic is setting in. Joseph had to trust the words of his seasoned veteran of a father: 'I know, my son, I know.' If we're in the same predicament, may we say, with hope and not despair: God knows.

Prayer: Lord, remind me once again that You are Sovereign. And I am not. Amen.

What you can't control

BIG PICTURE
Genesis 48:1–19
Job 42:1–6

FOCUS
'When Joseph saw his father placing his right hand on Ephraim's head he was displeased; so he took hold of his father's hand to move it … to Manasseh's head.'
(Gen. 48:17)

God knows

Promises for the future

BIG PICTURE
Genesis 48:20–22
John 14:1–3

FOCUS
'Then Israel said to Joseph, "I am about to die, but … to you … I give the ridge of land I took from the Amorites with my sword and my bow."' (Gen. 48:21–22)

I ALWAYS feel guilty when I hear Christians talk excitedly about heaven. Sometimes heaven – the term we use to describe what will be our eternal home with God – doesn't seem very real or tangible. At my worst, lowest moments, I can convince myself that heaven is little more than a ruse that we Christians use to fool ourselves that there is something after the finality of death. The concept of a perfect place, where there are no more tears or sorrow and where union with God is total, seems quite impossible to seriously think about. I was comforted by the honesty of the late David Watson, who wrote in his book *Fear No Evil* about the crisis he felt as a dying man and the fear that he had given his life in pursuit of a false notion. The daily choice to invest our lives into something that is largely invisible takes faith.

Perhaps Joseph felt like that, as he received the promise of an inheritance that was distant and one that he had left many years earlier. What use would a ridge of land be to him, in such a faraway place? But Jacob had eyes for the future and saw the day, soon to come, when Joseph and the other Hebrews would head for Canaan once more. Perhaps Joseph couldn't possibly conceive the value of what his father had pledged to him, so immersed was he in the hustle and bustle of the here and now.

Heaven is real. Our inheritance awaits us, whatever we 'feel' about it. You have a legacy. Don't forget that.

Prayer: Lord, You have promised us a life to come – may that be enough for our doubts and fears. Amen.

The value of our elders

Jacob, near to death now, still has his wits about him and is able to speak with incredible insight and accuracy about what lies ahead in the future for his sons and their descendants. There isn't space here to examine the details of his predictions but we must note one vital point: as the senior elder of his family, he calls for a listening ear – and gets it. He lived in an era when advancing years were not synonymous with frailty or irrelevance, but rather longevity was treated with reverence and respect.

Adolescents often go through a phase where they are convinced that their parents know nothing. Sometimes I think that we are an adolescent culture, because of the wanton disrespect that we show to our elders. And we, the Church, bear our own share of guilt, because too often, in an unseemly rush to be relevant to young people (an absolutely vital desire), we throw everything that older people might love into a proverbial skip; we trash their hymns, their traditions and smear all with the pejorative term: old-fashioned. Jacob spoke. People listened. We'd do well to emulate them.

… longevity
was treated with
reverence …

Jacob dies

BIG PICTURE
**Genesis 49:29–50:14
John 15:16**

FOCUS
'And the Egyptians mourned for him seventy days.' (Gen. 50:3b)

CHATTING the other day with a business associate who is not a Christian, he remarked that he felt I was the most non-religious minister he'd ever met. I was momentarily taken aback, instantly fearful that I had become someone who blended into the blur of living just the same as everyone else, with no distinguishable values that stand out and mark me as a follower of Christ and no lifestyle distinctives that make my life a living challenge to those who encounter me. He was quick to allay my fears and spoke warmly about humanness, openness and a lack of religious jargon that he had observed. I think I'm relieved.

What I do know is that I'd like to leave a legacy of making a good impression on people who don't currently share my faith. It's too easy to be on our best behaviour when we're around church people, because that's what's expected, only to lapse into living another way when we're doing the rest of everyday life. I've been around a few ministers who smiled beatifically and spoke with great warmth to the congregations on Sunday morning, only to notice how brisk and demanding they were in a restaurant *after* the service (and how mean they were with the tip, or lack of it). Jacob's funeral meant that Egypt mourned his loss; how wonderful it would be if we lived so well that when we pass from this earth we are missed by those who didn't necessarily share our faith.

Prayer: Lord, may I show something of You to those around me today. Amen.

OLD habits die hard. It looks like the brothers are up to their old tricks again, although we can't be certain. There's no evidence to suggest that Jacob really did leave a message for Joseph, insisting that his brothers' old betrayal remained forgiven. The way the text reads, it looks as though they put words in their dead father's mouth, as a hasty ruse to protect themselves. Perhaps a combination of grief for their dead father (and regret for all the years of emotional torture that they'd inflicted upon him), coupled with uncertainty about the future, meant that they came up with this ill-advised scheme. Certainly Joseph, in the response that we'll consider tomorrow, makes no mention of honouring his father's words: he weeps and gently reminds them that they *had* meant him harm in the past – the first time we hear any words of recrimination from his lips in the text. Perhaps Joseph wanted them to know that they had done great wrong – and so they shouldn't start their scheming again.

The brothers were gifted schemers – and so when they faced trouble, this was their sin of choice and the one that they easily drifted into, apparently at every stage of life. No matter how much we've moved on and have grown as Christians, we'd do well to observe our 'fault lines'. Notice that the Bible encourages us to confess our *faults* – our besetting weaknesses. That way we can be on our guard constantly and consistently.

Let's know ourselves – and know that we never retire from the possibility of sin.

Prayer: Lord, You know my faults – may I know them as clearly. Amen.

Still scheming

BIG PICTURE
Genesis 50:15–17
Judges 2:10–19

FOCUS
'So they sent word to Joseph, saying, "Your father left these instructions before he died … 'I ask you to forgive your brothers the sins and the wrongs they committed …'"' Joseph wept.'
(Gen. 50:16–17)

Let's know

ourselves …

Love covers

BIG PICTURE
Genesis 50:18–21
Matthew 5:7

FOCUS
'"So then, don't be afraid. I will provide for you and your children." And he reassured them and spoke kindly to them.' (Gen. 50:21)

LET'S assume for a moment that the brothers really are operating a cunning little scheme – which perhaps is quite simply a lie – as they go to Joseph with their post-death message from their dad. This could be the cue for a time of punishment, seeing as it seems that they have not learned their lesson. As we saw yesterday, there is mild rebuke in Joseph's response but that is all. There is no explosion of indignant temper, no 'Look what I've done for you and still you lie to me' speech. Rather, Joseph looks past their probable sin and sees the fear that is driving them. So he speaks kindly to them. And he doesn't suggest that they are doubting his word and integrity by being fearful – which they are – but, rather, he reassures them. Their scheming is apparently met by grace.

We don't need to 'sort everything out' when we see others making a mistake. Some Christians seem to be on a correction crusade, seizing any perceived weaknesses that they see in others and making the biggest possible deal out of them. But love covers a multitude of sins. We don't have to correct every little failing or call a summit meeting to work through any and every problem that emerges in our relationships. Sometimes we just need to let it go, lighten up and realise that, this side of eternity, we too are always in process. Imagine what life would be like for you if, every time you mildly irritated someone, they made a court case out of the moment. Be merciful.

Prayer: Lord, may I be as merciful to others as I would wish them to be to me. Amen.

ONE of the briefest, to-the-point statements about the character of God is found in the affirmation that *God is love*. In a sense, this is New Testament shorthand for everything that we know about God. At the end of our lives, could something similar be said about us?

We're almost at the end of our two-month trek with Joseph. We've walked with a man who learned grace the hard way. Emotional to the core, his early boasting of his dreams gave way to a deep trust in God when he was falsely accused and unjustly imprisoned. He was a seer, gifted by God with an uncanny sensitivity to the Holy Spirit. He forgave in the face of terrible rejection and, for the most part, managed to stay faithful both in power and poverty. He wasn't perfect, as his programme of national slavery demonstrates.

But one commentator sums up the man like this: Joseph loved. What a great statement that would be for *our* gravestones. Whatever our accomplishments, our successes and failures, the people we've met, or the places we've been to, all of these fade into insignificance before this great attribute. Will it be said of us that we have been loving?

Perhaps it's time to alter our ambitions. Maybe that alluring job that will mean more cash but less family time, isn't such a great deal after all. Maybe that moral temptation you're facing, shimmering and inviting though it is, will shatter others and destroy any possibility of a legacy of love for you in the process.

Joseph loved.

Prayer: Lord, may it be said of us that we loved. Amen.

Joseph: a man of love

BIG PICTURE
Genesis 50:22–26
1 John 4

FOCUS
'So Joseph died at the age of a hundred and ten. And after they embalmed him, he was placed in a coffin in Egypt.' (Gen. 50:26)

Joseph loved

Joseph: a man of faith and hope

BIG PICTURE
Hebrews 11:22
1 Corinthians 13

FOCUS
'By faith Joseph, when his end was near, spoke about the exodus of the Israelites from Egypt and gave instructions about his bones.' (Heb. 11:22)

YESTERDAY we considered that Joseph loved. And here, Hebrews provides a final postscript about him that surely offers vital partners to love: faith and hope. Joseph loved others, even when they were at their most unlovely but that love flowed from a source, which was his love for and his faith in God. To his dying day, Joseph remained sensitive to the revelation and strategy of God and so looked forward to a day of Exodus and called for his bones to be taken along for the trip. Faith leads him to hope for a better future for his people, even though tough times are coming, as a Pharaoh will rise up who didn't know Joseph (Exod. 1:8).

Thousands of years later, another man would sit down and pen a letter to some people of faith who were living in the crazy, amoral town of Corinth. That man, Paul the apostle, would remind them that only faith, hope and love will endure; only these three matter.

They matter for the whole of our lives; and they matter today. Will we choose to trust God, even if we're somewhere we don't choose to be? If we will, we must trust Him when we don't feel His presence or see any evidence of His being at work. Will we love, even if we're the victim of calculated spitefulness? And will we stay in hope; hope for prayers to be answered, hope for better days, hope that looks beyond the grave and sees an incredible eternity ahead?

Joseph lived well and died well, with an epic legacy. May the same be true of you and me.

Prayer: Lord, help me to trust You today as I face those things I don't want to face. Amen.

Will we choose to trust God?

Close encounters

Close encounters

HOW does a Messiah do His job? Faced with the mission to teach, model, demonstrate and dialogue the truth of the kingdom of God (the news that God's reign was coming to all people who would receive it, everywhere), what would Jesus do as He began His three-year ministry? Perhaps a public relations assistant would be necessary; and then, most vital, a diary secretary to organise His appointments. With limited time, He must be efficient.

Or … perhaps you just go and do life – and wait for people to come to you, which is exactly what Jesus did. As we trace no less than 52 spontaneous encounters in Matthew's Gospel – one of Matthew's favourite phrases is 'came to him' – we'll look afresh at the wonderful Jesus through these 'unplanned moments'. In a sense, of course, nothing was actually unplanned, because Jesus was walking according to His Father's will – but it is amazing what you can do when you're relaxed and open with your schedule!

Thanks for joining me.

Our God reigns

It was a song that helped through the turbulent season of my late teenage years: *Our God Reigns*. It was such a favourite, we wore the song out. But I needed the reinforcement of the message. As a new Christian, I was frantically trying to make sense of my fledgling faith, as I sought to live what was a brand-new life. It was confusing, but exhilarating. I had connected with the God who ran the universe.

As Jesus began His good-news tour in Galilee, the crowds quickly gathered and the news spread like wildfire: here was someone who could bring healing to those who had previously been beyond help. But this was far more than an attention-grabbing supernatural fireworks display. Jesus was staking a series of claims: there is a God; He is bigger than our most gigantic problems; His light can penetrate our darkest night.

As we begin our series of glimpses at Jesus and His 'impromptu' meetings, perhaps you feel stalked by sickness, fear, worry or financial need. I don't have a slick formula to guarantee that all will be resolved in the way you would like. But let's affirm this together: our God reigns.

… our God reigns

The extra mile

BIG PICTURE
Matthew 8:1–4
Mark 1:40–45

FOCUS
'A man with leprosy
came and knelt before
him and said, "Lord, if
you are willing, you can
make me clean."'
(Matt. 8:2)

RIGHT at the beginning of our eavesdropping on Jesus' close encounters in the Gospel of Matthew, we see a principle that is both totally obvious and so very easy to forget: people matter more than just about anything.

Jesus lived in a culture that was encumbered by endless social niceties; rules, expectations and traditions dominated just about every aspect of daily life, often choking out any possibility of spontaneity. The culture demanded that those who suffered from major skin diseases (the leprosy spoken of in the New Testament is a blanket term that covers a multitude of ailments) should keep their distance: out of sight, out of mind. This man was really ill: Dr Luke tells us that he 'was covered with leprosy' (Luke 5:12). The leper broke protocol by even approaching Jesus in the first place. But then, even though Jesus could have healed the poor man just by speaking a commanding word, He chose to deliberately touch him – an action that would have shocked any who saw it (not least the leper himself) and one that would have rendered Jesus ceremonially unclean. The action spoke a thousand words: this man was not just instantly healed, but totally included and welcomed.

Mark, in his account of this episode, shows us why Jesus did what He did: He cared. 'Filled with compassion, Jesus reached out his hand and touched the man' (Mark 1:41).

Love means that we will do more than is strictly necessary to express our love; that we will refuse to allow social niceties and the risk of offending others to stop us and we will take the risk that love often demands.

Prayer: Gracious God, take me beyond what is needed and show me how to love extravagantly. Amen.

Faith in unexpected places

PUTTING it bluntly, most of us think that our chosen brand of Christianity is more authentic than that of others. We have chosen our particular denominational affiliation because we feel most able to align ourselves with it doctrinally and because we are most comfortable with its style and culture of 'doing church'. Maybe also we have found a real sense of belonging; perhaps it has been a combination of all three factors. But whatever the reason for our settling where we have, we are there because it seems to be where we are called or will most benefit.

But there's a danger when that sense of homecoming becomes a lingering belief that others are not quite as 'spiritual' as we are; when we silently nurse the notion that, if all churches did it 'our way', then the world would be quickly reached. Such an attitude will ultimately lead to our impoverishment; our arrogance will blind us to the wonderful diversity of the family of God and we will miss the joy of learning from those who approach their faith differently.

Jesus, obviously moved by the simple, humble faith of the centurion, makes a statement that was a verbal stun grenade to Jewish ears. He congratulated a senior member of the oppressive Roman occupying forces, not only for his great faith but for a quality of faith unparalleled in the whole of Israel. Here is spirituality found in the most unexpected place. We'll be greatly enriched when we realise that God is hard at work where we least expect it. He calls us to respect what He's doing and those He's at work amongst.

BIG PICTURE
Matthew 8:5–13
Ephesians 2:11–22

FOCUS
'When Jesus heard this, he was astonished and said to those following him, "I tell you the truth, I have not found anyone in Israel with such great faith."' (Matt. 8:10)

Prayer: Open my eyes and my heart to see You at work in unfamiliar places: give me the heart of a learner. Amen.

… God is hard at work where we least expect it

Promises, promises

BIG PICTURE
Matthew 8:18–22
Luke 14:25–35

FOCUS
'Jesus replied, "Foxes
have holes and birds of
the air have nests, but the
Son of Man has no place
to lay his head."'
(Matt. 8:20)

IN OVER 30 years of being a Christian, I've probably
spent more than a few months of my life singing worship
songs (which most of the time I enjoy, although singing
the same song 20 times over has less appeal now). But I
am more cautious about what I sing these days, in case I
rush to declare things that I either don't mean or haven't
had time to think through. I don't believe that God is
impressed by superficial professions of undying love and
devotion: He wants reality to be at the heart of our praise,
as we worship 'in spirit and truth'.

One of my favourite songs is Matt Redman's *Blessed
be your name*. But it's a song that brings an abrupt reality
check – I'm never going to rush to state 'You give and take
away … blessed be your name' without engaging heart
and brain first. Words like that involve me singing by
faith; hopefully but not with certainty. It's my real hope,
if devastation or disaster came upon me, that I would be
able to bless God's name, but I can't be totally sure until,
God forbid, I am so tested.

Jesus invited some eager enthusiasts who wanted
to join His team to think again. It was vital that they
took a long, hard look at the road ahead, which might
include living without the security of a home and would
demand that they place everything – including loved
ones – in second place to the absolute priority of the
kingdom of God.

Let's hesitate without fear. The commitments we make
and the words we say must be real.

**Prayer: Let my words be true and my heart be thrilled
by the vision of Your kingdom, but sobered by the
sacrifice that it demands. Amen.**

Toxic holiness

SOME Christians try to get as far away from the 'big bad world' as possible. Using the church as an isolationist escape, they seek to live out their lives in the Christian ghetto, surrounding themselves with fellow Christians, insisting that they'll only read Christian books and listen to 'Christian music' (I use inverted commas here because I'm not sure that there is such a thing – just good music and bad music) and generally living in fear that they might be contaminated by the world. And indeed we live on a corrupt planet (2 Pet. 2:20). But true holiness is not like a fragile flower that needs to be cradled and nursed, in order to avoid it being blown to pieces by the wind. This is upside-down thinking. Rather, true holiness is a wonderfully 'toxic' force that carries the power to confront and overthrow evil. Unbridled purity unleashed in the world can act like an antiseptic, scattering the grubby powers of darkness in its wake. This is why Jesus describes His followers as the light of the world and the salt of the earth.

And here two men who have spent far too long being tormented by demonic forces find themselves irresistibly drawn into confrontation with Jesus, which is hardly surprising, considering who their Lord and Master was. The battle is over before it begins. The demons yell about judgment to come and desperately try to make a deal with Jesus: send us to the pigs. But notice that the men don't affect Jesus – He profoundly affects them and they taste freedom because He came their way.

Don't fear the world. Change it by being who you are.

Prayer: Father, help me to live today without fear and with expectation. Bring light, joy and Your kingdom to reign through me. Amen.

BIG PICTURE
Matthew 8:28–33
Matthew 5:13–16

FOCUS
'When he arrived at … the region of the Gadarenes, two demon-possessed men coming from the tombs met him. They were so violent that no one could pass that way.' (Matt. 8:28)

… true holiness [has] the power to confront and overthrow evil

The crowd can be wrong

BIG PICTURE
Matthew 8:34
Acts 21:27–36

FOCUS
'Then the whole town went out to meet Jesus. And when they saw him, they pleaded with him to leave their region.'
(Matt. 8:34)

THERE should have been the cultural equivalent of a street party, because freedom and new life had come to town. The two local madmen had been a frightening phenomenon, turning the place where they lived into an impassable no-go area. According to Mark, all attempts to subdue one of the men had failed, which must have been hideous for residents nearby. The silence of too many nights had been shattered by his blood-curdling screams. He must have made a terrifying sight, frequently bloodied by his self-harming (Mark 5:1–5). Now the yelling had stopped and that route was open again. But it came at a cost. For reasons that aren't explained, Jesus had sent the demons into around 2,000 pigs.

Pack the bunting and the balloons away, cancel the celebrations and replace them with an angry, hastily gathered city-wide protest. Get out of town, Jesus. If You stay, our economy goes south. The Son of God is hereby no longer welcome, by order of an entire city (with two noted votes against).

And as that crowd jeers and hisses, know that you don't have to be in the majority to be right. Sometimes being a Christian creates a sense of loneliness, especially in a culture where just about any god is welcomed and respected – except Jesus. He remains fair game for anyone who wants to take a kick at Him, and His followers can feel lost in the crowd. Perhaps there aren't many who would own the name of Jesus in your workplace, family or school. Take courage. Crowds often get things very wrong indeed.

Prayer: Jesus, help me to faithfully walk with You, when the crowd seems to be heading in the opposite direction. Amen.

Matthew 9:1–7 // Luke 5:1–26

Disabling people with disabilities

His name is Ian, he has a razor-sharp wit and was born with cerebral palsy. A lifelong wheelchair user, he has entertained and dismayed his friends in turn with stories of how people treat those with disabilities. Oblivious to the reality that his legs don't work but that his mind is perfectly in order, people shout at him (thinking he is deaf), pat him on the head (he has lost virtually all his hair and blames it on the never-ending patting), and talk to him in baby talk. He manages to laugh at the antics of the able-bodied.

One of the tragic indignities that people with disabilities have to endure is the idea that their problems are due to sin. And this story, taken out of context, could be used as ammunition for that; a cursory reading seems to have Jesus connecting sin, forgiveness and healing together. But that is not His point: He is simply stating that the One who has power to heal also has power to forgive. Let's be careful about theological quackery which bruises those who have been wounded. Let's do everything we can to help those who struggle.

… the One who has power to heal also has power to forgive

Sick and tired

BIG PICTURE
Matthew 9:10–13
Romans 15:7

FOCUS
'While Jesus was having dinner at Matthew's house, many tax collectors and "sinners" came and ate with him and his disciples.'
(Matt. 9:10)

THERE'S a tiredness that I often battle with which is peculiar to Christians. It has nothing to do with too little sleep and too much travel; this weariness often lands on me in the middle of a vacation, when I feel physically rested and refreshed. It is a profound exhaustion that creeps deep into my bones, forms a shadow over my heart and robs me of joy. It is the tiredness that comes from feeling that I can never be holy enough, never pray enough, never sacrifice enough. Whatever I do for God, something in my head tells me that it is not enough and that it will never be sufficient to please Him. During these seasons, God seems like a never-ending taskmaster, whip in hand and quite impossible to satisfy. I feel sick to my soul. Is God really like my high-school art teacher, who used to scrawl 'could do better' over my very best Picasso-like efforts?

When I look at this encounter that Jesus had, attracting notorious sinners like a magnet, I see a very different picture of the way God really is. The bad, the sad and those most shamed and smeared by failure eagerly sought Him out, not just for teaching but for lunch: they felt at ease in His presence. They liked and perhaps loved Him, finding unexpected acceptance and kindness. He explained that He was called to be a doctor, tending to the sick.

We're fully accepted and utterly welcome. The doctor is in the house.

Prayer: Save me from striving and help me to relax in Your company, loving God. Amen.

Fasting and feasting

SOME Christians find it easier to give than to receive; they're more at home with suffering than celebration, and fasting certainly comes more naturally than feasting to them. They are naturally disposed to feeling guilty when they're not and struggle with being blessed: they'd far rather be a source of blessing to others. They are the opposite of Jacob, who wrestled with God. His prayer was 'I will not let you go until you bless me'. They turn the prayer upside down: 'I will not let you bless me, let me go'.

So it was with John's disciples, as we see the remarkable sight of them raising an issue of holiness with the most Holy One that there has ever been (a sight that is worth noting: there are lots of Christians who try to be more 'holy' than Jesus, but their legalism is actually not holiness at all). Apparently they were disturbed because Jesus and His friends obviously were gaining a reputation for having a very good time with some very bad people. Jesus wasn't against fasting and taught that it would be a discipline that His followers would embrace (Matt. 6:16–18). But there is a time and a place for everything and this was the time to party! A whole new order of things was on its way, because Jesus wasn't patching up old religion, but ushering in a revolution – and that was reason enough for another banquet.

Are you nervous of laughter, suspicious of fun? Do you feel uncomfortable when someone is extremely generous to you? Think again, as you look at the celebrating Christ.

Prayer: Lord, help me to know how to fast and how to feast. Amen.

BIG PICTURE
**Matthew 9:14–17
Deuteronomy
16:13–15**

FOCUS
'Then John's disciples came and asked him, "How is it that we and the Pharisees fast, but your disciples do not fast?"'
(Matt. 9:14)

… there is a time

and a place for

everything …

Kindness beyond healing

BIG PICTURE
Matthew 9:18–19, 23–26

FOCUS
'... a ruler came and ... said, "My daughter has ... died. But come and put your hand on her and she will live." Jesus ... went with him and so did his disciples.'
(Matt. 9:18–19)

RAISING the dead is such a stupendous miracle. This episode, where a funeral is hastily cancelled and mourners sent packing because of the power of Jesus even over death, is so arresting that we could miss other delightful details in the story. Notice that Jesus demonstrates not only incredible power and authority, but all this is mingled with beautiful kindness too.

Jesus didn't have to go to the home of the dead girl at all. He just had to speak a word and death would be driven back, just as the sickness of the centurion's servant was dealt with; a long-distance miracle. But the synagogue ruler is obviously distraught with grief as he kneels before Jesus and so the Lord took the journey to his home, which would have meant conversation and comfort on the way. And then Jesus refuses to allow the little girl to become exhibit 'A' for the clamouring crowds and insists that they be removed before the miracle takes place. He is showing the power of the kingdom, but is no showman.

And then He takes her hand, cold and clammy and then suddenly warming as she stirs, her eyelids flicker and her watching parents believe the unbelievable. No wonder they were astonished.

But this is far more than a power encounter: here we see the reason for our prayers for the sick and dying. We ask God to intervene, not so that we can gawp at a miracle but because we care deeply for those who suffer. Compassion and care sit at the heart of every miracle.

Prayer: Lord, share some of Your heart with me – as much as I can bear. Amen.

I DON'T think I'm a particularly angry person, but I confess that there are times when I watch Christian programmes on television and I feel inclined to minister to the television set with an axe, which is extreme. It is foolish to generalise and tar everyone who has a television ministry with the same brush, but sadly there are a few televangelists who bring out the worst in me – and it has nothing to do with their pleading that I use my Visa card to give them money.

My problem is with the snappy, one-size-fits-all faith formula, where we are told four vital steps to healing, ten principles of prosperity (all of which wonderfully begin with the same letter) or 15 ways to get our prayers answered more efficiently. While there *are* principles to live by – give and you shall receive, for example – I don't think that faith should be reduced to a sure set of slogans. Relationships don't work that way – and neither does our relationship with God. If you're not convinced, try and figure out why it is that one person is healed and another dies of the same disease.

The ruler with the dead daughter did not have the same 'Just say the word' faith as the centurion. But the little girl was still raised. And the woman with the menstrual problem, reaching out to touch Jesus' garment, held the popular view that when the Messiah came healing would come through touching the hem of His prayer shawl. Each of the three expressed their desperation in different ways: each one experienced a miracle.

Don't be tempted to turn your Christianity into a simple package deal.

Prayer: Father, thank You that You have given us brains and hearts. Help us to use both. Amen.

Faith and formulae

BIG PICTURE
**Matthew 9:20–22
Romans 1:1–4**

FOCUS
'She said to herself, "If I only touch his cloak, I will be healed."'
(Matt. 9:21)

Don't … turn your Christianity into a simple package deal

Doing God a favour

BIG PICTURE
Matthew 9:27–31
Matthew 16:13–16

FOCUS
'Jesus warned them sternly, "See that no one knows about this." But they went out and spread the news about him all over that region.'
(Matt. 9:30–31)

THERE'S nothing more dangerous than a misguided zealot. We all know that terrible things have been done in the name of God. Aircraft have been driven into buildings and innocent passengers have been murdered on tube trains by zealots with a warped belief system. History shows us that Christians have too often bloodied their hands in the name of the Lord. The Spanish Inquisition, the blood-letting of Calvin's Geneva, the hanging of children for stealing bread in Victorian England: all of these were perpetrated by people who genuinely believed that they were serving God.

Jesus didn't want the healed blind men to help Him out – untimely publicity was the last thing He needed. The translation, 'Jesus warned them sternly', doesn't quite capture the weight and passion of His command to them – one translator renders this: 'Jesus looked severely, contracting His eyebrows and shaking His head at them as they are wont to do who wish to make sure that secrets will be kept.' Strong stuff indeed. But it was not enough and in their excitement and enthusiasm they dashed off and told everyone the epic news: they could now see.

All of this shows us that we humans have a remarkable capacity to believe that we know better than God. As we consider Peter trying to steer Jesus away from the cross, or building hotels (well, tents) on the mount of transfiguration, we realise that one of our most frequent prayers goes like this: despite it all, we know best.

Are there arguments raging between you and God, where you are convinced that your wisdom eclipses God's wisdom? Think again.

Prayer: Gracious God, be God in my life: I am abdicating permanently. Amen.

Matthew 9:32–34 // Luke 16:19–31

A smear campaign

'If I could just see a miracle, then I'd believe' is often stated by people who are frustrated that God doesn't give the world more convincing proofs of His existence. But what does it take to convince a committed sceptic? The Pharisees were treated to the stunning sight of a demon-tortured man set free. They couldn't deny the amazing miracle – the proof was right in front of them. There's no denying Jesus' obvious power – no wonder the crowd were so amazed. But the so-called religious experts launched into a terrible (and blasphemous) smear campaign, insisting that the root of Jesus' authority was satanic. Never mind that this would mean Satan would be casting himself out, if his underlings did the same: sometimes logic is the first casualty as people make unreasoned attacks on God.

I have not seen anyone's speech restored today. But as I look at the intricate engineering of the human body and the balance of the planet upon which we live, or consider yet another sunset and ponder so many answers to prayer over the years, I am drawn to worship: not fight against the truth that God really is God.

… God really
is God

When others are different

BIG PICTURE
Matthew 11:2–19

FOCUS
'Blessed is the man who does not fall away on account of me.'
(Matt. 11:6)

JOHN the Baptist always amazes me and not just because of his fashion or dietary choices (I've never been a lover of honey, but locusts sound even less appetising). He was the one who paved the pathway for Jesus, calling the errant people of God back to the Lord with his fiery repentance sermons. But he and Jesus were so very different. John was an ascetic and his wilderness-man lifestyle appeared harsh and even fanatical to some. Jesus, infamous in the eyes of the Pharisees because of His love of banquets and friendships with arch-sinners, seemed to come at life from the opposite extreme. Both men were roundly criticised, which proves that there is no pleasing some people.

But notice that as he languished in prison, John hit a crisis. Was this Jesus really the Christ? The little band of John's disciples therefore came as a delegation to look for confirmation that Jesus really was 'the One'.

Surely John was tempted to think that the coming Messiah would do things according to *his* expectations – indeed, that Jesus would be an extension of the ministry and lifestyle of John. Jesus knew that He was hard for John to take – hence His words, 'Blessed is the man who does not fall away on account of me' – the phrase means, literally, the man who is 'not scandalised by me'.

Perhaps you're struggling with someone right now because they don't 'do faith' according to your expectations. Are they wrong – or just different? Let's not try to make people in our own image. That's already been done – and can only be done – by God alone.

Prayer: Lord, forgive me for judging those who don't 'do' faith as I do. May I see them with Your eyes. Amen.

HERE'S a vital question for us all: what really matters to God? Christians are those who have decided to live the rest of their lives for God's purposes and pleasure. Far more than just being morally good or vaguely spiritual people, we 'make it our aim to please Him'. So what is it that really brings a smile to God's face – and what doesn't He care much about?

As the Pharisees got picky again about the disciples snacking on the Sabbath, Jesus pointed them back to what is really important. Jesus quoted from the enraged Hosea, who faithfully trumpeted God's call for a cancellation of all religious services, if they weren't accompanied by care for the poor. Mere ritual will never delight God: on the contrary, empty religious oblations that come from hearts void of compassion make Him angry. He calls for mercy rather than sacrifice. Both Old and New Testaments echo this call for social justice. Caring for our world is not an add-on to the gospel, but sits at the very heart of authentic biblical faith.

But beware the extreme path that some have taken, as they have dismissed corporate worship as pious irrelevance. They have no time to gather to sing, pray and share bread and wine – or so they say – quite wrongly. God doesn't reject the value of rest, renewal and worship – He just insists that it be genuine. Those who would love God in prayer and song must also love their neighbour in word and deed. Both matter. And both matter greatly to God.

Prayer: Lord, please give me Your wisdom to discern the essential amongst the inessential. Amen.

The heart of true religion

BIG PICTURE
**Matthew 12:1–8
Hosea 6:6**

FOCUS
'If you had known what these words mean, "I desire mercy, not sacrifice," you would not have condemned the innocent. For the Son of Man is Lord of the Sabbath.' (Matt. 12:7–8)

Mere ritual

will never

delight God …

Looking for a reason

BIG PICTURE
Matthew 12:9–14
Matthew 7:1–5

FOCUS
'Looking for a reason to
accuse Jesus, they asked
him, "Is it lawful to heal
on the Sabbath?"'
(Matt. 12:10)

I'VE met a few people on my travels who have apparently made a life choice to be offended. And religious people can be especially gifted at being prickly. The Pharisees deliberately went hunting for a reason to accuse Jesus. The irony of their complaint is startling: they condemn Him for bringing life and healing, while they go out on the Sabbath and plot His death without hesitation. But the compulsively offended often aren't too good with logic.

So why do we go looking for offence at times? Perhaps we've already made our minds up about someone – we've become judge, jury and executioner in our own little case against them and now we're just looking to be proved right in our prejudice. We hate to be wrong. Sometimes it is envy that makes us go to war: Jesus was able to perform a mind-stretching miracle for the man with the shrivelled hand, a slap in the face for the Pharisees who were impotent when it came to the supernatural. They could have done nothing for the man – not even to enhance their own credibility.

Notice that Jesus refused to buckle under the pressure of their sneering and pointed fingers and just went right ahead and did what they were pre-judging Him for doing – He healed on the Sabbath.

Be careful when you find yourself looking for trouble – you might just become unreasonable. There really is no pleasing some people. Let's not become one of them.

Prayer: Gracious Father, may I never seek for conflict or reasons to criticise. Cleanse my heart. Amen.

The encouraging God

BIG PICTURE
Matthew 12:15–21
1 Corinthians 14:1–5

FOCUS
'Here is my servant whom I have chosen, the one I love, in whom I delight.' (Matt. 12:18)

IT SEEMED like a crazy thing to say, news almost too good to be true. It was at the end of a Spring Harvest Big Top meeting; the worship band was playing quietly and it was my job to close the evening with prayer. But for ten minutes I had wrestled with a sense that God wanted me to encourage and exhort the people with a specific word, a prophecy, which comes to strengthen and build up the Church. I felt that God wanted to say something very succinct – that He wanted to thank His people, to express real gratitude for their hard work, their faithfulness in times of struggle, their trust when prayers had seemed unanswered, their showing up on Sundays sometimes when they least felt like it and their countless acts of service and practical love shown to their communities and to the wider world. Thanks, says God. It seemed outrageous – why should God say thank you? He is after all, the One who gives us breath and so He owes us nothing. But as I shared what was on my heart, I heard the sound of sobbing breaking out around the big tent. Many were stunned – and thrilled – that the Lord would express His appreciation.

But that is exactly what God is like. He delights in His Son and in His sons and daughters. He tears open the sky at the baptism of Jesus and shouts His affirmation. And He is revealed as the One who will say 'well done' to many as His opening greeting on the last day. Working hard and staying true? Know that God appreciates it.

Prayer: Lord, I thank and praise You that we matter to You – even if I don't understand it. Amen.

He delights in His Son and in His sons and daughters

The astonishing Jesus

BIG PICTURE
Matthew 12:22–37
James 1:26–27

FOCUS
'All the people were astonished and said, "Could this be the Son of David?"' (Matt. 12:23)

SOMEONE once said that astonishment should be the permanent condition of the forgiven sinner. Jaws dropped and eyes stared wide in amazement as Jesus healed this man who had been so tortured by demons and had lost his sight and speech. Trapped in a dark world, unable to express his basic needs to others, only able to hear their derision because of his strange behaviour, now the man could see and speak once more: it was a beautiful day, an astonishing miracle.

But for the Pharisees, it was traumatic. Ironically, they become the newly blind. All they can see is that their power base is being undermined, as the people begin to wonder if Jesus is the Messiah. They resort to further dirty tricks: unable to deny the miracle, they once again suggest that Jesus is a satanist. It was a terrible smear campaign, but perhaps the most tragic part of it was that the Pharisees probably believed their own rumour mill and doubled their efforts to be rid of Jesus. Remember – these are highly dedicated, religious people who genuinely wanted to see revival in Israel. Zeal is not a guarantee that we are right.

Sometimes passionate people rush to make hasty judgments and, like the Pharisees, we can be terribly wrong in our rush. I look back over 30 years of ministry and have more than a few regrets about opinions that I have loudly shared (and sometimes preached). My so-called radicalism led me into reactionary arrogance. I wish I could take some of those verdicts back. I can't. But I can engage brain and heart before speaking too quickly today.

Prayer: Father, I praise You for Your astonishing Son – may I grow more like Him daily. Amen.

There is none so blind …

Over the last few days we've been considering the terrible blindness of the Pharisees, who, on the lookout for offence, criticised Jesus for healing on the Sabbath (although their next move – plotting an assassination – apparently was acceptable Sabbath behaviour). Now, having tried to discredit the signs and wonders that He did, they come requesting another sign. What do these men want – is there any way they can be satisfied? The answer is no.

The power of self-deception is frightening. We can so easily believe that our flawed opinions, shaky theology and consistently bad behaviour are actually fine, if we try hard enough to convince ourselves. When we dig our heels in, refuse to listen to others and absolutely insist that we are in the right, we edge towards danger. As the old song puts it, 'There is none so blind as him who will not see.'

As Jesus tells the somewhat humorous parable of the homeless demon, He is teaching a vital principle – self-deception only gets worse when we allow it to take root in our lives. As the Pharisees fixed their stubborn jaws and hardened their hearts, they descended into greater darkness. Stay open.

The power of
self-deception
is frightening

We are family

FOCUS
'Pointing to his disciples,
he said, "Here are
my mother and my
brothers."' (Matt. 12:49)

KAY and I are so grateful for our wonderful immediate family, but we have struggled at times because we don't have close ties with our wider family. We have aunts and uncles that we've not seen for decades; there's no problem, but the distant family has become just that – distant. We've looked enviously at friends who have huge family reunions, where Christmas or Thanksgiving (in America) is the perfect reason for a boisterous get-together. In fact, we've been welcomed as friends at family reunions with over 100 in attendance. We've often come away grateful for the time we've shared, but feeling just a little envious. Perhaps you share our dilemma.

All of which makes the family that is the Church more precious to us. It sounds like a cliché; more a great title for that catchy song than a reality: 'We are family'. But it's what we are called to be as Christians, together in the community called the Church. The Church is not a fast-food joint, a biblical bakery where I can grab a snack and run; it's a family. In pointing to His disciples and unusually describing them as His mother and brothers, Jesus points the way to a newly-formed family that is not centred on race or ancestry. Yet it is a blood tie that joins us – as disciples, we are one through Jesus' shed blood on the cross and we share a wonderful common ambition – to do the will of God. Of course families have tensions, misunderstanding, good times and bad times; they know joy and despair and they are far from perfect. That's us. Flawed, but family.

Prayer: Father, thank You for Your family – the Church. Amen.

The search continues

IN THE early years of my Christian faith, I had plenty of enthusiasm, energy and commitment. I zealously (and often clumsily) shared the gospel as often as I could and probably attended more Christian meetings than was actually healthy. But looking back, although I was eager to learn, I didn't *think* my faith through a great deal. I wanted quick answers to my many questions and, dangerously, accepted at face value almost everything I was told. How grateful I am that I was part of such a caring church that helped me in those early faltering steps.

But there came a time when I began to ask some deep questions about the doctrines that I'd swallowed without hesitation. This was a scary place – suddenly some of the bold, clear lines that I'd accepted became a little blurred and I wondered for a while whether I was losing my grip on faith. One or two people discouraged me in my agonising and pressed me to 'just believe'. But thinking and questioning are part of belief.

Flanked by such a huge crowd that He makes a boat His pulpit, Jesus tells a series of parables. A parable is not designed to 'dumb down' truth, to make it obvious to everybody: rather it is a device to launch a search, to provoke those who hear to wrestle with ideas, to struggle, to pray and to solve the mystery. To question an idea that we've been told is not to doubt – rather it ensures that the notion is solid enough to survive our questions. Let's engage our brains as well as our hearts as we continue in faith.

Prayer: Lord, may Paul's words be true of me – transform me through the renewing of my mind. Amen.

BIG PICTURE
**Matthew 13:1–10
Romans 12:2**

FOCUS
'The disciples came to him and asked, "Why do you speak to the people in parables?"'
(Matt. 13:10)

… thinking and questioning are part of belief

Bible feeding

BIG PICTURE
Matthew 13:11–23
Psalm 119:11–16

FOCUS
'… the … good soil is the man who hears the word and understands it. He produces a crop, yielding a hundred, sixty or thirty times what was sown.'
(Matt. 13:23)

WRITING these Bible notes can be a challenge – quite a few readers have contacted me to offer prayerful support (and occasionally sympathy!) because they realise how much work has to be done to produce what we hope and pray is a practical, inspiring devotional. Certainly my admiration has increased for the late Selwyn Hughes, who crafted *Every Day with Jesus* literally every day for over 40 years.

But there's a wonderful benefit personally to this work: it demands that I consistently put my heart and mind into Scripture. And in so doing, I try to make sure that I am not just reflecting and thinking with my reader – you – in mind – but that the Word of God impacts me first. Kay, my wife, often notices a faraway look in my eyes – and one not caused by jet-lag. The distant look is because I'm learning to mull over the words of Scripture that I'm writing on – and the discipline of that biblical meditation has strengthened me. As I allow that living seed to take root in my life, something mysterious happens that is far more than so-called self-improvement. I am changed, challenged, strengthened and directed. Far more than words, through the words of Scripture God breathes life into me once more.

But of course that growth is challenged. Jesus talks about the seed being threatened by trouble (which we all know about), persecution (about which we may know) and the worries of life and materialism (again, a battle we all share). Through it all, we need to determine to give Scripture a central place in our daily lives. That way we'll produce a bumper crop.

Prayer: Father, thank You for Your Word. As I feast on it, please feed me. Amen.

Asking questions

LAST Sunday, after I'd preached, a lady approached me. She stammered her words, apologised for taking my time and told me that she felt like running away rather than speaking to me. When I asked her why she was ready to flee, she responded with a statement that unsettled me: 'I'm intimidated.'

She hurried on to say that this wasn't something that was my fault, that she was just nervous about talking with someone who stands on a platform, but it still challenged me. I want to be utterly approachable and make people feel able to ask the most awkward questions of me, if that's what they'd like to do. I've been to churches where asking questions is viewed as a sign of rebellion by insecure leaders who ought to know better. Or to not know something is seen as a sign of immaturity. And so questions stay unanswered.

There are so many things about the character of Jesus that make Him so attractive: His patience, wit, boldness, tenderness and creativity all combine together to make Him the greatest. No wonder people flocked to Jesus and children felt so at ease with Him.

The aspect of His character that is surely so winsome is His being so approachable. The disciples felt able to quiz Him, to ask for clarification in their stumbling search for truth. A question is a sign of strength, not weakness. It shows we realise that we have not yet arrived, that we still have a quest to know. Children are often good at questioning: we can lose that child-like skill with the advent of so-called 'maturity'.

Go ahead, question away.

Prayer: Father, none of us has a monopoly on truth. May I question and answer with Your grace. Amen.

BIG PICTURE
**Matthew 13:36–43
Acts 17:11**

FOCUS
'Then he left the crowd and went into the house. His disciples came to him and said, "Explain to us the parable of the weeds in the field."'
(Matt. 13:36)

A question is a sign of strength, not weakness

Tell Jesus

BIG PICTURE
Matthew 14:1–12
Psalm 73

FOCUS
'John's disciples came
and took his body and
buried it. Then they went
and told Jesus.'
(Matt. 14:12)

THE madness of Herod had sparked a devastating event: the execution of John the Baptist. Herod was a coward, pushed around by public opinion and unwilling to admit that his 'I'll do anything' vow was reckless and wrong. So John lost his head.

John's disciples were surely traumatised. Their mentor, leader and friend was gone now and all because of the wiles of a dancing girl. Confusion must have overwhelmed them. Having taken care of his funeral, they did something that we'd do well to emulate: they went to Jesus and poured out their hearts to Him.

Sometimes sadness silences my prayers. I don't feel like praising God, because a dark emotional cloud seems to blind me to what I should be thankful for. Disappointment seems to short-circuit my faith. It's not so much that I want to abandon God: it's just that, as far as I'm concerned, we're not talking. That stalemate can go on for quite a while – longer than I'd like to admit.

But I'm learning that some of the greatest prayers are when I just tell God what's upsetting me. I might not labour over the prayer for hours – in fact, some of my most effective praying has been when I've said, in just a sentence or two, what's really on my mind. I'm convinced that God is far more interested in real conversation than He is with my speeches when I pretend to be ecstatic. The old hymn sounds sentimental, but says it so well. Are you weak and heavy laden? Take it to the Lord in prayer.

Prayer: Lord, may I learn to pour out my heart to You, in all and any circumstances. Amen.

WEEKEND

Inconvenience and compassion

Any minute now, even as I write this, my telephone is going to ring. A friend of mine is in trouble and has told me that he's calling. The trouble is, I have to write this: my deadline is looming.

Jesus was in danger. John's death signalled increased opposition, hence Jesus' need to retreat to safety. His time had not yet come. But there was no keeping His location a secret and the crowds hunted Him down. When they found Him, advertising His whereabouts, they weren't hurriedly shooed away, which might have been perfectly reasonable. Despite being endangered, Jesus has compassion upon them.

I find compassion easier when I make an appointment for it. It's so much easier for me to help when I have clarity of mind, time to spare and the physical and emotional energy that I need. But when I'm busy, distracted or exhausted, then someone's need can too quickly become an unwelcome interruption. Most needs don't keep schedules. We need to cultivate a willingness to be interrupted.

We need to cultivate a willingness to be interrupted

Got to go. Believe it or not, the phone just rang. It was *not* my friend, but someone else who needed to talk. Living what I write can be a challenge!

Send them away

BIG PICTURE
Matthew 14:15–21
Psalm 139:7–12

FOCUS
'… the disciples … said,
"This is a remote place
and it's already getting
late. Send the crowds
away, so they can go
to the villages and buy
themselves some food."'
(Matt. 14:15)

OVER the weekend we saw that need often doesn't make an appointment, but presents itself at 'inconvenient' times. As do miracles. Sometimes something wonderful happens when we least expect it. When I'm tired, hungry and just want to go home, I discover that this is the time when God surprises me.

It's often happened in Timberline Church, where I serve as a teaching pastor. We have five services every weekend, which means that the preacher gets to share the same sermon – same outline, content (and spontaneous humour!) five times over. When I get to the end of the last service, I don't have very much energy left. And yet that's often the time when someone stops me as I leave to ask for prayer. Or perhaps when I'm almost out of the door, sparkling moments of encouragement, reports of answered prayers or other wonderful incidents happen.

So it was with the feeding of the 5,000. It's clear that the disciples would have cancelled that particular meal if they could. They didn't like the place (it was remote), they didn't like the time (it was late) and all they wanted was to be somewhere else. But it was then that one of the greatest miracles took place.

After initially nudging the disciples towards performing the miracle (a ploy that didn't work) Jesus took over and the massive crowd was fed with food to spare. Perhaps you find yourself in a place and time that you don't like and your prayer is simple: get me out of here. Pray that, by all means – but don't think that God can't meet you *there, now*.

Prayer: Lord, please meet me where I am now and remind me there are no no-go areas to You. Amen.

PONDER the sight of a group of men screaming their lungs out in a storm. These were the very same chaps who, only a couple of hours earlier (or even less), had watched wide-eyed as 5,000 people were fed from just five loaves and two fishes. And the day had started with a large number of healing miracles. So, this had been one fine day: healing in the morning, miraculous multiplication in the late afternoon – but yelling with fear in the evening. Had they learned nothing? Perhaps it was the fact that Jesus had not been in the boat with them that initially set them up for fear. Then when He comes strolling atop the waves, they break into full-blooded yelling. But you would have thought that the disciples, having seen so much of the authority of Jesus over utterly impossible situations, might have mustered up a little more faith rather than just giving themselves to loud hollering and acting like they've seen a ghost – literally.

That's the way we are. God can answer our prayers this morning and we can wander into sin or plunge into fear by mid-afternoon. Yesterday's triumphs don't guarantee success or faithfulness today.

Perhaps we should all be a little more encouraged about ourselves. If these disciples, who had a front row seat to see such stunning stuff, can doubt and be confused the very same day, then perhaps we who 'have not seen' as they had can relax a little when we have our struggles. We're not 'only human' – but we are *still* human.

Prayer: Dear Lord, as I ask for mercy on my humanity, may I extend that mercy to others. Amen.

One fine day

BIG PICTURE
**Matthew 14:22–36
John 20:24–29**

FOCUS
'… Jesus went out to them, walking on the lake. When the disciples saw him … they were terrified. "It's a ghost," they said and cried out in fear.' (Matt. 14:25–26)

Yesterday's

triumphs don't

guarantee

success or

faithfulness today

Tradition versus obedience

BIG PICTURE
**Matthew 15:1–9
Isaiah 29:13**

FOCUS
'… some Pharisees and teachers of the law came to Jesus … and asked, "Why do your disciples break the tradition of the elders? They don't wash their hands before they eat!"' (Matt. 15:1–2)

TRADITION can be valuable. I used to be so desperate to be 'radical' as a Christian that I dismissed whatever had been done by others in the past, longing to find the fresh, new thing that God was doing. I now know how foolish that was: tradition can be a rich inheritance; hints from others about how to live for God.

But *traditionalism* can be a trap, when it makes faith cumbersome and complex, or allows it to get in the way of what God wants to do. The Pharisees' anger about Jesus' disciples not washing their hands before eating was not about hygiene, but strict ritual.

Under Old Testament law, Aaronic priests were required to ritually wash their hands before stepping into the tent of meeting, and the elders of a city were required to ritually wash their hands if there was an unsolved murder case – but religion adds to God's requirements. The Scribes and the Pharisees insisted on a complicated routine to be employed repeatedly during everyday meals. Water, enough to fill ten eggshells, was required – the water was first poured on both hands, held with the fingers pointing upwards, and then had to run up the arm as far as the wrist, where it had to drop off at the wrist because it was now unclean. The process was then repeated with the fingers pointing down, and finally each hand was cleansed by being rubbed with the fist of the other. A really strict Jew would do this before a meal and in between each course …

Tradition is the living faith of the dead; traditionalism is the dead faith of the living. Let's know the difference.

Prayer: Lord, grant us discernment and wisdom in deciding what to hold onto and what not. Amen.

THE man came up to me at the end of the service, a huge grin on his face. 'You came to our church a few years ago,' he said, 'and you got me into a lot of trouble.' I was puzzled. What on earth did I do to prompt this congenial-looking chap to do something that had landed him in hot water?

I asked him to clarify. 'Well, I told our minister that I really liked you and enjoyed your preaching. But he was not amused and said that it was a shame that not everybody else in the church felt the same way.' Apparently I had gone down like a lead balloon.

I searched my memory banks and recalled the evening. I remember driving away after the service thinking that the time had gone well, that there had been a warm reception to my ministry. Now I realised that I had been completely deluded. As I stammered to know how best to respond, I felt that hollowness in the pit of my stomach that comes with the realisation: not everybody likes me – on the contrary.

We all want to be liked. I know some people who say that they couldn't care less, but I struggle to believe them. It's just the way life is. As Jesus continued to expose the empty hypocrisy of the Pharisees, He succeeded in making more enemies and critics – which the disciples seemed uncomfortable about, hence their nervous report.

Don't go out of your way to make enemies. But know that you're not everyone's cup of tea and get on with life anyway.

Prayer: Lord, may I be concerned mostly with the opinion that matters – Yours. Amen.

Not everyone likes you

BIG PICTURE
**Matthew 15:10–20
Galatians 1:9–11**

FOCUS
'Then the disciples came to him and asked, "Do you know that the Pharisees were offended when they heard this?"'
(Matt. 15:12)

… get on with

life anyway

Irony?

BIG PICTURE
**Matthew 15:21–28
2 Peter 3:15–17**

FOCUS
'He replied, "It is
not right to take the
children's bread and
toss it to their dogs."'
(Matt. 15:26)

'IT'S what the Bible says and that's that.'

I've heard that said often – but the Bible demands a careful look at its contents before we jump to conclusions. Having just taught that no food is unclean, Jesus takes His ministry into 'unclean' Gentile territory. There's a strange encounter with a distraught mother. Let's face it – Jesus' words seem harsh. This desperate woman, traumatised by her daughter's torment, approaches Him for help. At first greeted with silence, she then seems to be demeaningly rebuffed. It hardly seems caring …

Look again. It's total conjecture, but perhaps Jesus is teaching by irony here. Having just done battle with the Pharisees, whose rituals would have even barred many Jews from God, now perhaps Jesus seeks to shock His disciples into seeing what exclusivism really looks like. It drives people in desperate need away. The Jews called the Gentiles 'dogs', a term that Jesus uses here – but He doesn't use the harsh word coined by the Pharisees, but another meaning 'little pet dog'. Is this gentle humour?

Perhaps Jesus was testing His disciples – would they act like the Pharisees, or encourage the woman to press Jesus for help? Perhaps they were being shown what the outworking of the Pharisees' ideas really looked like. Is the woman's faith under scrutiny too? She certainly passed the test, insisting on His help, which she wonderfully received.

This episode is hard to understand and demonstrates that we need to look closely at Scripture and think it through carefully. A cursory glance could lead us to disastrous conclusions.

Prayer: Gracious God, may I see You clearly through Your Word. Amen.

Simple faith

Yesterday we saw that unthinking faith can be dangerous. The Bible has been used to justify some terrible actions throughout history and so a careful approach to it is vital. In the wrong hands, it's volatile material! But in calling for a faith that enquires, I don't want to suggest that we *complicate* faith. There's something refreshing – and disturbing – about the contrast between the nit-picking of the religious leaders, and the simple, heartfelt worship that came from the crowds. Perhaps the Pharisees were so used to talking through every minute detail, they talked faith to death and allowed cynicism and self-interest to blind them to the glorious.

But the ordinary people in the crowds were wide-eyed with amazement and offered heartfelt praise to God. Nothing too complicated about that. And once again, these were Gentiles, confirming that Jesus had always intended to reach masses of those so-called 'dogs' during this trip.

… I want simplicity of faith that worships even when I don't … understand …

I want a faith that is informed, rigorous and nurtured by study and discussion with others. But I want simplicity of faith that worships even when I don't fully understand and where praise is not paralysed by endless analysing.

Prayer: Gracious Father, may I be captivated by You and what You are doing. Amen.

Déjà vu

BIG PICTURE
Matthew 15:32–39
Acts 7:44–53

FOCUS
'His disciples answered, "Where could we get enough bread in this remote place to feed such a crowd?"' (Matt. 15:33)

KAY and I have been blessed with remarkably good health up until now. In nearly 30 years of marriage, we've only had a couple of skirmishes with what looked like serious illness. We've been through just a few of those nail-biting seasons when we had to wait a few days for the results of tests, where a bad report could have spelled disaster.

But I marvel sometimes at my own capacity to *not* learn the lessons of those testing times. How quickly I forget how to trust God, how to pray when I'm fearful and how to seek help and support from close friends when the climb gets steep. It seems like I find myself back in the classroom of discipleship, having to learn the same old lessons over once more.

So it was with the disciples, who had seen very clearly how to feed a hungry crowd: the feeding of the 5,000 was a wonderful education.

Yet, when exactly the same need arises (although this time with 1,000 less male mouths to feed), they act as if they'd never been to school and the previous miracle had never happened. They ask the question: 'Where can we get enough bread?' that their previous experience should have answered.

Perhaps you're in a situation right now which makes you feel like you are at your wits' end. The need is overwhelming and there seems no answer on the horizon. Stop right there – perhaps you've been this way before. What did you learn back then that you need to recall – and apply – today?

Prayer: Lord, help me to recall the lessons I learn – particularly when I need them. Amen.

ONCE in a while it's a good idea to realise that we can be quite wrong. And that is especially important for Christians, who are people of passion and conviction, not easily swayed. Our understanding of the truth isn't perfect: the Bible is trustworthy, but our interpretation of it isn't fail-safe. Right now, we probably nurse ideas about our faith that aren't quite right.

Certainly that was the experience of the disciples and they spent three years personally living in the closest friendship with Jesus Himself. As the Pharisees and Sadducees arrive for a showdown (a strange coalition, as these groups hated each other and believed totally different ideas), we see that almost everybody has missed the point. The Pharisees are wrong, with their sign-seeking and legalistic obsessions. The Sadducees are wrong, because they don't believe in the resurrection of the dead – so they are going to be surprised by the Easter event, 'the sign of Jonah'. And the disciples completely missed the boat as well. They misunderstood Jesus, thinking that He was telling them off because they hadn't picked up the shopping! Often in the ministry of Jesus, people misconstrued His words by interpreting them literally rather than spiritually. Nicodemus thought that Jesus was talking about an actual physical birth and the Samaritan woman thought He was referring to actual water from the well.

We can be wrong – and I'm not just talking about our understanding of Scripture. Our opinions, our views on what's happening around us, our insistence on what takes place in our churches – we can get it wrong. That knowledge should keep us humble – and teachable.

Prayer: Lord, please help me to act wisely and to be able to admit when I am wrong. Amen.

We can be wrong

BIG PICTURE
Matthew 16:1–12
Matthew 12:38–42

FOCUS
'Do you still not understand? Don't you remember the five loaves for the five thousand and how many basketfuls you gathered?' (Matt. 16:9)

That knowledge should keep us humble – and teachable

Let me tell You, Jesus …

BIG PICTURE
Matthew 16:13–23
Mark 8:31–38

FOCUS
'Peter took him aside and began to rebuke him. "Never, Lord!" he said. "This shall never happen to you!"'
(Matt. 16:22)

WE SAW yesterday that we can be quite wrong. Today we see that Peter, who had received such incredible heavenly revelation about the identity of Jesus, now gets it very wrong too. Perhaps we were right yesterday, but that doesn't guarantee us being correct today. And Peter missed the mark badly, giving Jesus such a telling-off. How quickly the 'rock' became a stumbling block!

Why did Peter miss the point? Part of it was due to his theological understanding of what the Messiah would do. Peter probably expected Jesus to be the triumphant rescuer of Israel – and perhaps hoped to share in that glorious victory. Defeat and death (and still worse rejection by Israel's official leadership) were not on his agenda.

And then perhaps Peter was also motivated by his genuine love and care for Jesus – the thought of losing Him was just too appalling. In Mark's version of this episode (8:32), the writer uses a word that implies that Peter felt pity for Jesus. Certainly Peter was insistent. It's as if he is saying, 'Death in Jerusalem? Over my dead body …'

Whatever the motives, Peter was wrong. He was thinking in mere human terms rather than seeing God's plan, and he earned himself a stern rebuke.

Perhaps we have a track record for being right; we're respected for our wisdom and when we offer an opinion, people listen and trust our perspective. That's a wonderful and dangerous position to be in. We can start to get a little too confident in our rightness – and before we know it, we're blurting out bad ideas rather than seeing things God's way.

Prayer: Gracious Father, please give me Your wisdom but always remind me that it remains Yours. Amen.

THE lady was indignant as she described her church. 'I don't suffer fools gladly,' she told me. I stayed silent and thought: God does. He's got me and you, lady, for starters …

In a week where we've been considering the sobering truth that we often get things wrong, it's encouraging to consider the wonderful patience and kindness of Jesus. As He has to put up with His blundering disciples and their failures in faith, we realise that He spent three long years training them for the rigours to come. This obviously had its huge frustrations and He wondered how long He would 'put up with' them. But put up with them He did, tending their bruises, correcting their misunderstandings and nudging and encouraging them towards strength, so that this hapless little band would emerge as world changers.

Jesus 'puts up with us' too and not just when we make serious mistakes. We tend towards distractions, we have a propensity to get upset about things that don't matter much and we can meander around in endless circles. We truly are like sheep, as the Bible describes, and sheep aren't known to be that bright. Yet He is endlessly patient with us, committing Himself to be with us until the very end.

Surely that means that we who have been shown such patience should pass it around and be a little more long-suffering when those around us don't deliver as we'd like or expect. We've been accepted – so let's accept each other.

As we forbear with each other (a nice way of saying, 'put up with each other') we share what we ourselves have received – and are receiving.

Prayer: Help me to value people as You do, remembering that we all have to put up with each other. Amen.

The patience of Jesus

BIG PICTURE
Matthew 17:14–18
Matthew 5:22

FOCUS
'"O unbelieving and perverse generation," Jesus replied, "how long shall I stay with you? How long shall I put up with you? Bring the boy here to me."'
(Matt. 17:17)

We've been accepted – so let's accept each other

What did we do wrong?

BIG PICTURE
Matthew 17:19–20
John 21:1–23

FOCUS
'Then the disciples came to Jesus in private and asked, "Why couldn't we drive it out?"'
(Matt. 17:19)

IT WAS an inspiring lecture about preaching, but I parted company with the lecturer at one point.

'If you say something that's wrong and realise it a few sentences after you've said it, keep going. Don't go back to your statement – it just draws more attention to it.' I disagree and I'm sad to admit that there have been lots of times when I've finished preaching, sat down and then had to return to the pulpit to correct something I'd said that was wrong, or apologise for what I felt was an untimely comment or bad attitude.

We've been seeing this week that we can all be wrong. But there are some people who never acknowledge their mistakes, preferring to gloss over them and move on. Perhaps pride prevents them from conceding that they may actually have made a mistake. I've met people who have insisted that they have heard from God, even when it was obvious that they hadn't. Unable to admit their error, it seemed their whole faith would collapse if they did so.

When we act like that, we will never grow. Failure is part of life for us all. We share an unfortunate bond – we all mess up. But what we do with our failures determines the kind of people that we will be. The disciples must have been embarrassed by their inability to help the tortured boy; but to their credit, they went to Jesus to ask why they had failed. They learnt that they needed to grow in faith. When we fall over, let's learn from the trip.

Prayer: Lord, please help me to admit my mistakes and to learn from them. Amen

Matthew 18:1–6 // Mark 10:13–14

Greatness and humility

In Jesus' day, children had no status or power. They were totally dependent upon others, easily brushed aside by the disciples of Jesus, who saw them as social nobodies with nothing to offer in terms of advancing the kingdom cause. They were simply a time-consuming distraction, to be sent packing. This dismissive attitude made Jesus angry.

But then, with a group of disciples still eager to establish a 'pecking order' of greatness, Jesus summoned a child. Power to heal or prowess in teaching aren't listed by Him as attributes of greatness. He doesn't describe a great warrior as one who has authority over the demonic. Instead, He places His hands on the shoulders of a child – one so dependent: a true example of simple humility and trust.

Humility and simplicity don't come naturally to us. We're almost programmed to need to be noticed, congratulated and even celebrated. But that need can become a hunger that is never satisfied and we end up living driven, insecure lives, starving until the next compliment comes our way. Like the disciples, we need to be changed by God's Spirit today.

… we need to be changed by God's Spirit today

Forgiveness

BIG PICTURE
Matthew 18:21–35
Genesis 4:1–24

FOCUS
'Jesus answered, "I tell you, not seven times, but seventy-seven times."' (Matt. 18:22)

I RECENTLY had to give my old car a Christian burial, figuratively speaking. She was a trusty steed, with over 300,000 miles on the clock. About 150,000 miles ago I gave up worrying about dents and scratches, so she looked like she'd been in a war zone but, until recently, had continued to drive beautifully. Until the power-steering fluid started leaking, that is. At first it was a steady drip, requiring occasional attention. In the end I got to the point where any journey over 20 miles would require me to stop and top up the fluid. It was time to say goodbye, not least because the fluid bill could have made a healthy car payment.

Forgiveness is the lubricant of all relationships and, us humans being what we are, we must know that we are required to use it frequently. As Peter was hoping to only have to forgive on a limited and sporadic basis, (a later rabbinic discussion suggested three times as reasonable) he discovers that 'seventy-times-seven' (NASB) grace is needed. Our willingness to forgive should be as limitless as the extravagant vengeance of which Lamech once boasted – Genesis 4:24 is being deliberately echoed in the figures seven and 77. This isn't a maths calculation adding up to 490 times, but a call to limitless forgiveness. But when we refuse to forgive often, our relationships seize up, splutter out – and finally die.

Of course, this shouldn't surprise us. How often God forgives us! We're called to pass that grace around, as Jesus' parable of the king and the servant shows. Don't be surprised when others fail you. We live in a seventy-times-seven world.

Prayer: Lord, may I forgive today as You have forgiven me. Amen.

Divorce

DIVORCE is a difficult subject to approach biblically, because it is so hotly debated and is such a sensitive issue. As I write today, I am prayerfully conscious that some of my readers have walked through the pain of divorce and don't need to get a nasty cut from me by my carelessly 'swinging the sword' that is the Word of God. Let me say right away that if divorce has been part of your journey I'm so sorry for the pain that you have experienced. Whatever times of rejection, conflict, mistakes, bad decisions, attempts at reconciliation, forgiveness and faithfulness or betrayal have been in your life, I'm sure that it has been very difficult. As I write these words, I am pausing to pray for you.

I can't outline the Bible's teaching on divorce in a few paragraphs. But I can say this: Jesus had an incredibly high view of the sanctity and importance of marriage, to the degree that the disciples were shocked and wondered if singleness might be the only workable option. Speaking to a culture where a man could divorce his wife for just about any reason (including burning the dinner) but the wife had no right of divorce, Jesus emphasises the dignity and preciousness of the marriage relationship. It is far more than a human invention, being part of God's creation design. In a culture that largely dismisses marriage, or sees it as easily disposable, we are called to the faithfulness, hard work and seventy-times-seven forgiveness that we considered yesterday. Sometimes divorce may seem to be the only option. But in affirming that, let's also declare that God is utterly *for* marriage.

Prayer: Lord, thank You for marriage and all that You created it to be. Amen.

BIG PICTURE
**Matthew 19:3–12
Genesis 2:20–24**

FOCUS
'Some Pharisees came to him to test him. They asked, "Is it lawful for a man to divorce his wife for any and every reason?"' (Matt. 19:3)

… God is utterly

for marriage

When the question is answered …

BIG PICTURE
Matthew 19:16–22
Philippians 4:12

FOCUS
'Now a man came up to Jesus and asked, "Teacher, what good thing must I do to get eternal life?"'
(Matt. 19:16)

HAVE you ever asked a question, knowing that you didn't want to hear the answer? Here are a few: 'Do you like my hair?' 'Did I offend you?' 'Is there anything I can do?' 'What did I do wrong?' 'Do I owe you anything?' And then that perennial favourite, 'Do I look fat in this?'

The man who approached Jesus with a question about eternal life seemed to have been in that 'Tell me, but I'm not sure I want to know' position, if his response to the answer is anything to go by. His question was skewed. He thought that by being 'good' he could earn his way into eternity.

But then Jesus challenged the man about his materialism. That doesn't mean that all who are rich have to give everything away (although we must acknowledge that we are *all* stewards of whatever we have; not only is all we have God's in a general sense, but the way we use our money is a matter of obedience for us all). What is clear is that money was this man's sticking point. It was not that he had money, but sadly money had him. Wealth seems to have a special allure, demanding our loyalty and even worship. The rich young man walked away, face downcast.

Is money a 'sticking point' for me? And if cash isn't the issue, then is there another area of my life where I refuse to issue God with an 'access all areas pass'? Perhaps we could all do well to follow the rich man's example at least in one action and ask God to show us our sticking points.

Prayer: Lord, where in my life have I presented You with a 'No Entry' sign? Please show me. Amen.

Sober assessment

I'M NOT a fan of television game shows. Whenever a programme comes on that involves someone (or a family) being poised to slap a big red buzzer, thus proving that they are the quickest draw when it comes to answering questions, then I usually change channel.

But lately I've been wondering if I tend to hit the proverbial red button too quickly.

Yesterday we pondered a big question: is there an area of our lives where we absolutely refuse to allow God to take charge? It's a big question – and also one that we can be tempted to answer too quickly. It's too easy to give a superficial response, assuming that our lives are surrendered to God and drowning out any challenge that we might sense by moving on. We need to hit the pause button and respond seriously.

When Jesus challenged James and John, who had set their mother up to claim the seats of greatest honour for them in the coming kingdom, He asked them a question that they answered rather too quickly: could they drink His cup? Were they willing to suffer as He would?

Immediately they affirmed that they were – and they did suffer – James would die at Herod's whim (Acts 12:2) and John would be exiled to the island of Patmos. But that would be after they denied Him and fled and, whatever they suffered, it didn't compare to the 'cup of suffering' that Jesus drank to the full. But in their eagerness for greatness and glory, they answered too quickly.

Join me as I reread yesterday's piece. And let's all take time to carefully answer the challenge.

Prayer: Lord, may I be ready to consider and not quick to make foolish claims. Amen.

BIG PICTURE
**Matthew 20:20–28
Matthew 26:47–56**

FOCUS
'"You don't know what you are asking," Jesus said to them. "Can you drink the cup I am going to drink?" "We can," they answered.'
(Matt. 20:22)

It is easy to give a superficial response ...

267

The ability to ask

BIG PICTURE
Matthew 20:29–34
Daniel 3:16–18

FOCUS
'Jesus stopped and called them. "What do you want me to do for you?" he asked.' (Matt. 20:32)

EARLIER this week I was doing some careful stocktaking of my own faith journey, as I suggested yesterday. Suddenly it hit me: I don't ask God for things as I used to, especially in the realm of healing. As a new Christian I was delighted and excited to go to God with my needs (and those of others). I had a real anticipation about what God might do and saw some marvellous answers to prayer.

Sadly, some of that simplicity has been lost and I think I know why. For one thing, I've been appalled by the acrobatics and shenanigans of some television evangelists whose emotional appeals make God look like a cosmic vending machine. The idea that your healing is more likely if you flash your Visa card in the direction of one of 'God's appointed messengers' is nauseating. And then, to be brutally honest, there have been disappointments that have eroded my confidence. Watching a good friend walk through horrendous suffering and then die, long before what seemed to be his time and despite prayer and fasting by literally thousands of people, has made a casualty out of my ability to ask. Perhaps I don't ask any more because I can't bear the potential disappointment.

Whatever the reasons, I want to learn to ask again. As Jesus was hotly pursued by these yelling blind men, He asked them a question that has a screamingly obvious answer – what did they want from Him? Their blindness was plain to see, but He wanted them to articulate their request, to be very specific.

Let me ask: have you asked God for something lately?

Prayer: Lord, may I learn to ask – and to accept the answer 'No' when necessary. Amen.

This is getting out of control

Yesterday we thought about asking and if there's one thing that most children are gifted at, it's asking and receiving. When our children were younger, they thrilled me with their ability to enjoy and receive gifts. If we gave them a treat, there would be no embarrassed awkwardness, no affirmation that they were not worthy, having not cleaned their rooms since birth. They would ask and receive.

And they knew how to say thank you, too. They didn't take for granted the good things they enjoyed, but freely appreciated what they had.

So it is in the Temple. Wonderful healings are happening as people in dire need are brought to Jesus. Much to the disgust of the disgruntled religious authorities, offended as religious people often are at the outbreak of signs of life, the children were not only shouting in the Temple area, but shouting the praises of God. They yelled out their hosannas to God for all that He was doing.

Let's not forget to say thank you. Let's not worry when life means a little chaos and mess. And let's take a leaf out of the children's book and holler our praises now and then.

Let's not
forget to say
thank you

Authority

BIG PICTURE
Matthew 21:23–27
Proverbs 1:7

FOCUS
'So they answered Jesus, "We don't know." Then he said, "Neither will I tell you by what authority I am doing these things."'
(Matt. 21:27)

JESUS was meek and humble, often returning kindness when He was insulted. But never allow that truth to make you think that He allowed Himself to be controlled and manipulated. His encounters with the chief priests and elders, who were obviously convinced that they and they alone had the 'franchise' on all things concerning God, shows Jesus' delightfully clever ability to make sure that He stayed one step ahead of His critics. This episode unfolds like a verbal chess game – with Jesus emerging as a victor and brilliant tactician.

The reason for the interrogation about authority was obvious: the religious big guns thought that they alone had the right to represent God. Knowing that they were edging Him towards a trap, Jesus set them a conundrum about John the Baptist, one that threw them into a political storm. Whatever their answer, they were bound to lose: if they denied John's ministry, they'd upset popular opinion; to affirm John would be to affirm all that he said about the coming Messiah. Checkmate.

And then, when they refused to be drawn, Jesus insisted that, seeing as they wouldn't answer His question, then He didn't have to answer theirs. Game over.

Here Jesus shows incredible wisdom. He sees through the question to the motive behind it and with winsome brilliance skips out of their trap. I'm inclined to think that, faced with the same situation, I would have been intimidated by these leaders and would have blurted out a stammering defence. All of which makes me want to pray that God will give me – and you – real wisdom in our conversations today.

Prayer: Lord, thank You for all the abilities You shower upon us. May my words reflect You today. Amen.

Smooth talking

I SO appreciate encouragement. Sometimes I receive emails from *Lucas on Life Every Day* readers, many of them sharing how God has used these notes to bless their lives. I'm grateful that people take the time to do that: encouragement is vital for us all. It helps us to keep plodding on when we feel like we are on an uphill climb.

But there's a real difference between encouragement and flattery. The Pharisees switch tactics, send some of their disciples to Jesus (surely hoping that He wouldn't know who their masters were) and try to catch Him off guard with some smooth talking. It is a cunning ploy: let Jesus know that He's wonderful because He's not a 'man pleaser' and then hit Him with a question about taxation. The hope was surely that Jesus would declare Himself as a greater authority than even Caesar – which He was – and then He would shoot Himself in the foot by teaching that tax paying was unnecessary. The ploy fell flat, of course, but it was a clever attempt, because to support the Roman tax might have been considered by Jewish nationalists to be unpatriotic and to condemn them would have been dangerous – particularly for a Galilean popular leader.

So what's the difference between flattery and encouragement? It's surely all about motive. Flatterers will say anything to ingratiate themselves; they will exaggerate and lie in order to get on someone's good side; or, as in the case of these suave smooth talkers, they will praise in order to make someone lower their defences.

Encourage someone today. But stick to the truth and do it for their sake, not yours.

Prayer: Gracious Father, may I have clean motives in what I say – whoever I am talking to. Amen.

BIG PICTURE
**Matthew 22:15–33
1 Thessalonians
2:5–6**

FOCUS
'"Teacher," they said, "we know you are a man of integrity and that you teach the way of God in accordance with the truth. You aren't swayed by men ..."' (Matt. 22:16)

Encourage

someone today

Legacy

BIG PICTURE
Matthew 26:6–13
John 12:1–7

FOCUS
'I tell you the truth, wherever this gospel is preached throughout the world, what she has done will also be told, in memory of her.'
(Matt. 26:13)

I MUST be getting older fast. Recently I've been considering the question: what is my legacy? If I die today, is there anything that I have done that will be worth celebrating? It's John who tells us two crucial details about this story; firstly he specifically identifies the woman who gave such an extravagant and costly offering to Jesus – it was Mary of Bethany. And then he identifies Judas as the snivelling complainer who seemed so appalled at such a 'wasteful' offering – the word used here means 'dead loss'. Apparently the other disciples joined in with the litany of protest. Discontent spreads easily, even when it's started by a thieving hypocrite who couldn't care less about the poor – Judas.

But how daunting it must have been for Mary to hear her act of devotion criticised as it was. There are moments when I think we all hear a little voice in our hearts: 'What's the point of all this hard work, this effort towards holiness? Why bother with church, when people can be so obnoxious? It's all a waste of time.'

At times like that, it's good to remember the marvellous words of Jesus: 'She has done a beautiful thing to me.'

And the fragrance of her offering lingers still. Mary of Bethany has a legacy, a life that is celebrated wherever the good news of the gospel is told. Perhaps you've been tuning into that same voice, which taunts you and wants to nudge you to give up your efforts, pack away your sacrifices and do something more 'sensible' with your life. Think again: beautiful things done for and to Jesus live long.

Prayer: Thank You, Lord, for Mary's example – pouring out all she had for You. May I do the same. Amen.

Victim – or victor?

HE IS arrested. At first glance, it seems that the Lord of all is now a prisoner of a few, sold out with a kiss by the betrayer, Judas. He is led away to face unspeakable pain, bound and shackled, no longer the captain of His own destiny. Others are in control. Or are they?

Sometimes ultimate power is demonstrated by willing surrender. Jesus has friends, like Peter, who are ready to fight for Him. Peter is clumsy and not great with a sword, but he's willing. Far more importantly, Jesus has battalions of angels available to His beckoning: just say the word and these soldiers would be dead, struck down by divine vengeance. But He's walking in a higher plan, to a different drumbeat: He lets them do their worst, so that Scripture might be fulfilled. They all think that they're in charge, calling the shots. But in His weakness, He is showing himself to be the strongest of them all. They shove Him roughly, big men, or so they think, but it is only this way because He chooses it to be so. He does not react to their evil, but responds calmly, knowing that, for now, it must be.

When we offer forgiveness in the face of cruelty and show mercy rather than rage, we demonstrate real strength. Refusing to fight fire with fire is no sign of weakness, but of true character.

While His captors descended into being out-of-control, snarling dogs, Jesus maintained an inner poise that showed who *really* was in charge. Never let meekness be confused with weakness.

Prayer: Lord, please forgive me for the times I have reacted badly. Amen.

BIG PICTURE
Matthew 26:47–56

FOCUS
'Do you think I cannot call on my Father and he will … put at my disposal more than twelve legions of angels? … how then would the Scriptures be fulfilled …?'
(Matt. 26:53–54)

Never let meekness be confused with weakness

Prelude to denial

BIG PICTURE
**Matthew 26:57–68
John 18:15–18**

FOCUS
'But Peter followed him at a distance, right up to the courtyard of the high priest. He entered and sat down with the guards to see the outcome.'
(Matt. 26:58)

WHY do people give up on God? Most of us know someone who is a so-called 'prodigal' – a person who has marched or drifted away from God. Why did Peter, the one who was willing to swing the sword to defend his friend Jesus, end up betraying Him when placed under very little pressure? He doesn't seem short of courage, because he was the one most ready to put up a fight.

Perhaps Peter cracked under the accumulating pressure of tiredness and bewilderment. His violent swashbuckling outburst was rejected by Jesus – he was told to sheath his sword so that God's purposes could be fulfilled. So what was he to do? He followed at a distance; unlike John, who had contacts on the inside of the high priest's house (John 18:16) and eventually found himself up close and personal with some of the personalities who lived and worked in the high priest's courts – including one of the high priest's servants, who also happened to be a relative of the chap who temporarily had his ear amputated by Peter's sword-swinging (John 18:26).

Perhaps, finding himself at the heart of this evil powerhouse, Peter allowed fear to conquer him. Even though Jesus had clearly warned him about the battle – and the denials – to come, it seems that when we're exhausted, we can easily forget almost everything that is right and true. Tired, disappointed and emotionally strung-out people do things that they'd never do under normal circumstances – and live to regret them. Take special care if you're in that vulnerable place.

Prayer: Lord, please comfort and support any who feel vulnerable today – use me, if possible. Amen.

Matthew 27:11–14 // Isaiah 53:6–8

Silent before his accusers

My mouth has got me into quite some trouble over the years. I can't tell you how many times I wish I'd actually allowed my brain cells to do some work before my mouth got motoring. But one of my greatest challenges comes when I am falsely accused. The moment I catch a hint of unjust attack, my mouth goes into overdrive and I inevitably fall victim to my own verbosity, regretting my word spillage for days.

Jesus, barraged by false charges, stands in silence, much to the 'great amazement' of Pilate. We saw a couple of days ago that Jesus maintained poise throughout His ordeal: now, as He resists the temptation to bark His defence and confound His accusers, He keeps His mouth firmly shut. In fact the Greek text is very precise, as if the writer is stunned by Jesus' epic self-control: 'But Jesus made no reply, not even to a single charge – to the great amazement of the governor.'

Today, I'm praying for me, not only that I'll know what and how to speak, but also that I'll be more comfortable with being quiet. The world will be a better place without my sharing some of my opinions and outbursts. Make me like You, Jesus.

Prayer: Gracious God, please make all of us more like Your Son – slow to speak. Amen.

… He resists the temptation to bark His defence …

The power of a crowd

BIG PICTURE
Matthew 27:19–31
1 Kings 19:1–18

FOCUS
'But the chief priests and the elders persuaded the crowd to ask for Barabbas and to have Jesus executed.'
(Matt. 27:20)

BEING a Christian can feel quite lonely. Perhaps, as far as you know, you are the only professing believer in your workplace or home. Maybe you're a student: you are surrounded by others, many of whom have passionate ideals about politics, the environment or a host of other vital social issues, but they don't follow Christ and some of them are rather bewildered and even bemused by those who do. You wince when yet another anti-Christian sideswipe comes from a broadcaster or famous personality; you're swimming against the tide. But remember this: the crowd can be terribly wrong.

Put a pack of people together, fill their minds with terrible ideas and the result can be devastating. As the chief priests and their cronies acted as evil cheerleaders, whipping the ordinary people into a blood-lust, we see just how easy it is for almost everyone to be deceived. And then a gaggle of Pilate's troops, surely egging each other on, descend into crude brutality as they perform a parody of a coronation, kneel before Jesus in mock allegiance and then, spit and fists flying, band together in a blasphemous battering. Anyone who has seen the wandering groups of binge drinkers on the streets of Saturday night Britain will know this: put some people into a crowd and they change. Encouraged by their pals, fuelled by alcohol and eager to make a mark, they will become violent, embarrassing or abusive.

Stand up for God, whatever the crowd says or does. And be careful when you're being tempted to run with the herd.

Prayer: Dear Lord, give courage to all those who stand out from the crowd for You. Amen.

An unspeakable pain

THERE'S a pain that many feel today, but sadly there's no doctor who can help and no medical procedure that can relieve. This malady is an epidemic problem and strikes the affluent as well as the poor. No vaccination is currently available and some experts are suggesting that the spread of this virus is increasing. Technology, far from helping to solve the issue, is probably making things worse. The pain of which I speak may be creating a dull ache in you today even as you read this. I'm talking about loneliness. Nowhere else is the trauma of loneliness seen more than at the cross.

Matthew's Gospel doesn't focus too much on the physical suffering of Jesus, but is more concerned to show the black hole of rejection that Jesus died in. A little mercy is shown by the soldiers as they offer an anaesthetic drink, but everyone else – religious leaders, robbers, passers-by – all 'hurl' and 'heap' insults upon him. Jesus was utterly rejected by his own people. He was alone. Loneliness is one of the bitter fruits of sin, as we find ourselves separated from God and alienated from each other. Christ bore that pain and now through him, as the psalmist says, the lonely can truly be set 'in families' (Psa. 68:6).

Perhaps we could deliberately and prayerfully peer beyond the horizons of our own schedules, priorities and needs today and ask God to make us aware if the pain of loneliness is tormenting anyone that we might meet today. Our smiles, interest, encouragement, offers of prayer and empathy could make all the difference.

Prayer: Lord, thank You that You faced the ultimate lonely experience for all of us. Amen.

BIG PICTURE
Matthew 27:33–44
Psalm 68:1–6

FOCUS
'In the same way the robbers who were crucified with him also heaped insults on him.'
(Matt. 27:44)

… the lonely can truly be set 'in families' …

No fear

BIG PICTURE
Matthew 28:1–20
Psalm 23

FOCUS
'Then Jesus said to them, "Do not be afraid. Go and tell my brothers to go to Galilee; there they will see me."'
(Matt. 28:10)

IN THE winsome film *The Lion King*, there's an encouragement to take the phrase *Hakuna Matata* as our mantra for life. 'It means no worries for the rest of your days,' as the catchy song explains. I love both the song and the sentiment, but there's a problem: no real reason is given for us to choose not to worry. *Don't worry, be happy* is another popular song that proposes a lovely idea, but without explanation.

As Jesus meets His beloved friends, He exhorts them not to be afraid – but for very good reasons. His is not superficial, 'don't worry, it will all be all right' advice – in fact the pathway ahead for the apostles would be fraught and perilous. There's no false promise of no trouble ahead. Rather, the apostles can go forward in confidence because Jesus has beaten even the power of death and has ultimate authority. Also, He doesn't just send the disciples out, but rather promises to go with them by His Spirit. These are solid reasons for our fears to be stilled: there is a God who has beaten even our greatest enemy – the power of death itself – and He is with and for us.

Over the last couple of months, we've been looking at encounters that people had with Jesus. As we draw our study to a close, let's remember and celebrate the wonderful truth that Jesus' encounters with His people are not over: they continue, to this very moment. May that reality calm our hearts and steady our nerves, and cause us to go into today – and tomorrow – with faith and hope.

Prayer: Dear Lord, please be with me today. May I be aware of Your presence always. Amen.

He is with

and for us

He never said …

INTRODUCTION

He never said …

IT'S been said that God made humans in His image and that, ever since, we've been trying to return the favour. Just as the children of Israel, impatiently waiting for Moses to return from his mountain-top conference with God, made a golden calf 'god' for themselves, so we too can be guilty of 'making God' – by putting words into His mouth that He never said in the first place. Part of the problem is that ideas become catch phrases. They are often attributed to the great and the good and, before we know it, they become accepted as being helpful wisdom for our lives. We don't have to look far to know that some of this 'wisdom' is anything but. 'If it feels good, do it!' is hardly a great line to offer the sex-obsessed, binge-drinking culture of Britain today. So let's take a closer look at some of these sayings that sound so sensible – but often aren't.

God bless you!

IF THERE'S one phrase that makes me nervous, it's the catch-all term 'Everyone knows that …' Through catchy sayings that ease their way gradually into popular consciousness, we build up a body of 'wisdom' that is apparently the way to do life. And because 'everyone' seems to follow these ideas, however misguided, we can swallow wholesale some rather terrible and even dangerous notions. As we'll see, popular wisdom has so much to say about God, relationships, money, pain, leadership, marriage and parenting, to name but a few vital areas. It seemed that almost 'everybody' (until recently) thought that what one newspaper columnist described as 'a national obsession with sex' was acceptable. Lately, some secular commentators have woken up to the terrible devastation that this has wreaked on our society. Almost everybody was wrong for too long. We need to expose the myths around what 'everybody' thinks.

One saying that *is* popular (although it's often a mantra of despair rather than an affirmation of faith) is *God knows*. Indeed He does. As we come to the Scriptures, we encounter the 20/20 vision that God alone has. In a culture where the idea of absolute truth is almost frowned upon, Scripture shows us how we are called to live and points us to the power that we need to live God's way.

Wisdom is priceless. Given a once-in-a-lifetime opportunity to choose *anything*, Solomon picked wisdom, longing to know the difference between right and wrong – a core skill for life that so many lack. As we journey together, let's join Solomon in his prayer.

Prayer: God of all wisdom, grant me understanding to know right from wrong. Strengthen me to choose what is right. Amen.

Everyone knows

BIG PICTURE
1 Corinthians 1:18–30
1 Kings 3:1–15

FOCUS
'Where is the wise man?
Where is the scholar?
Where is the philosopher
of this age? Has not
God made foolish the
wisdom of the world?'
(1 Cor. 1:20)

God knows.

Indeed He does

You deserve it

BIG PICTURE
Ephesians 2:1–10
Psalm 103:1–10

FOCUS
'For it is by grace you
have been saved, through
faith – and this not from
yourselves, it is the gift
of God – not by works,
so that no one can boast.'
(Eph. 2:8–9)

THE stunning actress flicks her beautiful blonde hair, waves the expensive shampoo at the camera and tells us, the gullible public, why it is that we absolutely must buy what she's hawking. It's not because the sudsy stuff is soft, perfumed, kind to hair, or will turn all who use it into gorgeous facsimiles of her. No, the reason to buy is just this – because 'you deserve it'. 'You get what you deserve' is an idea that is drummed into most of us from an early age: so much so that when tragedy strikes, the first question that jumps to mind is often, 'What did I do to deserve this?' And the reverse of course is true: there are still so many who believe that there is a point of goodness that we can reach that can earn us an eternity of bliss with God.

We don't earn pain or paradise. Pride has no place around God's banqueting table, because we only find ourselves there because of what God has done through the work of Christ. If we don't grasp that truth (and it takes a real work of God to help us to do so, so deeply engrained is our 'you get what you deserve' thinking) then we'll swing wildly between insecurity and arrogance. We'll either be so unsettled by fear that we skip between being found and lost on an hourly basis, depending on our performance, or we'll become smugly self-sufficient, convinced that we can pay our own way.

It's an outrageous scandal and an affront to human pride – but we are saved by grace alone.

Prayer: I bring nothing to save myself, Lord. You have given everything for me. I give everything today to You. Amen.

Life's too short

I don't hear much preaching about eternity these days – and I include my own preaching ministry in that. Perhaps we're at the far end of the reaction against dreamy-eyed piety where life on earth becomes not much more than a waiting-room for heaven, and environmental concern is dismissed by 'forget that, it's all going to burn up anyway' kind of thinking. We've rightly discovered that God wants us to use our days on earth to make a serious difference in our world – and the fact that God is going to renew the heavens and earth obviously doesn't negate our responsibility to be stewards of our planet's resources.

Although eternity is difficult for us to grasp, the truth is that today is not all there is. Perhaps this becomes especially comforting when we lose someone we love. We still grieve, not for them, but for us, because we miss them. It's important to know that. A grieving mother whose son died was rebuked by a 'helpful' Christian: 'Don't you know he's with Jesus?' She wisely replied 'That's the point – he's not here with me.' Because there's more ahead, we grieve, but not as those who don't have hope.

… God wants us to use our days on earth to make a serious difference in our world …

Real men don't cry

BIG PICTURE
John 11:17–37
Acts 20:17–38

FOCUS
'Jesus wept.'
(John 11:35)

I CRY at television commercials – and not just because some of them are so excruciating. Throw up some compelling images combined with a few minor-key violin chords and I'm reaching for the Kleenex. Combine that with a little accumulated tiredness and I can easily turn into a blubbering wreck. Say something nice to me and I'll cry. Be horrid and I'll probably struggle to contain the tears too. A couple of days ago, I learned of the passing of someone who has been a good and faithful friend to me for nearly three decades. Passing the sad news on, I found myself in tears and quickly apologised and hurried away, embarrassed by my own inability to control myself.

The notion that emotion and tears are not compatible with real masculinity is nothing short of mad. To think that someone who sheds tears is demonstrating weakness is bizarre. While we don't all have to wear our hearts on our sleeves and some people – women as well as men – will prefer to express what they feel in private, nonetheless we want to avoid false ideas that will inhibit us.

Jesus sobbed as He saw the trauma created by Lazarus's death. Paul's farewell with the Ephesian elders, aware as they were that they would never see each other again, was loaded with emotion. In both cases, tears were the 'amen' to spoken words of love: Jesus and Paul were moved as they demonstrated the depth of their care and concern. Cry if you need to. Be yourself. And know that real men – and women – can be free to express what's on their hearts.

Prayer: Creator God, You designed me. Save me from defining myself according to what my culture insists that I be; release me to be who You have made me to be. Amen.

IN HIS compelling (and wonderfully honest) autobiography *My Story*, the late Selwyn Hughes speaks about some of the 'Christian taboos' that were around during his early years of faith and ministry. Fifty years ago it was considered 'worldly' for Christians to pursue academic qualifications and degrees – and he found that there was no such thing as Christian counselling – with some tragic results, because people who needed significant professional help could not find it in a Christian context. But back then, holiness was basically about superficial non-conformity – so if the 'world' did something, then Christians would define themselves by *not* doing it. It doesn't take too many brain cells to realise that this is flawed thinking.

That said, we are called to live according to what God calls us to, rather than the lifestyle that others insist upon. Some people can be almost evangelical with their poor living, insisting that everyone around them joins them in their sins and excesses, mocking them as mindless puritans if they don't.

Where does the pressure to run with the crowd come from? Sometimes we fit in because we don't want to be too conspicuous and aren't willing for the flak that we'll catch if we say so. Then we sometimes do what everyone else is doing because we're not confident in our convictions. But according to Paul, most often we're not changed because we're not being renewed in our minds. That's why the Bible is so important. We're all being brainwashed. But we Christians know what we're washing our brains in. Don't become a Roman.

Prayer: Living, loving God, renew me, change my mind and transform me, that I might be conformed only to You. Amen.

When in Rome do as the Romans do

BIG PICTURE
Romans 12:1–2
2 Corinthians 6:14–18

FOCUS
'Do not conform any longer to the pattern of this world, but be transformed by the renewing of your mind.'
(Rom. 12:2)

… we're not

changed because

we're not being

renewed in

our minds

If a job's worth doing, it's worth doing well

BIG PICTURE
Galatians 2:1–21
1 Timothy 4:12–16

FOCUS
'When Peter came to Antioch, I opposed him to his face, because he was clearly in the wrong.' (Gal. 2:11)

SOME Christians can be intimidating, especially the apparently perfect ones who have prayer lives that operate like efficient machines, who have smilingly perfect children and seem to be endowed with rippling muscles of faith. I'm glad for their strength, but am prone to want to give up when I'm around them, because I'm just not that consistent, strong or good. Sometimes I genuinely wonder why God ever called me into ministry and leadership – I'm sure that there are plenty of people around who wouldn't make nearly as many mistakes as I do.

But the truth is there are times when, if a job is worth doing, it's only going to be done by those who will sometimes do it badly, because the army of God is made up of flawed, in-the-process people who sometimes perform magnificently but often make a hash of things. The Bible is the story of women and men who often did less than a great job, but nonetheless were called by God to make a great contribution. Peter is surely a case in point. The great apostle, graced with heavenly insight and situated as a key figure in the life of the Early Church, still occasionally made a complete lash-up of things, noticeably in Galatia, where he and Paul had a face-to-face standoff over his inconsistent behaviour. And Timothy, trusted with key leadership, had to be nudged away from youthful insecurity and fear.

Don't wait until you've graduated into being a total expert in most things before you attempt something for and with God.

Prayer: Use me, Lord, imperfect that I am. Override my blunders and build Your kingdom through my stumbling efforts. Amen.

I'VE just spent three productive days in a small leadership group that is fun, creative, boisterous – and incredibly diverse. Here sits a politically conservative gentleman who loves to play bowls, next to a former Labour councillor and Spurs supporter. An East London lad, the son of a maintenance man, is parked next to an educational consultant who is also related to a former organist of St. Paul's Cathedral. And the way this crowd do their spirituality is so diverse too: here are three Anglicans, two new-church types, a Salvation Army leader and a couple of Baptists.

One of the marvellous things about the Church – when she is at her best – is the fact that people who would never normally pass the time of day find themselves in the same family together. Blue-rinsed grandmothers can chat with blue-rinsed, multi-pierced teenagers; prosperous City types can share the time of day – and more – with others from far less privileged circumstances. Part of the wonder of the Church is found in her potential to bring so many utterly diverse people together.

The idea that we've got to think, act, dress or sound alike in order to be compatible is overturned through the community of Jesus, where we all meet at the common ground of the cross. It will always take work, but we must strive to calm tensions that can be created by ethnicity, tradition, worship styles and doctrinal nuances. The world is splintered and horribly divided and sometimes the Church reflects that alienation. Thank God for His family; and let's celebrate our differences rather than be fearful of them.

Prayer: Help me, Lord, to build true family with people who, naturally speaking, would not even be my friends. Amen.

Birds of a feather flock together

BIG PICTURE
**Galatians 3:26–29
1 Corinthians
12:12–26**

FOCUS
'There is neither Jew nor Greek, slave nor free, male nor female, for you are all one in Christ Jesus.' (Gal. 3:28)

… let's celebrate

our differences

rather than be

fearful of them

If at first you don't succeed, then try, try, try again

BIG PICTURE
Exodus 18:1–27
1 Corinthians 12:27–31

FOCUS
'Moses' father-in-law replied, "What you are doing is not good."'
(Exod. 18:17)

EARLIER this week we saw that our best efforts will always be imperfect. Today, as we think about words that are normally used to prompt perseverance and tenacity, we see the other side of the coin. Sometimes, having another try is *not* what we need to do: there are occasions when we need to concede that we are failing (or consistently delivering shabby results) because we are trying to do things that God hasn't called or equipped us to do.

I used occasionally to lead sung worship – complete with guitar. Perhaps one of the most excruciating experiences – for the congregation and for me – was leading worship in a service where a few thousand people were present and Jack Hayford, who composed the well-known song, 'Majesty', was the speaker. Jack graciously smiled (probably through gritted teeth) as I single-handedly murdered his greatly-loved song.

A few crimson-faced experiences – and the painful assistance of friends who told me the truth – assisted me towards the revelation that worship leading was not my primary gift (and that's putting it mildly). I stopped doing what I was decidedly average at to concentrate on what I felt God was mainly calling me to do.

The trouble is, like Moses, we are sometimes the last people to see that either we're plugging away at what God hasn't asked us to do, or working so hard that we're not making room for the gifts of others. It takes the kindly straight talking of a Jethro to bring us to our senses. Is it time to face some hard facts?

Prayer: Lord, keep me where You have called me. And help me stay open and tender to those who would help me when I wander. Amen.

If God seems far away, guess who moved

Sometimes faith – the act of believing – gets tiresome, at least to me. Christians are those people who are endeavouring to live their whole lives centred around one core essential truth: Jesus is alive. But the fact that we currently can't see Jesus makes that daily commitment difficult, especially when the going gets tough. But added to that tension is the idea that if I can't *feel* that God is with me, then He isn't and I've probably done something to create distance between us. The truth is that our feelings and emotions are not dependable indicators that signal the presence – or absence – of God.

Years ago, Adrian Plass shared one short sentence with me that changed the life of the yo-yoing emotionally turbulent person that I am: 'Your feelings are not the barometer of your spirituality.' The psalmist, who spends a lot of his time complaining and lamenting, at times felt utterly deserted. And all we humans share in that pain. But Scripture celebrates the wonder of faith that thrives even though often we trust in the darkness. Sometimes there is joy: sometimes not.

… Scripture celebrates the wonder of faith …

Perhaps God seems far away today. But He hasn't moved and perhaps you haven't moved either. Trust what is true, rather than what *feels* true.

An Englishman's home is his castle

BIG PICTURE
Matthew 26:36–46
James 5:16

FOCUS
'Then he said to them, "My soul is overwhelmed with sorrow to the point of death. Stay here and keep watch with me."'
(Matt. 26:38)

FOR those *Lucas on Life Every Day* readers who live outside the UK, I need to point out that the vast majority of English people don't live in castles, don't 'take tea' at four o'clock in the afternoon and don't wear bowler hats, carry umbrellas or fight our way through pea-soup London fog. Most of that is from bygone days, images kept alive by Hollywood.

But the notion lingers that your home is your castle: a totally private, off-limits place which permanently has its drawbridge up and where any advice from others about what happens in one's marriage or family is unwelcome interference, a raider to be repelled at all cost.

The fact is that all is not well inside the castles. Marriages are falling apart at an unprecedented rate (where there was a marriage in the first place). But the castle saying suggests that we should just sort ourselves out without help from any trusted outsider.

Kay and I used to have what we called 'the donkey strategy'. That meant that if, say, I was acting like a mule (I am the best example of this in our partnership) then Kay had the right to pick up the phone to a couple in our church whom we trusted implicitly and ask them to come round to give me a little talking-to. The strategy was never actually used, although I confess that the phone was lifted to Kay's ear once or twice …

Jesus was not ashamed to ask for the support and prayers of His friends during His great Gethsemane struggle. And James describes a 'confessional culture'. If you need to, cry for help.

Prayer: Loving Father, help me to be humble enough to ask for help, wise enough to know where to ask and bold enough to act on what I hear. Amen.

Let's say grace

PRAYERS of thanks shared together are a great idea, as long as they're meaningful. A word of blessing offered before a meal can be a positive punctuation point in the day and surely is an acknowledgement of genuine gratitude. Where it goes wrong, of course, is when 'saying grace' descends into being a mindless mantra or speech, an unthinking ritual to hurry through before we dive into the sausages. And my mind goes into a spin when we ask that a plate laden with trans-fat and calories is 'blessed to our bodies' by a God who is apparently expected to command all the fat to be gone …

I was amused when dining in the home of a Christian family recently. There came that rather awkward moment when all the food was served and I paused before picking up knife and fork – was this a 'grace' family? I asked one of the teenage children if they usually prayed before meals. 'Oh yes,' she chortled, 'especially when we have guests.'

I know some people who are so worried that giving thanks for food may just become a religious habit that they now religiously *don't* give thanks; all rather bizarre. 'Saying grace' should not be used as a sign of holy authenticity, must be heartfelt, should include making sure that we are giving consistently to those who are hungry today (and would sing 20 hymns if they could have just once what we take for granted). And as we'll see tomorrow, when it comes to gratitude, why should we stop at food? Be thankful.

Prayer: Lord, thank You, for all things good. Help me never to take what I enjoy for granted. Amen.

BIG PICTURE
**Matthew 14:13–21
Colossians 4:2**

FOCUS
'And he directed the people to sit down on the grass. Taking the five loaves and the two fish and looking up to heaven, he gave thanks and broke the loaves.'
(Matt. 14:19)

When it comes to gratitude, why should we stop at food?

I don't owe anybody

BIG PICTURE
John 11:38–44
Colossians 1:3–14

FOCUS
'So they took away the stone. Then Jesus looked up and said, "Father, I thank you that you have heard me."' (John 11:41)

KAY and I have friends whom we always enjoy spending time with, because they have a habit of noticing when we're all having fun and marking it with a comment of thankfulness. There have been numerous times when we've been together and we have found ourselves saying 'Isn't this great?' We refuse to allow a lovely event to pass by unnoticed.

Gratitude is a lifestyle and not just a moment. Some people grumble their way through life, or see no reason to be thankful to anybody for anything – what they enjoy, as far as they're concerned, is simply the fruit of their own hard work. They have no sense of appreciation or indebtedness. It's all rather bleak – the atheist has no one to thank for anything!

I like G.K. Chesterton's attitude, insisting that food is not the only blessing to celebrate: 'You say grace before meals. All right, but I say grace before the concert and the opera and grace before the play and the pantomime and grace before I open a book and grace before sketching, painting, swimming, fencing, boxing, walking, playing, dancing and grace before I dip the pen in ink …'

Just as Jesus was thankful not only for food but for His whole relationship with the Father, so perhaps we'd do well to stop today and express our appreciation – 'Count your blessings' as the old hymn quaintly but rightly exhorts us.

What are we more prone to – gratitude or grumbling? Wonderfully, when we pause to be thankful for something, our own enjoyment of it is increased. So what's on your list of 'reasons to be glad' today?

Prayer: You bless me, loving God. Help me to notice and remind me to give thanks. Amen.

He prays so beautifully

BIG PICTURE
Matthew 6:5–15
Mark 12:38–40

FOCUS
'They devour widows'
houses and for a
show make lengthy
prayers.' (Mark 12:40)

REFLECTING on the subject of giving thanks and gratitude over the last couple of days has made me remember an incident, years ago, when 'giving thanks' turned a meal that I shared into a disaster. I think the meal was baked beans on toast (for non-UK readers, baked beans on toast is a fabulous British breakfast delicacy …). Unfortunately, the chap who had cooked the meal (well, toasted the bread and warmed the beans in a saucepan) sadly held the view that the best prayers were *long* prayers.

I sat, meal parked on my knees (there was no dining table) while he prayed fervently, loudly and poetically about practically every issue under the sun, including the state of the Church, overseas missions, a variety of world leaders (health and wisdom) and for the spiritual state of the local area. I was praying that God would somehow keep the food hot throughout this extended time of intercession. And then, just when I thought that a lukewarm breakfast was actually about to be consumed, he decided to lay hands on my head and pray for me again, which he did forcefully – knocking my plate to the floor. Now we had to start all over again …

God isn't interested in what my friend Gerard Kelly calls 'Pray and display' prayers. The Pharisees were convinced that 'real' prayers should be extended. Sometimes we need to set aside a good amount of time for quiet prayer. But when we get locked into that idea, we pray for the wrong reasons and may not pray at all. Let prayer come from the heart. And don't set your clock: it's not a competition.

Prayer: Lord, teach me how to pray, authentically, diligently and intimately. Amen.

God isn't interested in … 'Pray and display' prayers

Prayer is the answer

BIG PICTURE
2 Corinthians 7:2–7
Philemon 7

FOCUS
'But God, who comforts the downcast, comforted us by the coming of Titus, and not only by his coming but also by the comfort you had given him.' (2 Cor. 7:6–7)

I'M BRACING myself for a few complaints as I write this, but here goes anyway: prayer is *not* the answer for everything. There have been times in my life when I've been struggling and a fellow Christian has patted me on the back and murmured, 'Just pray about it', as if that will solve everything. Don't misunderstand me – prayer must be the primary part of our response to pressure and pain. But there are times when I don't need to pray – I need to talk to a real live human being, I need to go for a walk on the beach and throw stones into the sea, I need to laugh, watch a film, have a meal with my wife, go for a run or hear a joke.

Paul was a great man of prayer. But he discovered that God uses human beings – in this case the visit of Titus – to lift our spirits and brighten our days. I know that sometimes what I think is prayer is actually worrying about my needs. Far from withdrawing into seclusion and battling alone, I need the clearer perspective that others can give.

When I walked through clinical depression some years ago, I felt guilty about taking the medication that was prescribed for me, as surely 'prayer was the answer'. In fact, being a Christian at that time made me feel worse – not only did I feel unendingly sad, but ashamed with it. But my hesitation was illogical. If I had broken my arm, I would have worn a sling and not insisted that prayer alone was the answer. I need God. And I need people too.

Prayer: You know me, Lord. Show me when to pray and when prayer is not what I need to pursue. Amen.

Romans 15:1–13 // 1 Thessalonians 4:13–18

It's hopeless

I'm sitting here, staring at my computer screen, which stares back at me, expecting me to type something sensible. Nothing is coming. It's a grey day outside and the absence of sun seems to echo the emptiness in my own soul. But then, my instant messenger beeped and I heard news of a friend who had battled cancer fearlessly. She died late last night. She very much wanted to live. But at the end, sensing that her time had come, she gathered her family around her bedside for a wonderful goodbye. That lady, faith-filled and feisty all the way, is home now. She died well.

I've shed a few tears, not least for her husband and family who will miss her terribly. But I'm reminded once more of what this Christian faith is all about: God with us through sun, rain, healthy vibrancy and disease. We're the people who grieve, but then smile quietly, for there's more. Death is beaten. Christ is risen. Even in the greyest of days, such as that family are experiencing now, there is the certain hope of the resurrection to come. As I look out of the window, the sun peers around the clouds.

God with us through sun, rain, healthy vibrancy and disease

I don't suffer fools gladly

BIG PICTURE
2 Corinthians 11:16–33
Ephesians 4:1–6

FOCUS
'Be completely humble and gentle; be patient, bearing with one another in love.' (Eph. 4:2)

TYPICALLY a comment made by a high-achieving, 'my time is precious' type, the 'I don't suffer fools' phrase is obviously a huge insult. With this one short acerbic missile, people can know that (a) we think they are fools (b) their presence makes us suffer and (c) we resent their presence – they make us far from glad. It packs quite a knock-out punch, a truly poisonous put-down.

The fact is, we're all fools, which gives none of us reason to be haughty. Paul resorts to a little sarcasm as he writes to the high and mighty Corinthians and pokes gentle fun at their thinking themselves to be so very wise. And earlier in his letter he reminds them who they really are and where they came from: 'But God chose the foolish things of the world to shame the wise; God chose the weak things of the world to shame the strong.' (1 Cor. 1:27).

The fact is that God *does* suffer fools gladly – He keeps company with us. And nowhere is that perseverance shown more beautifully than in the relationship between Jesus and His disciples, especially in Mark's Gospel. As the bumbling Twelve stagger from one misunderstanding via another gaffe to another crisis, we see Jesus' patience being stretched – but He sticks with them.

As Paul writes to his friends in Ephesus, we see the reality of church life (and all relationships) where sometimes we just have to 'bear with one another in love'. God is kind to us, in all of our stumbling ineptitude. Let's pass that attitude on to others around us.

Prayer: Lord, You put up with me. Help me to love when I'm irritated and when I feel superior to those frustrating me. Amen.

IT'S a delicious temptation that sneaks up on us when we're proven to be right. We all live with a lingering suspicion that we're in the right most of the time anyway: to have it confirmed by the bitter experience of another can turn us into smug people who have to chalk up a victory with the words no one wants to hear: 'I told you so.' Hannah, so horribly accused by Eli of being a drunk in the house of the Lord, refuses to even give a hint of reproach and self-justification when she brings young Samuel to be dedicated to God's service. Rather than rubbing Eli's nose in his mistake, she makes no mention of it. Being magnanimous is a sure sign of spiritual maturity. To quote another saying, we don't all need our 'pound of flesh' when others are shown to be in error and we were right all along. It's more kind to be told that we are correct than to highlight the fact that we were.

'I told you so' is often hollow, because sometimes our telling is not enough for people – they had to find out the truth for themselves, even if their searching led them into difficulties. And we may have to face the fact that our words of advice or instruction were less than convincing because we haven't lived in a way that commands a respectful hearing and a positive response.

It takes grace to be proven wrong and to admit it – and grace to be proven right and not make a fuss. Gloating is an ugly pastime.

Prayer: Lord, give me grace when my advice is ignored, especially when I'm right and shown to be so. Amen.

I told you so

BIG PICTURE
1 Samuel 1:1–28
Proverbs 24:17

FOCUS
'I prayed for this child and the Lord has granted me what I asked of him.'
(1 Sam. 1:27)

It takes grace to be proven wrong and to admit it …

A leopard never changes its spots

BIG PICTURE
2 Peter 3:14–18
2 Corinthians 3:17–18

FOCUS
'But grow in the grace and knowledge of our Lord and Saviour Jesus Christ. To him be glory both now and forever! Amen.' (2 Pet. 3:18)

WHAT is the moment of greatest failure in your life that you wish had never happened? For Peter, the dreadful episode of his denial of Jesus caused him to weep bitterly at the time (Matt. 26:75) and I'm sure prompted more than a few tears of regret later, when he remembered. Perhaps we can all look over our shoulders at something and shudder. And we can be tempted to define ourselves according to that incident of shame, as if everything that we are is summed up by that single failure.

But it was Peter who was able to write so movingly of God's grace and the wonderful truth that we are all invited to grow and change. What we were does not have to define what we are or will be. There's real hope for us here.

And the hope is not just for us. Perhaps there's someone close to you whom you tend to define by their worst moments: they lied, so now you are convinced that they always will lie; the past, as far as you are concerned, indicates what is most likely in the future. But when we take that attitude, we lock people up and help them lose hope. If we don't expect them to change (or believe that they have) they can feel that all of their good choices are useless, since we already have them tagged negatively.

The denier became the apostle Peter. The wild-eyed persecutor became Paul. You can become more than you are: and so can others around you. We *can* change.

Prayer: Change me, God. Move me beyond what I have been at my worst. Help me to see the best in others. Amen.

THERE have been many occasions in my life when I have performed with distinctive mediocrity and one of these was during my short-lived career as a cricket scorer. The glorious English game, surely designed to confuse Americans (!), is so relaxing to watch it can actually heal insomnia, at least in my opinion. As the man armed with the score book and pen, it was my job to meticulously record the details of the game, which was difficult, due to my actually being asleep at times. There's not much hope of an accurate result if the scorer is also a snorer.

One of the myths that many hold in life is that there is somehow a score to be kept and when you've been hurt, you have a right to 'even the score', which usually calls for vengeance, which is rarely just. I've met too many people who have been hurt terribly, but then who keep the hurt going by allowing bitterness to seep into their souls. Of course, forgiving those who have cut us deeply isn't easy and is more about a journey rather than a one-off action: indeed we risk seriously abusing someone if we try to hurry them to a place of forgiveness. Then there are those who feel that to forgive is to somehow lessen or even justify the original crime – but it isn't. When we refuse the jailhouse of bitterness, we are leaving our cause with God, making room for His justice and insisting that we will not create further harm for ourselves. The forgiver is the first person to benefit from forgiving. We don't have to keep score.

Prayer: Forgiving, merciful God, make me like You. Rid my heart of bitterness. Amen.

Don't get mad, get even

BIG PICTURE
**Ephesians 4:17–32
Romans 12:9–21**

FOCUS
'Be kind and compassionate to one another, forgiving each other, just as in Christ God forgave you.'
(Eph. 4:32)

… forgiving …

is [like] a journey

Don't rock the boat

BIG PICTURE
Galatians 2:1–21
Ephesians 4:15

FOCUS
'When Peter came to Antioch, I opposed him to his face, because he was clearly in the wrong.' (Gal. 2:11)

I SIT on a board where we have one particular member who is gifted when it comes to asking awkward questions. He examines the balance sheet carefully, notices the tiniest details and can always be relied upon to see things from a completely different camera angle to most. And he's always kind and gracious in the way that he approaches things. He is the best board member we have, too faithful to ever descend into simply being a weak 'yes' person. He's willing to rock the boat. We love him for it.

There's another side to the coin of kindness that we looked at yesterday – and that is, because we are called to be kind, forgiving people, this implies we will never have a contrary opinion to anybody and that if we disagree, we probably have a bad attitude. We confuse meekness with reluctance to rock the so-called boat and keep silent when in fact we should speak out. Ironically, I've seen that this unwillingness to disagree usually leads to a delayed reaction of greater, more explosive content, as we bottle up our concerns until breaking point. And then it gets really ugly …

It goes without saying that we follow the Jesus who was willing to capsize a vessel of religious arrogance and pomposity, if that was what was needed. Never shrinking back from controversy and yet never arguing for the sake of it, Jesus was clear, firm and refused to back off when some suggested that His teaching was creating turbulence.

Be kind. Listen. Pray more than you talk. Be willing to admit you're wrong. Don't crusade to win. But if the boat needs rocking …

Prayer: Lord, give me the ability to agree with encouragement, to disagree with grace and to hear as well as speak. Amen.

1 Samuel 2:27–36 // Amos 5:1–17

Ask no questions, tell no lies

It's also called turning a blind eye – when we know that something is very amiss, but, using the excuse that we need to mind our own business, we ignore what's happening and evil continues. Eli was found guilty when it came to the rampant sinning of his sons – even though he was warned, he refused to bring them to book for their outrageous behaviour. And he and his household were judged as a result.

We are *not* called to be tracker dogs, ever on the hunt for something bad that's hidden; but at the same time, when we know that someone is being hurt and we refuse to do something about it, then, in a sense, we join with the perpetrator.

Could this principle be applied to us when we ignore the needs of our starving world? We can't take the weight of the whole planet on our shoulders. But as we consider children being trafficked, clothing made in sweatshops and chocolate that is bitter-sweet because it's made from cocoa beans picked by child slaves, then we have a responsibility to ask questions about the oppression and injustice. And 'to turn a blind eye' is no excuse for any of us. Those who are holy cannot look away.

… we have a responsibility to ask questions about the oppression and injustice

I made it

BIG PICTURE
Philippians 3:1–21
1 Corinthians 9:24–27

FOCUS
'Not that I have already obtained all this, or have already been made perfect, but I press on to take hold of that for which Christ Jesus took hold of me.' (Phil. 3:12)

TODAY I discovered that a new autobiography is hitting the shelves. Called *Welcome to my World*, it's written by Coleen McLoughlin, who is just 20. The single distinguishing feature about this attractive young lady is the fact that she is engaged to be married to British footballer Wayne Rooney, a chap famous for his fancy footwork and fiery temper. Coleen admits that she hasn't achieved a great deal in her life so far – speaking to a British newspaper about her new book, she said as much: 'I am not a pop star, I am not an actress, I haven't got one thing I can say I have done. I'm a face in the public.' And yet … she has written a story of her life, which may be just a little premature.

Of course, whatever the length of our life journeys and the achievements we may have totted up along the way, we still haven't arrived yet. Paul (who never got round to writing his autobiography, what with all that world-changing to do) declared that, even with all of his great accomplishments for the kingdom of God, he was still moving on each day. No smug sense of self-congratulation here: just a pause for breath before he jogged on to the next epic episode.

Most people grow quickly in the early Christian years, fuelled by an intense hunger to learn, to know God, to get their lives on track. But then we can slow our sprint to an amble, or worse still, settle down on the side of the track for a ten-year nap. Still moving?

Prayer: Lord, thank You for the gift of today. Today, may I grow. Today, may I love. Today, may I know You. Amen.

I did it my way

IT'S one of the most commonly requested songs for funeral services – Frank Sinatra's 'My Way'. At first glance the song celebrates free-thinking independence: the uniqueness of every individual. But it's never going to be a song that I want to go out on, because its message is the opposite of the Christian gospel. A Christian has figured out that *our* way usually leads to disaster and despair. We balance the truth that we are, each one of us, unique, yet made in the image of God, but the story doesn't end there. The Fall means that we have become like wandering sheep – and sheep aren't noted for their brilliance. *My* way is a fight to get through life without the resources that God has given to really live; *my* way means treading the treacherous paths that fickle hearts and wayward hormones steer us to; *my* way means that I am on my own, without reason for goodness or indeed purpose for anything. *My* way puts me first, last and foremost.

And it's an impoverished way. Sinatra's song apparently celebrates the dubious fact that being human is the ultimate achievement – that apart from himself man has nothing – and then implies that reliance on God is a second-rate activity for the weak, for these are not the words of 'one who kneels'.

Paul, knowing what a mess of life he made when he was named Saul, sets out what should be our ultimate ambition in life: to please God. For him, death is not 'the final curtain', but the beginning of the wonderful life to come.

Prayer: Show me where 'my way' has become my song. Help me to yield, gladly, to doing life Your way. Amen.

BIG PICTURE
2 Corinthians 5:1–10
Colossians 1:9–14

FOCUS
'So we make it our goal to please him, whether we are at home in the body or away from it.'
(2 Cor. 5:9)

… our ultimate ambition in life: to please God

Jump right in

BIG PICTURE
Psalm 119:105–112
2 Timothy 3:10–17

FOCUS
'Your word is a lamp to my feet and a light for my path.' (Psa. 119:105)

ONE of my many weaknesses is that I don't tend to read the instructions on packaging, a habit that I inherited from my mother. One fond childhood memory is of when she managed to fill the kitchen knee deep in soap suds, because she hadn't read the instructions on the washing powder, or indeed noticed that it was labelled *concentrate*. It's probably a sign of an impatient soul – it just seems to take up so much time to discover how that latest time-saving device works, especially, as in the case of one gizmo I purchased recently, it comes with a 132-page user's manual. Yesterday I spent an hour scrubbing a barbecue, very ineffectively, until I read the manual, which told me in three seconds what to actually use. Result: a gleaming barbecue and one red-faced amateur cleaning operative (me) who could have saved so much wasted effort just by pausing to read the small print.

The Bible, which at times is wonderful, exasperating, illuminating and confusing, provides the vital know-how we need for life. It comes from the heart of the Maker Himself, who knows humanity through and through. It is instruction from the vantage point that God alone enjoys: through Scripture, He has become willing to share the benefit of His experience with us. We ignore His directions at our peril.

Don't jump right in, even with both feet. Make the reading of Scripture your habit, not just because it's what kosher Christians do. It could prevent a sudsy kitchen or far worse.

Prayer: Help me, all-wise God, to know, understand and apply Your Word today. Amen.

FEARING that I am becoming a fully-fledged workaholic, we decided to take a long-overdue day off today. The computer was turned off and, as we are in Colorado at the moment, we headed for the hills. The sun broiled my forehead (I now look like a lobster with specs), we wandered around little gift stores and art galleries, drank coffee and had a delightful time doing nothing much. We spotted a herd of mountain goats at the side of the road and pulled over to watch them. Driving back through the mountain gorge, I found myself going faster than I needed to – not speeding, but just heavy-footed enough to show me that I was more anxious to get back than just enjoy the beautiful journey. And I wondered – why do I spend my life racing on to the next thing, rather than enjoying and celebrating the moments? Days like today come too rarely but I realised that I can cancel out the joy of them by fretting endlessly about all that I have waiting to do: ministry appointments, emails to reply to and all of the rest of the paraphernalia of life. I'm Martha with a laptop.

It was busy, passionate and incredibly effective Paul who was able to declare that contentment was a state of being that he had learned. Rather than figuratively ripping out great chunks of his calendar – and life – and wasting them, he learned to find joy daily. I'm still in the early stages of that most vital education. Meanwhile, as that professed workaholic, I've just realised that I'm back in my study once again, writing this to you …

School continues.

Prayer: Help me to live and not just to rush; to relish, rather than hurtle on. Amen.

Hurry up

BIG PICTURE
**Philippians 4:10–20
Luke 10:38–42**

FOCUS
'I have learned the secret of being content in any and every situation, whether well fed or hungry, whether living in plenty or in want.'
(Phil. 4:12b)

… Paul …

learned to

find joy daily

Hard work never killed anyone

BIG PICTURE
Exodus 16:23–36
Matthew 11:25–30

FOCUS
'He said to them, "This is what the LORD commanded: 'Tomorrow is to be a day of rest, a holy Sabbath to the Lord.'"'
(Exod. 16:23)

PERHAPS it's my nervous confession of yesterday that prompts it, but I'm challenged by the notion that some people just work so hard that they are sinning. It all sounds very noble, all that expended energy and effort, but let's pause for a moment (if we can) and think about just why it is that some of us work too much. Some of it is a thinly disguised pride, the notion that no one can quite fulfil a task like we can. Sometimes we can be driven by simple greed: we want more, so we'll push ourselves to the limits and beyond to get it. And surely it's possible to use work as an escape route that tunnels us away from having to face some uncomfortable issues in our lives: if we just submerge ourselves in activity, then we won't have to look into the mirror for too long.

Whatever the reason, the idea that work never killed anybody is one of the most blatant lies ever circulated. Premature heart attacks in stressed-out executives, marriages murdered by punishing schedules, children raised without a father or mother because the office became that parent's new family … the casualty list goes on.

God created the Sabbath, not as a merely religious idea, but because He has designed us to need pause if we are to maintain rhythm in our lives. It was Rob Parsons who said it so pointedly: 'No one ever said, "I wish I'd spent more time at the office" on their deathbed.' Amen. Now what can I change? How about you?

Prayer: I want to work to live, Lord and not live to work. Show me the difference. Amen.

There's no smoke without fire

Asked a question by a lady after I preached recently, I answered politely but apparently not to the enquirer's liking. A few weeks later I discovered that there's a rumour (started by her) circulating the internet, accusing me of being discourteous. I'm as capable of rudeness as anyone, but in this case, I was not guilty. But it's too late. The rumour is out.

There's something delicious about gossip. Is it the thrill of being in the know, privy to information not known by others, that makes a careless whisper so inviting? Or perhaps gossip enables us to feel a sense of relief about our own shortcomings. We are perversely comforted by news of the jumbo-sized failures or small indiscretions of others, proof that we are not alone in our sins.

Gossip is a violent act. When we gossip, we're mugging a defenceless person, punching them hard and then disappearing into the shadows. We accuse but give no right of reply and assassinate the good character of another. And we also make fiction into fact, which is called lying.

Gossip is a violent act

Sometimes there *is* smoke when there's no fire. Just because a rumour is prevalent doesn't make it right. Careless talk hurts.

307

If in doubt, don't

BIG PICTURE
Acts 15:1–35
Romans 14:1–8

FOCUS
'Some men came down
from Judea to Antioch
and were teaching the
brothers: "Unless you are
circumcised, according
to the custom taught by
Moses, you cannot be
saved."' (Acts 15:1)

THIS was a popular saying that did the rounds when
I was first a Christian. Designed to make sure that we
didn't edge our way into sin, the idea was that, if you had
any concerns about something, you should err on the side
of caution and not do it. This ruling especially applied if
any other Christian might be offended by such behaviour.
Sounds like good advice? Perhaps not.

While some of us walk perilously close to the cliff
edge when it comes to freedom, the idea that hesitation
should prevent us from doing anything just won't stack
up. If the Early Church had taken that view then the
gospel would have never reached the Gentiles – it all
must have seemed incredibly risky and radical at the
time and some among them were very opposed to it.
If Barnabas had used this little mantra, then perhaps
he wouldn't have taken the risk to welcome the newly
converted, ex-persecutor Saul. If Jesus had used the 'if
in doubt' clause, then He wouldn't have allowed His feet
to be bathed with perfume or had lunch with sinners (the
Pharisees hated that) or talked with the woman at the
well (which went down badly with just about everybody
at the time).

That's not to say that we ride roughshod over cautions
that our conscience provides. But the conscience isn't
infallible. Surely, in order to be 'fully convinced in our own
minds', we should ask ourselves why it is that we are
concerned about a course of action and check what the
Bible says about that issue. Our hesitations aren't always
trustworthy.

**Prayer: Help me to be sensitive, bold, teachable and
radical. Amen.**

I'VE written on this before in *Life Every Day*, but it's worth revisiting because, as we saw yesterday, sometimes we feel badly about something but it may not necessarily be that we are wrong. Perhaps our conscience has been wounded and therefore we feel guilt, but are quite wrong to feel so. The person who has been told that sex is unclean may well have trouble in enjoying the physical expression of their love in marriage; those raised in churches where fun and laughter are considered not truly spiritual may feel troubled by a relaxed atmosphere on Sundays.

So it was that a lady in our church had a panic attack over having a Christmas tree in her home. She had been part of a group which taught that to celebrate Christmas was evil. Her conscience had been programmed to make her feel bad but what she was doing was not wrong at all.

Told always to let my conscience be my guide, I searched the Scriptures to find the verse that taught this and even employed the use of a rather large concordance in my hunt. Then I discovered that these immortal words of wisdom came not from Jesus, Paul or Moses but rather from Jiminy Cricket in a little chat with the wooden and potentially wayward Pinocchio.

The conscience is a gift and we should listen to it: our feeling troubled might well indicate that we really are getting into trouble. But the conscience is not infallible and needs to be 'fed' with the pure truth of Scripture.

Prayer: Lord, renew my mind with Your truth and protect my conscience I pray. Amen.

Always let your conscience be your guide

BIG PICTURE
1 Corinthians 10:23–33
1 Peter 3:13–22

FOCUS
'Eat anything sold in the meat market without raising questions of conscience, for, "The earth is the Lord's, and everything in it."'
(1 Cor. 10:25–26)

The conscience

is a gift …

It's not spiritual

BIG PICTURE
Colossians 3:12–17
Exodus 23:1–9

FOCUS
'And whatever you do, whether in word or deed, do it all in the name of the Lord Jesus, giving thanks to God the Father through him.' (Col. 3:17)

IT'S been a while since I've cried at the end of a film but it happened today, and this was no weepy so-called 'chick flick'. *Hotel Rwanda* is the harrowing and inspiring story of Paul Rusesabagina, a hotel manager who saved over 1,200 people by sheltering them in his four-star hotel during the 1994 Rwandan genocide. The Hutus massacred over a million of the Tutsi tribe, after the nation's president was killed in an air crash and crazed machete-waving gangs took to the streets. All of this bloodshed is terrible enough – but the added horrific twist to the tale comes as we realise that so many of the people who joined in the slaughter were professing Christians.

Rwanda was one of the most evangelised of the African countries – over 80 per cent of the population claimed to be Christian in the 1990s. This stemmed from a revival in the 1930s where widespread conviction of sin, public confession and evangelism had spread across Uganda, South Africa, Kenya, Tanzania, Burundi and the Congo, as well as Rwanda. The revival had some impact on ethnic issues, especially the attitudes of white missionaries; a favourite saying of the day was 'the ground is level at the cross'.

But the teaching of the Church was narrow and focused on blessing, experiences and 'spiritual' concerns and it failed to teach the Lordship of Christ over all of life. Roger Bowen, of the Rwanda Mission said: '… missionaries preached a form of pietism that encouraged withdrawal from the public life of the nation or a naïve, uncritical support of the party in power.' *All* of life is spiritual; let God into every part of it.

Prayer: Give me faith that can engage with the toughest issues; a faith for Mondays as well as Sundays, Lord. Amen.

Let's make
a deal

IF I'M honest, I think I might have been tempted to negotiate with the rich young ruler. After all, he was obviously a highly committed, godly sort of chap, who showed great potential. Sadly, it wasn't just that he had money – money had him in a stranglehold. Nonetheless, I think I might have been willing to thrash out a mutually acceptable deal for both parties … how about giving away half … or maybe just ten per cent. 'Don't pass up this special, today-only offer, Mr Rich Young Ruler, sir … sign here, if you please …'

But Jesus called this loaded young man – and He calls us – to follow Him with everything we've got. That doesn't mean that everyone has to give away everything they own to be a follower of Christ – that would make this one encounter into a legalistic template for everybody. And yet, in another sense, we *do* have to give everything up – to Jesus and not just in theory. All that we have and all that we are, needs to be made available to Him. And if you're like me, that means we need to review the reality of our availability from time to time and respond to opportunities to discover whether our commitment still works and is more than words.

Jesus doesn't want to be an add-on, an extension, or a useful number to dial in case of emergencies, but invites us to make Him the centre of our existence, daily. Anything less won't work. He won't make a deal, because He loves us too much.

Prayer: Make 'take all of me' a reality and not just a statement of aspiration, Lord. Amen.

BIG PICTURE
**Mark 10:17–31
Luke 14:25–34**

FOCUS
'At this the man's face fell. He went away sad, because he had great wealth.' (Mark 10:22)

Jesus doesn't

want to be

an add-on …

I may be wrong

BIG PICTURE
John 14:1–7
Romans 1:18–32

FOCUS
'Jesus answered, "I am the way and the truth and the life. No one comes to the Father except through me."'
(John 14:6)

BEING convinced of anything isn't terribly fashionable these days. The idea that there is such a thing as absolute truth smacks too much of fundamentalism and religious extremism. Our culture is more enamoured of easygoing, live and let live relativism (where all truth is relative – if it works for you, then fine; just don't force your ideas on me). But it only takes a second to know that there are truths that don't waver, no matter how much we try to ignore or mock them. Boiling water always burns, ice is cold, the wrong road won't take me home and it rains a lot in England.

Just as we saw yesterday that Jesus makes the supreme claim to be Lord of our lives and isn't interested in bargaining, so today we can affirm that He is the truth embodied and that, in Him, we know the truth that sets us free. No longer do we need to look up at the vast expanse of a night sky and wonder about the secrets of the universe – Jesus stands astride all the pompous speculations of clever humanity and, without hesitation, declares Himself to be the answer to all our questions.

That doesn't mean that we, His followers, are never wrong – far from it. We hold the Word of life in our hands, but how often we fumble around with it, misinterpreting what it says. The Bible has been used throughout history to perpetuate some terrible crimes. So we walk as humble learners and listeners. But we do follow the One who definitely knows the way.

Prayer: You are the Christ, the Light, the Truth, the Way. Lead me today. Amen.

Play it safe

Christmas is my very favourite time of the year. The shops get busier, the turkeys get nervous, children's excitement builds and, sadly, the credit card balances climb. But look past the soft, warm glow of candlelight and the familiar Yuletide melodies and remember that Christmas was about high drama and danger. There's nothing 'safe' about a child being born in a cave, then becoming a refugee because a crazed king is pursuing a campaign of infanticide. This was the coming of the One who would invite others to risk everything to follow Him: walking on water, tackling mad demoniacs, running the gauntlet of lynch mobs and irritating the religious power players of His day – none of this was 'safe'. Having met this Jesus, Paul exchanged a promising career for one that was a little more risky, as he explained to the Corinthians …

Sometimes I'm tempted, not so much by great sin, but with a quiet life. But the call of Jesus to us all is one of adventure, faith and challenge. When was the last time we had a go at something really risky for and with God?

Sometimes I'm tempted …
with a quiet life

313

Actions speak louder than words

BIG PICTURE
John 15:9–17
Colossians 3:17

FOCUS
'As the Father has loved me, so have I loved you.'
(John 15:9)

THERE'S something about a crowd – especially a crowd of Christmas shoppers – that I sometimes find mildly depressing. Look at the faces as they hurry by, too many bulging bags in hand. There are one or two bright spots – giggling children, couples newly in love looking for gifts. But the majority seem woodenly fixed on getting the job of giving done as quickly as possible. The practice of exchanging gifts years ago used to be an act of thoughtful musing and creative energy – but we can reduce Christmas gift buying to a tiresome chore that just has to be done. Never mind if it's something they don't want: they can take it back … keep the receipt. How much did they spend on us last year?

Even sending Christmas cards can be reduced to a quick, work-through-the-list project where we allow the pre-printed sentiment to say it all and simply sign our names to someone else's bad poetry. A few thoughtful handwritten words of love and appreciation from us would be a greater labour of love – whether or not the words actually rhyme. A woman asked her husband if he loved her. 'Of course I love you. I told you on our wedding day and if I ever change my mind, I'll let you know.' Now there's a divorce in the making.

Jesus came and proved His love for us in the hugely sacrificial choices He made. Actions matter most. But He chose to use words of love, encouragement and grace as well. Actions and words are not mutually exclusive: both matter. Say it with words – and deeds – this Christmas.

Prayer: Give me a moment to use words to bless and build today, loving God. Amen.

Buy now, pay later

ADMITTED to the hospital for a minor procedure recently, I asked the anaesthetist how quickly his little injection would take to knock me out. He advised me that if I counted to three, I would be asleep by the time I reached two. Intrigued by this process, I opened my mouth to count and never got past 'One'. I was gone.

A credit card is one of the fastest anaesthetics available. There's something seductively painless about handing over a piece of plastic rather than cash, coupled with the knowledge that the bill is probably a month away, deferring the pain for a while. But that bill can deliver a severe bite. With some stores charging an incredible 19–32 per cent (which is corporate racketeering and should be made illegal), we'll soon discover the real hurt that comes when we insist on extreme credit card use. Credit companies are desperate that we borrow – it's the fastest way to pick our pockets.

And unbridled greed is a black hole – it's never satisfied and we can live life on a treadmill where, no matter how much we have, we lust for more.

Christmas is a time when shopping can turn into a frenzied activity and we throw regular caution to the wind, justifying our unreasonable spending with the excuse that others will enjoy our generosity. But perhaps those we love – and who truly love us – will be more greatly blessed if they know that we are not making foolish decisions as we pursue their gift. Before you flash that card, try counting to 19 – or whatever your interest rate is …

Prayer: My money is Yours, Lord, my Provider. Help me to use it thoughtfully, generously, as a steward of Your gifts. Amen.

BIG PICTURE
**Ezekiel 18:1–17
Ecclesiastes 5:10–11**

FOCUS
'He withholds his hand from sin and takes no usury or excessive interest.' (Ezek. 18:17)

… no matter how much we have, we lust for more

Ho ho ho …

BIG PICTURE
John 8:31–47
2 Timothy 4:4

FOCUS
'Then you will know the
truth, and the truth will
set you free.' (John 8:32)

A MINISTER friend of mine got himself into serious hot water recently because he mentioned that Santa Claus is a myth. I remember the day I discovered that the big chap in red wasn't real, as I was seriously alarmed at the thought of this rotund stranger showing up in my bedroom in the middle of the night. It didn't matter to me that he came bearing gifts – I just had no guarantees about the moral consistency of this household invader and besides, when I'd met Father Christmas at the local store, he'd smelled of whisky. I didn't want the bearded one in my house, thank you very much and I was delighted to know that he was just a fairy tale.

Don't write in and tell me that I'm being a spoilsport, any Santa fans. If you want to tell your children the story, that's of course your choice. Despite my own nervousness, Santa was a part of my children's upbringing. He didn't last long, as I got caught sneaking into their rooms in the middle of the night with a sackful of gifts and my muffled 'ho ho ho' wasn't terribly convincing.

Be careful that Jesus doesn't become another fanciful character to be rejected when adulthood dawns, alongside Pinocchio, Goldilocks and Paddington Bear. Let's make sure that for all of us, not just those with children, the Christmas story is really shared among us at this time of the year. Jesus is better than any character that Disney can dream up. And He's for real.

Prayer: Living Christ, let the heart of this season refresh me again and be at the centre of my celebrations. Amen.

The customer is always right

ALL the Christmas shopping seriously gets to me, as the crowds of Mutant Ninja shoppers get bigger and ever more aggressive in their search for the perfect gifts. So spare a thought for those who work in retail at Christmas, because they are all too frequently on the receiving end of rudeness and sometimes outright abuse. It's sad when people believe that possessing a credit card gives them a licence to be snappy and unkind – but that is the consumer culture we live in.

And it doesn't take too much to upset some people. The Starbucks Corporation were recently sued for $138 million by an irate New Yorker. The coffee giants released an internet coupon offering a free coffee to anyone who had a friend or family member who worked for the company. Of course, there's no way to prove such a relationship and no limit on how many coupons could be printed, so Starbucks withdrew the offer hastily before going broke. But the lady with the lawsuit became terribly upset when she was denied her free cappuccino: her lawyer said that she 'felt betrayed' when the coupon was refused – a slight overreaction?

It's too easy to be nice when we're 'under surveillance' at church – and then snarl at each other on the way home, growling in the restaurant, thinking that, as long as we don't have that fish badge in our lapel, then we can get away with it. Paul calls his friends to good behaviour when he is with them and therefore watching and when he's absent. Make the season happier. Be nice.

Prayer: Help me to be an ambassador for You, Jesus, becoming like You … always. Amen.

BIG PICTURE
Philippians 2:12
Ephesians 4:29–32

FOCUS
'Therefore … as you have always obeyed – not only in my presence, but now much more in my absence – continue to work out your salvation with fear and trembling.'
(Phil. 2:12)

It's too easy to be nice when we're 'under surveillance' at church …

If you want to hear God laugh, tell Him your plans

BIG PICTURE
Psalm 37:1–40
Philippians 2:13

FOCUS
'Delight yourself in the
LORD and he will give
you the desires of your
heart.' (Psa. 37:4)

IF YOU'RE reading this at Christmas, think of me as my annual gift panic level will be rising. I really want to get gifts that they will love and enjoy.

But picture this – how would it be if, knowing that my wife Kay would really enjoy a particular perfume, I deliberately chose a scent that she couldn't stand, just to test her love for me? It's a twisted notion and one that could lead to *me* wearing the perfume – the whole bottle at once. Yet some people think about God that way, as if He loves nothing more than to sneer at our hopes and dreams, and delights to trash our cherished ambitions. Obviously there are times when our will collides with God and when that happens, we'd do well just to submit quickly to His loving rule and reign in our lives. But let's know too that much of the time God is changing us to be those who desire precisely what He desires – thus, my calling to speak, broadcast and write is precisely what I love doing.

As we delight ourselves in the Lord, it's not that anything goes, but He can give us the desires of our hearts because we grow to long for what He's planned for us anyway. Paul picks up this idea as he speaks to the Philippians about God wonderfully being at work within their lives, so that they do His 'will and good pleasure'.

Is there something wholesome that you love and long for? It might be an indication that God is leading you in that direction.

Prayer: Work Your will in me, Lord, that I might delight to follow You. Amen.

Happy Christmas

It's the standard greeting that we exchange at this time of the year – Happy Christmas. And lest I begin to sound like Ebenezer Scrooge, let me make it clear that it's my hope that yours, dear reader, will indeed be happy. But for some, Christmas is the saddest season. Looking back at better, warmer days feels so painful; loved ones are so sorely missed and the apparent joy of others can make us feel our own sadness more acutely.

Perhaps you know what I mean. I don't have a magic slogan to make your sadness disappear – I wish I did. But I pray that the comfort of God will be yours; that there will be a time when you laugh without shame or apology and when, if you don't have a family to call your own, a friend will call, a meal will be offered and a conversation will be shared. And for those of us who take these blessings for granted, perhaps we can be on the lookout to be the answer to that prayer and make someone's Christmas just a little happier. As we serve up some kindness to others, we find Jesus sitting at our table.

As we serve up some kindness to others, we find Jesus sitting at our table

Behind every good man stands a good woman

BIG PICTURE
Luke 1:26–38
Mark 3:1–6

FOCUS
"'I am the Lord's servant," Mary answered. "May it be to me as you have said.'"
(Luke 1:38a)

I CONTINUE to be amazed at the blatant sexism that seems to plague the Church. We still suffer from an acute shortage of competent female leaders, preachers and Bible teachers, not because women lack gifting in these areas, but rather because they have not been released into a context to see their gifts develop and grow. Just this last week I was informed by an intelligent-looking Christian leader that God uses women in some areas of leadership, 'when He can't find a man to do the job'. Self-restraint prohibits me from sharing what I felt like saying in response to such a blatantly prejudicial comment, which fuels nothing less than the oppression of women.

Too often the slogan is used of good men who are supported by good women – but in the case of Mary and Joseph, it was the man who played the supportive and obscure role, and initially misunderstanding what was going on when he discovered that Mary was pregnant. Mary, the woman, emerges as the compliant, trusting risk-taker for God, submitting to the angel's announcement of a forthcoming virgin birth, in a culture where unmarried pregnant women would suffer as social pariahs – or worse. She asks for clarification, but never demands an explanation and ultimately speaks one of the most beautiful statements in Scripture: 'I am the Lord's servant – may it be to me as you have said.' What a contrast to the wooden stubbornness exhibited by the male religious 'experts' of Jesus' day – their refusal and resistance ignited anger in Jesus. Sometimes, a very good man stands behind an even better woman.

Prayer: Lord, bless and strengthen women everywhere who know Your call but battle with prejudice that hampers their fulfilling that call. Amen.

SOMETIMES we can get the impression that God only uses a selected 'elite' for His purposes – those who preach well, pray beautifully and seem to have sorted-out lives. But in the Christmas story God includes some 'dodgy' characters in His purposes. The revelation of Jesus' birth comes to humble shepherds on the hills. In His day, shepherding was considered a dishonest, dirty trade, because shepherds often trespassed onto land to which they had no legal access. They were known to sell milk and lambs, pocketing the money rather than passing it on to their employers. No wonder some rabbis taught that herding was a disreputable occupation. Shepherds were often bad, which perhaps explains why Jesus would later call Himself the *Good* Shepherd (John 10:11,14).

Fishermen enjoyed moderate respect and a carpenter was an esteemed trade, but Jesus grew up to spend most of His time with demoniacs, prostitutes, tax collectors, sinners and adulterers, as well as those who were tragically stigmatised by reason of their disabilities, like the blind, deaf, disabled, diseased and the lepers. In their day, these were the social throwaways – but not in Jesus' eyes. People were divided into rigid boxes – but Jesus refused to acknowledge such categorisation and actively worked to undermine and overthrow such prejudicial thinking.

Recently I found myself in a ministry situation where most of the other leaders were Oxbridge educated, from upper class backgrounds. My Essex boy accent stood out in the crowd. It wasn't that they made me feel an outsider at all: my discomfort came from within. But I'm comforted by this: God calls all sorts to build His kingdom.

Prayer: I'm not the best, Lord, but I am Yours. Amen.

Only the best will do

BIG PICTURE
1 Corinthians 1:26–31
Amos 7:14–15

FOCUS
'Brothers, think of what you were when you were called. Not many of you were wise by human standards; not many were influential; not many were of noble birth.' (1 Cor. 1: 26)

God calls all sorts to build His kingdom

Christmas is for the kids

BIG PICTURE
1 Corinthians 10:1–12
Matthew 1:18–25

FOCUS
'For I do not want you to be ignorant of the fact, brothers, that our forefathers were all under the cloud and that they all passed through the sea.' (1 Cor. 10:1)

IT'S amazing just how confused our culture is. A leading supermarket chain decided to issue a press release last Easter, thrilled as they were that people were buying chocolate eggs, but concerned that most people don't know the actual significance of those yummy eggs. And so they put out a press release, which, incredibly, got Christmas confused with Easter, announcing that the practice of giving eggs was to commemorate Jesus' *birth*. Sensing that they'd got that a little wrong, they then issued a second press release declaring that Easter is the celebration of Jesus' *rebirth*, whatever that is supposed to mean. Finally a third press release got it right, as they told the world that Easter is the celebration of Christ's death and resurrection, establishing now the difference between Christmas and Easter. I'm not attacking the supermarket chain – surely we, the people of God, carry a huge responsibility for the ignorance that people today have concerning the gospel. Perhaps if we had not spent so much time making the truth about God seem so boring and irrelevant, the world would show a little more interest.

But if there's confusion about Easter, then certainly most seem to have missed the whole point of the Christmas story, thinking it to be more about family gatherings, log fires, fat chaps dressed in red, a bumper time for the high street stores and fun and games for the children.

The good news is that we are not alone in the bleak midwinter of a life bereft of God. Pass it on.

Prayer: Lord Jesus, You came. It cost You dearly. Thank You. Amen.

Children should be seen and not heard

BIG PICTURE
Matthew 18:2–5
Mark 10:13–14

FOCUS
'And whoever welcomes
a little child like this in
my name welcomes me.'
(Matt. 18:5)

A FEW days ago I had a conversation with a Christian leader who, like me, has to travel a lot. However, unlike me, his children are still very young and his wife wants him to make some radical changes in their lifestyle so that he will be home more. He told me he was praying about it so that he might discern what God was saying and I said (as gently as I could), that perhaps God was already speaking loud and clear. His family needed his attention and care and he should not miss those beautiful episodes that slip through our fingers too quickly: the netball game, the school parents' evening, those bedtime stories. I tried to balance my own travel carefully when my children were young, but regret that too often I didn't get it right and would give anything to walk through some of those lost days once again. Yesterday we saw that Christmas is far more than a gift-fest for the children – but today, let's redress the balance and say that Christmas is a time of wonder and joy for the young. Far from seeing children as unimportant and incidental, Jesus showed just how valuable they are, not in their potential for the future, but in His delight in them now.

Indignant and angry with His shoo-away disciples, Jesus suspended the summit talks with the Pharisees and turned to what He saw as more important matters – a hug of blessing for a child. Let's make His priority *our* priority.

Prayer: For children everywhere – those safe and well fed and those hungry, vulnerable to abuse and exploitation: bless them, save them and reveal Yourself to them. Amen.

Let's make

His priority

our priority

Go on, it's Christmas

BIG PICTURE
1 Peter 1:13–16
2 Corinthians 7:1

FOCUS
'Therefore, prepare your minds for action; be self-controlled; set your hope fully on the grace to be given you when Jesus Christ is revealed.'
(1 Pet. 1:13)

CHRISTMAS is the time of year when many use the season as a reason for madly irresponsible behaviour. Office parties notoriously provide the opportunity for crazy decisions made in a merry moment that will destroy marriages which have taken a lifetime to build. And Britain's binge-drinking culture will sadly worsen as too much alcohol is poured down too many throats and all in the name of Christmas, the celebration of the birth of the One who came to save us from our hapless stupidity.

We can easily be seduced by the nudge to 'go on' because it's Christmas, or be fooled by the hackneyed notion that a little bit of what we fancy does us good. But think again. Sin is never a good idea, because it is the great catastrophe that destroys. Sin is a bad idea, not because God is a cosmic killjoy, but because He loves us so much and longs that we don't blight and damage our lives. Holiness is what all humans, Bible carriers and binge drinkers alike, are called to. Ajith Fernando states that 1,400 of the 2,005 verses in Paul's writings have something to say about holiness, godliness, or Christian character.

And holiness is the beautiful lifestyle that is the opposite of that catastrophe. Grace allows us the wonder of what fantasy writer J.R.R. Tolkien of *The Lord of the Rings* fame describes as a euchastrophe, a *good* upheaval, a Eucharistic revolution.

Enjoy the season and celebrate it well. But let's not use the birthday of Christ to subconsciously print us a licence to act in a way that is not worthy of Him.

Prayer: Help me to live well and in a way worthy of Your name during this season, loving God. Amen.

When you wish upon a star

I never cease to be amazed what sensible people will believe. As they reject the claims of Jesus Christ out of hand, there are some who will seemingly put their faith in almost anything, including lucky charms or the position of the planets as they correspond to our birth date. Perfectly intelligent people mock the claims of Christ yet pore over their horoscopes daily. And what this implies is that all truth is relative: if your little belief system works for you, then that's good enough. It doesn't have to be actually true, just as long as it makes you feel a little better. I'm not sure what owning a rabbit's foot is supposed to do for us – it didn't exactly bring much good luck to the long-eared amputee who lost it.

The Christian faith is not based upon hopeful myths and superstition, but upon the revelation of the all-powerful God who is the Creator of all, and the Christ who came as a helpless child lived to show us how to live, and died to enable us to live the same way, in relationship with the Father. This Christmas, the light of the world shines still.

Perfectly
intelligent
people mock
the claims
of Christ …

All ways lead to God

BIG PICTURE
John 14:5–14
Matthew 4:12–17

FOCUS
'Jesus answered, "I am the way and the truth and the life. No-one comes to the Father except through me.'
(John 14:6)

I CURRENTLY have two GPS devices in my car. Make that three. I've written before about the slightly irate German lady who lives in the navigational system of my car. Cold and humourless, she barks commands at me and never congratulates me when I arrive at my destination without mishap or 'diversion' (a nice word for getting lost). My other GPS is in my PDA: there lives a jolly-hockey-sticks plummy English lady who trills away endlessly about where I should turn at the next roundabout. Armed with these two mechanical sisters, together with my third GPS (Kay, armed with a map), you'd really think that I'd be able to find my way around. Alas, I am still frequently lost, much to the consternation of all three sisters. What could be more fun than hearing both computerised voices chanting the mantra, 'Turn around when possible'? And I need to turn around when I get lost. If I want to go to Cleethorpes and end up on the wrong road, it doesn't matter how sincerely I believe that I'm in the right: I'll still end up in Cambridge instead.

Perhaps this Christmas Eve we'll gather in churches and chapels to light candles, sing carols and worship the Christ who came to bring light into our darkness. Christmas Eve is perhaps my favourite day of the year, loaded as it is with hope, as we wonder again at the rescuer who came for the lost. Perhaps this is the day to gently, lovingly share with others that we care about, the news that He came for us and He came for them. If He's right – and we followers of Christ affirm that He is – there is no other way.

Prayer: Allow me to share my confidence in You with kindness, compassion and conviction, Lord. Amen.

Charity begins at home

LAST year, our Christmas Day was transformed by one gift that we received. Our daughter and son-in-law, Kelly and Ben, were working in Banda Aceh, Indonesia, where over 200,000 people died in the tsunami on Boxing Day 2004. They decided that, rather than giving our family gifts, they would take the money and buy shoes for some tsunami orphans. They took the children to the shoe store and then out to an ice-cream bar and filmed the whole event and sent it to us as a gift to open on Christmas Day. I've watched it a hundred times since and I cry every time. But when we first viewed that six-minute film on Christmas Day last, we realised afresh that the greatest joy comes not from receiving, but from giving. There is something delightful about the broad smiles of those who have cried too many tears in the past.

I hope that you are given some gifts you'll enjoy, and if you are on your own, may you know the comfort of God in perhaps what is the unwelcome quietness. But why not pause this Christmas, in the midst of all the celebrations or in the quiet solitude and ask God to make this coming year one where we bring smiles again around the world to those who desperately need our gifts the most. Read the story of the One who came to give everything – including His life – and pledge to walk in His footsteps. Giving is not just a Christmas habit and charity doesn't begin at home.

And may the joy and wonder of this day bring light to your heart.

Prayer: Praise You, living Christ, for You have come to us. Life can be lived and death defeated. I give thanks in Your name. Amen.

BIG PICTURE
Luke 2:1–20
Luke 12:27–34

FOCUS
'While they were there, the time came for the baby to be born, and she gave birth to her firstborn, a son.'
(Luke. 2:6–7)

… the greatest

joy comes not

from receiving,

but from giving

Don't worry, be happy

BIG PICTURE
Philippians 4:1–7
Matthew 6:25–34

FOCUS
'Do not be anxious about anything, but in everything, by prayer and petition, with thanksgiving, present your requests to God.'
(Phil. 4:6)

IT'S a catchy little ditty that conjures up images of sipping an ice-cold drink on a Caribbean beach: 'Don't worry, be happy'. And it's easy to sing when your body smells of coconut suntan oil and the warm blue ocean is nipping your feet. But when Paul talked about learning to be contented and fleeing anxiety, we remember that he was parked on death row – and he didn't know what was ahead. So is this some stick-your-head-in-the-sand positive thinking strategy that Paul came up with?

Absolutely not, because Paul and the Lord Jesus have more to say than just 'don't worry'. If that were the extent of the message, it would be hollow rhetoric, in a world where there is plenty to worry about. Paul immediately points his friends in Philippi to what should be the reason for their lack of anxiety – and that is the practice of praise and thanksgiving. They are able to share what would normally terrify them with the living God who cares. Outside of faith in God, I can't think of a single reason not to worry. If the planet is just in the hands of humans, then the track record so far doesn't point to a positive future and I'll start biting my nails to an Olympic level right away. But there is a God. He wants us to share our nervousness and needs with Him and then learn how to trust Him. Peace like this doesn't come overnight: Paul had learned the art of living in grace. May we learn too.

Prayer: Teach me trust, faith, prayer and contentment, Lord. Amen.

If you can dream it, you can do it

BIG PICTURE
Acts 16:1–10
Proverbs 3:5–6

FOCUS
'When they came to the border of Mysia, they tried to enter Bithynia, but the Spirit of Jesus would not allow them to.'
(Acts 16:7)

POSSIBILITY thinking is big these days, with no shortage of humanistic gurus who want to tell us that we can achieve the impossible if we just buy their book. The so-called 'self-help' pop-psychology publishing industry is booming, encouraging us to dream the impossible dream and achieve unthinkable success. And there's a danger that we can try to turn Jesus into a saviour/coach/trainer who will lead us along the yellow brick road to materialistic and emotional nirvana. But the invitation of Christ is not that we come to Him to see all *our* dreams come true, but rather that we allow Him to dream *His* kingdom dreams through us. Sometimes the statement, 'I can do all things through Christ who strengthens me' has been misquoted by those who think that God is just about enabling them to do what He's never actually called them to do.

To become a follower of Christ is to lock ourselves onto His agenda and not insist that He follows ours, as Paul discovered during this missionary journey which led him into Europe. As we've already seen, that doesn't mean that all of our hopes and aspirations will be trashed, because some of those have been birthed by the God who is always at work in us, whether we are aware of it or not. But perhaps as another year draws to a close, let's say to God: what are You up to in this coming year, Father, and can I play? As we make ourselves available to His purposes and place ourselves on readiness to serve Him every day, then He can dream *His* dreams through us.

Prayer: What are You doing this year, Lord? Can I join in? Amen.

… what are You up to in this coming year, Father, and can I play?

God helps those who help themselves

BIG PICTURE
John 15:1–17
Philippians 2:1–7

FOCUS
'I am the vine; you are the branches. If a man remains in me and I in him, he will bear much fruit; apart from me you can do nothing.'
(John 15:5)

NEW Year's Eve is famous for resolutions, fireworks and champagne at midnight and, for some, a real sense of fear about what the coming year might bring. Perhaps, as you stand on the threshold of another 12 months, you already have a sense that it might herald a time of struggle for you. Perhaps you're worried. Have you got what it takes to get through the difficulties ahead?

It's no cliché to say that we don't have to have what it takes. God has the goods. Jesus became nothing – that doesn't mean that to be human is nothing, rather it states how He lived His life. John's Gospel reports continually that Jesus did nothing by Himself, He only spoke the words that the Father gave Him and only did the things that the Father was doing. Read John's Gospel through in one sitting sometime and marvel at the step-by-step relationship between Jesus and the Father.

But just as Jesus became nothing and lived in total dependency, so He calls us to do the same. And then, in John 15, He bluntly announces, 'without me, you can do nothing'. This is wonderful, liberating news. It means that we don't have to try, but as we walk in friendship with God into the New Year, He can and will help us, come what may. Take a good look at what challenges and even threatens you about the coming year. Tell God about it and share your nervousness with Him. And then ask for His dynamic help. He's with you.

Prayer: Look with me, Lord, at what I fear, and come with me, Lord, through what I fear. Amen.

1 Peter 3:8–22 // Acts 1:1–9

Preach the gospel and, if necessary, use words

In recent years preachers have made use of a popular phrase usually attributed to St Francis of Assisi, famous for chatting with squirrels, who said, 'Travel everywhere, preach the gospel and use words if you have to.' This can lead us to have an unbalanced view about what evangelism is, as if we are never called to open our mouths. Francis sold everything and gave all he had to the poor – a wonderfully radical lifestyle. And of course Jesus *did* more than He *said*, often activating a search in those who witnessed His actions rather than simply just explaining them immediately. But evangelism will usually involve verbal explanation; this seems consistent with the Greek word *euangelizomai*, which always seems to bear a verbal content. Graham Tomlin calls us to both words *and* actions: 'Without actions, no one listens. Without words, no one understands.'

Healings, as marvellous as they are, require explanation: they startle, but do not necessarily inform and can be wrongly interpreted. Some assigned Jesus' power to a satanic source. Surely we are called to go into this next year living the life and also explaining the reason for the hope that is within us; words and actions both.

'Without actions, no one listens. Without words, no one understands.'

Whatever

Philippians 1:27–30
Colossians 3:17

FOCUS
'Whatever happens,
conduct yourselves in a
manner worthy of the
gospel of Christ.'
(Phil. 1:27)

WHATEVER. It's one little word that is often used these days to express a 'couldn't care less' attitude: whatever. If you want to let people know that you are bored, indifferent, or simply can't be bothered to respond to what is being said to you, it's a fairly devastating put-down: whatever. But 'whatever' is not the catchphrase of the Christian. At this time, when so many are thinking about New Year's resolutions, perhaps we should take the opportunity to do a little stock-taking in our own lives. Rather than sliding into a new year clutching at unhelpful attitudes or habits, we should do some sober assessment and make some decisions about how we'd like to do life for God in the coming 12 months.

Of course, Paul the apostle had a 'whatever' attitude of his own: 'Whatever happens, conduct yourselves in a manner worthy of the gospel of Christ' (Phil. 1:27). His loyalty to Jesus wasn't dependent on a particular desired outcome that he insisted for his life. And remember, he wrote to the Philippians from what, for all he knew, might have been death row for him. His future was uncertain, he might have been tempted to feel that God had abandoned him, and he could have said, 'If God doesn't get me out of here soon, I'm giving up on Him.' But instead, he said, 'Whatever.' May God give us grace to say our own amens to Paul's prayer. And may I thank you for joining me on the *Life Every Day* journey. Have a wonderful New Year. And stay with Christ. Whatever.

Prayer: Lord, thank You for the year that's gone. May I love and serve You in this new year. Whatever. Amen.

… stay with

Christ. Whatever

National Distributors

UK: (and countries not listed below)
CWR, Waverley Abbey House, Waverley Lane, Farnham, Surrey GU9 8EP.
Tel: (01252) 784700 Outside UK (44) 1252 784700 Email: mail@cwr.org.uk

AUSTRALIA: KI Entertainment, Unit 21 317-321 Woodpark Road, Smithfield, New South Wales 2164.
Tel: 1 800 850 777 Fax: 02 9604 3699 Email: sales@kientertainment.com.au

CANADA: David C Cook Distribution Canada, PO Box 98, 55 Woodslee Avenue, Paris,
Ontario N3L 3E5. Tel: 1800 263 2664 Email: swansons@cook.ca

GHANA: Challenge Enterprises of Ghana, PO Box 5723, Accra. Tel: (021) 222437/223249
Fax: (021) 226227 Email: ceg@africaonline.com.gh

HONG KONG: Cross Communications Ltd, 1/F, 562A Nathan Road, Kowloon.
Tel: 2780 1188 Fax: 2770 6229 Email: cross@crosshk.com

INDIA: Crystal Communications, 10-3-18/4/1, East Marredpalli, Secunderabad – 500026, Andhra Pradesh.
Tel/Fax: (040) 27737145 Email: crystal_edwj@rediffmail.com

KENYA: Keswick Books and Gifts Ltd, PO Box 10242-00400, Nairobi.
Tel: (254) 20 312639/3870125 Email: keswick@swiftkenya.com

MALAYSIA: Canaanland, No. 25 Jalan PJU 1A/41B, NZX Commercial Centre, Ara Jaya, 47301 Petaling
Jaya, Selangor. Tel: (03) 7885 0540/1/2 Fax: (03) 7885 0545 Email: info@canaanland.com.my

Salvation Book Centre (M) Sdn Bhd, 23 Jalan SS 2/64, 47300 Petaling Jaya, Selangor.
Tel: (03) 78766411/78766797 Fax: (03) 78757066/78756360
Email: info@salvationbookcentre.com

NEW ZEALAND: KI Entertainment, Unit 21 317-321 Woodpark Road, Smithfield,
New South Wales 2164, Australia. Tel: 0 800 850 777 Fax: +612 9604 3699
Email: sales@kientertainment.com.au

NIGERIA: FBFM, Helen Baugh House, 96 St Finbarr's College Road, Akoka, Lagos.
Tel: (01) 7747429/4700218/825775/827264 Email: fbfm@hyperia.com

PHILIPPINES: OMF Literature Inc, 776 Boni Avenue, Mandaluyong City.
Tel: (02) 531 2183 Fax: (02) 531 1960 Email: gloadlaon@omflit.com

SINGAPORE: Alby Commercial Enterprises Pte Ltd, 95 Kallang Avenue #04-00, AIS Industrial Building,
339420. Tel: (65) 629 27238 Fax: (65) 629 27235 Email: marketing@alby.com.sg

SOUTH AFRICA: Struik Christian Books, 80 MacKenzie Street, PO Box 1144, Cape Town 8000.
Tel: (021) 462 4360 Fax: (021) 461 3612 Email: info@struikchristianmedia.co.za

SRI LANKA: Christombu Publications (Pvt) Ltd, Bartleet House, 65 Braybrooke Place, Colombo 2.
Tel: (9411) 2421073/2447665 Email: dhanad@bartleet.com

USA: David C Cook Distribution Canada, PO Box 98, 55 Woodslee Avenue, Paris, Ontario N3L 3E5,
Canada. Tel: 1800 263 2664 Email: swansons@cook.ca

CWR is a Registered Charity – Number 294387
CWR is a Limited Company registered in England – Registration Number 1990308

Courses and seminars

Publishing and new media

Conference facilities

Transforming lives

CWR's vision is to enable people to experience personal transformation through applying God's Word to their lives and relationships.

Our Bible-based training and resources help people around the world to:
· Grow in their walk with God
· Understand and apply Scripture to their lives
· Resource themselves and their church
· Develop pastoral care and counselling skills
· Train for leadership
· Strengthen relationships, marriage and family life and much more.

Our insightful writers provide daily Bible-reading notes and other resources for all ages, and our experienced course designers and presenters have gained an international reputation for excellence and effectiveness.

CWR's Training and Conference Centre in Surrey, England, provides excellent facilities in an idyllic setting – ideal for both learning and spiritual refreshment.

CWR Applying God's Word
to everyday life and relationships

CWR, Waverley Abbey House,
Waverley Lane, Farnham,
Surrey GU9 8EP, UK

Telephone: **+44 (0)1252 784700**
Email: **info@cwr.org.uk**
Website: **www.cwr.org.uk**

Registered Charity No 294387
Company Registration No 1990308

Two more years' worth of Jeff's wisdom and wit

Life with Lucas Book 1:

- Friends rediscovered
- Stop looking for the will of God
- Faith on the far side
- The Church – a blushing bride
- A walk on the wild side
- Unsung heroes change their world

Life with Lucas Book 2:

- Independence Days?
- Friendly Fire
- Rediscovering Jesus
- Singing in the Rain
- Elijah – Prophet at a Loss
- Seven – Those Deadly Sins